Early praise for

THE ART OF LANGUAGE INVENTION

"David J. Peterson's *The Art of Language Invention* accomplishes a minor miracle in taking a potentially arcane discipline and infusing it with life, humor, and passion. It makes a compelling and entertaining case for language creation as visual and aural poetry. I cherish words, I love books about words, and for me this is the best book about language since Stephen Fry's *The Ode Less Traveled*. And, best of all, there's a phrasebook!"
— Kevin Murphy, co-creator and showrunner of Syfy's *Defiance*

"If you want to know how someone makes up a language from the ground up, you'll find out how in this book—and the glory of it is that along the way you'll get the handiest introduction now in existence to what linguistics is. In fact, read this even if you *don't* feel like making up a language!" — John McWhorter, author of *The Language Hoax*

"Accessible, entertaining, and thorough, Peterson has created an invaluable resource for authors, dedicated fans, and casual enthusiasts. This is the book I wish I'd had when I started writing."
— Leigh Bardugo, *New York Times* bestselling author of *Shadow and Bone*

"This book not only lucidly ushers language invention into its own as an art form, it's also an excellent introduction to linguistics."
— Arika Okrent, author of *In the Land of Invented Languages*

"George R. R. Martin created Khal Drogo, and David Benioff and Dan Weiss believed in me, but David Peterson gave me life." — Jason Momoa

PENGUIN BOOKS

THE ART OF LANGUAGE INVENTION

DAVID J. PETERSON was born in Long Beach, California, in 1981. He began creating languages in 2000, received his M.A. in linguistics from the University of California, San Diego, in 2005, and cofounded the Language Creation Society in 2007. The inventor of numerous languages for television, film, and novels, he is best known for creating Valyrian and Dothraki for HBO's hit series *Game of Thrones*, adapted from George R. R. Martin's *A Song of Ice and Fire* series. He is the bestselling author of *Living Language Dothraki: A Conversational Language Course Based on the Hit Original HBO Series Game of Thrones*. He has also created languages for many other television shows, such as the CW's *The 100*, Netflix's *The Witcher*, and Showtime's *Penny Dreadful*, as well as films such as Marvel's *Doctor Strange*, Netflix's *Bright*, and Legendary's *Dune*.

The Art of Language Invention

From Horse-Lords to Dark Elves to Sand

Worms, the Words Behind World-Building

DAVID J. PETERSON

 PENGUIN BOOKS

PENGUIN BOOKS

An imprint of Penguin Random House LLC
penguinrandomhouse.com

Published in Penguin Books 2015
This edition with revisions and a new chapter published in Penguin Books 2021

Ayeri's Tahano Hikamu script used by permission of Carsten Becker. © Carsten Becker, 2014.
Sondiv (or Atrian) language from *Star-Crossed* television series. Courtesy of CBS Studios Inc.
The Dothraki and Valyarian languages from the HBO original series *Game of Thrones*. © 2011 Home Box Office, Inc. All rights reserved. HBO® and related service marks are the property of Home Box Office, Inc.
Dark Elf language appears courtesy of Marvel Studios.
Phrases from the SyFy television program *Defiance* appear courtesy of NBCUniversal Media, LLC.
Minza text from Conlang Relay 13 used by permission of Herman M. Miller. © 2006 Herman M. Miller.
Rikchik language used by permission of Denis Moskowitz. Copyright 1997–2014 by Denis Moskowitz.
Sakhi'i Widoshni (Naming Ceremony) illustration used by permission of Trent M. Pehrson. © 2014 Trent M. Pehrson.
Kēlen's Ceremonial Interlace alphabet used by permission of Sylvia Sotomayor.
Da Mätz se Basa language from 13ᵗʰ Conlang Relay used by permission of Henrik Theiling.
Chakobsa language appears courtesy of Legendary.
Trigedasleng (or Grounder) language from *The 100* television series. Courtesy of CBS Studios Inc.
Ménìshè language appears courtesy of Freeform.
Ravkan language appears courtesy of Netflix, based on the book *Shadow & Bone* by Leigh Bardugo.

LIBRARY OF CONGRESS CATALOGING IN PUBLICATION DATA
Peterson, David J., 1981–
The art of language invention : from Horse-Lords to Dark Elves to Sand Worms, the words behind world-building / David J. Peterson.
pages cm
ISBN 978-0-14-312646-1
1. Languages, Artificial.   I. Title.
PM8008.P48 2015
499'.99—dc23   2015003967

Printed in the United States of America

Set in ITC Stone Serif Std Medium and Arial Unicode
Designed by Sabrina Bowers

For Erin

Contents

The Art of
Language
Invention

Introduction

The first time I heard a language of mine spoken on-screen was at a cast and crew premiere event for the first season of HBO's *Game of Thrones*. It was a lavish, but, comparatively speaking, poorly attended event. George R. R. Martin was there, but many of the seats reserved for cast members in the Ray Kurtzman Theater remained vacant throughout the screening of the first two episodes of the series. Needless to say, they didn't know how big this thing would get (who did?), but I appreciated the extra legroom—and the front-row seat.

My initial reaction to hearing Dothraki, the language of the long-braided, horse-riding warriors, though, was one of dismay. The first line one hears in the series is in the pilot, when Illyrio Mopatis, welcoming Khal Drogo and his band into his courtyard to arrange a marriage, says *Athchomar chomakaan*—"Welcome" when said to one person. I misremembered how I'd translated it, though, and thought he should have said *Athchomar chomakea*—"Welcome" when said to more than one person. So even though Roger Allam's performance was fine and it was I who was mistaken, I was a little miffed. After the screening had finished we all got in line to congratulate David Benioff and Dan Weiss on a successful premiere, and when they asked me how the Dothraki speakers did, my face must have betrayed me, for David said to me, "You know, we [i.e. he and Dan] were talking, and we realized, if any of the actors made a mistake, who would know it—except for you?"

This is actually a question I've gotten a lot since. That is, if there's an actor performing in a created language that no one speaks, who will know if they make a mistake aside from the one who created the language? From experience, I can tell you that the actors always know (and it frustrates them when the takes with errors make their way into the final cut), but let me focus on the audience.

If you, as a viewer, sit down and listen to one line from a created language and nothing else, it's nearly impossible to tell if it's a created language, a natural language one doesn't know (one that exists in our world), or gibberish—to say nothing about whether or not the actor gets all the words right. If that's the extent of the linguistic material in the production, it doesn't matter what work went into creating the line.

As the number of lines increases, though, the odds of the casual audience member picking up on inconsistencies increase. It's not every fan who pays attention to what actors are saying in a language they don't understand, but there are those who do. Furthermore, television shows and movies aren't plays—that is, they aren't events that happen at one moment in time and are never seen again. If the general public is anything like me, *most* of the television and movie viewing they do now isn't done live—and if a show is worth its salt, they'll watch it again and again and again and again.

As a language creator, I always had a bit of a different perspective. When I was creating Dothraki, I wasn't creating it simply to fill out the requisite non-English dialogue. I had an idea that *Game of Thrones* could be big, and could occupy a special place in television history—just as George R. R. Martin's books already do occupy a special place in the history of fantasy. The work I was doing, then, would need to be something that would stand the test of time. Because even if a fan who's never heard of the books can't tell if one actor makes a mistake in the premiere on their first viewing, fans five, ten, twenty years from now *will* be able to tell. And, of course, if mistakes crop up, they won't belong to the show, the producers, or the actors: they'll belong to me.

When I was a kid, the original *Star Wars* trilogy had just completed its initial run in theaters, and *Star Wars* was *everywhere*. I had a toy sand skimmer (which I broke), a toy TIE fighter (which I also broke), and a read-along *Return of the Jedi* picture book with accompanying record which would play the sound of a ship's blaster when you were supposed to turn the page. (If you're too young to be familiar with record players as anything other than "vinyl," type "Pac-Man record read along" into YouTube to familiarize yourself with the concept. That was my childhood.)

In short, aside from *He-Man*, *Star Wars* was pretty much *the* thing if you were a child of four in 1985. At that age, when I watched movies, I didn't really pay careful attention to the dialogue, and wasn't able to follow stories that well. Consequently when the *Star Wars* trilogy was rereleased in 1995, I rewatched it eagerly. Once I got to *Return of the Jedi*, I was struck by what I thought was a particularly bizarre scene. In the beginning of the movie, Princess Leia, disguised as a bounty hunter, infiltrates Jabba the Hutt's palace in order to rescue Han Solo. She pretends to have captured Chewbacca, and engages Jabba to negotiate a price for handing him over. In doing so, Leia pretends to speak (or evidently *does* speak, via some sort of voice modification device) a language Jabba doesn't. He employs the recently acquired C-3PO as an intermediary. As near as I can tell, this is how the exchange goes (transcription is my own; accent marks indicate where the main stress is):

LEIA: *Yaté. Yaté. Yotó.* (SUBTITLE: "I have come for the bounty on this Wookiee.")

C-3PO relays this message and Jabba says he'll offer 25,000 for Chewie.

LEIA: *Yotó. Yotó.* (SUBTITLE: "50,000, no less.")

C-3PO relays this message and Jabba asks why he should pay so much.

LEIA: *Eí yóto.*

The above isn't subtitled, but Leia pulls out a bomb and activates it.

C-3PO: Because he's holding a thermal detonator!

Jabba is impressed by this and offers 35,000.

LEIA: *Yató cha.*

The above isn't subtitled, but Leia deactivates the bomb and puts it away.

C-3PO: He agrees.

Order is restored.

I want you to remember that I was in seventh or eighth grade at the time that I was rewatching this. I was not a "language" guy at that point by *any* stretch of the imagination. I never dreamed that a human could invent a language, and even if I had, I probably wouldn't have been able to come up with a good reason for one to do so. Furthermore, up to that point, I'd never studied a second language, and the prospect filled me with dread (I had enough trouble understanding my Spanish-speaking relatives who always spoke too fast for me).

But even so, I knew something was wrong here. How on earth does Leia say the same thing twice and have it mean something different the second time? Even if we take C-3PO for an unreliable translator (he is quite loquacious, after all), that applies only to the last two phrases. How could one expect to have an unreliable *subtitle*? Subtitles are supposed to lie outside the world of the film. If you can't rely on a subtitle provided by the film's creators, how can you rely on anything?

In trying to resolve this conflict, it occurred to me that the only plausible explanation for this aberrant phenomenon is that the language itself was correct, but worked differently from all other human languages. In our languages (take English, for example), a word's meaning can be affected by the context it's in, but if you control for context, the word will always mean the same thing. Thus, if you're telling a story about your dog, and you use the word "dog" several times throughout the story, it will still refer to a fur-covered animal that barks and covets nothing so highly as table scraps. This is fairly standard and uncontroversial.

What would happen if a language didn't do that, though?

Take, for example, the word I have transcribed as *yotó* above. What if it changed its meaning over the duration of a discourse? Naturally, one would have to define a discourse, but I think it's fair to consider this conversation featuring Leia, Jabba, and C-3PO a single discourse, so we can leave that concern aside for the moment. What if the word *yotó* has several definitions? Specifically, what if the first time it's used in a conversation it means "this wookiee"; the second time it's used it means "50,000"; and the third time it's used it means "no less" (or the rough equivalent of those)? The same, then, applies for all other words in the language. That would resolve the ambiguity. How could one possibly use such a language? Well, they *are* all aliens (*Star Wars*, recall, takes place a long time ago in a galaxy far, far away). Maybe they're just better at this stuff than humans. Why not?

This was where my brain went while rewatching *Return of the Jedi* for the first time. At some future date I may have shared this with a friend, but if I did, the response was likely an eyeroll. This quirk was just an unimportant detail in an otherwise fantastic movie. Why bother about it?

And so that's pretty much where my thought experiment died. I didn't take it any further, and no one was really interested, so I didn't think about it again until college.

But that, of course, was a different era—a pre-internet era. Who does a teenager have to share news with other than their family, friends, and teachers? Who do they come in contact with? In 1995, that's pretty much only the people who live near you and with whom you interact on a daily basis. How would you ever get ahold of anyone else? How would I have known that someone in the Bay Area, let's say—less than five hundred miles away—had the same idea I'd had and also found that exchange interesting? In 1995, there was no way.

Then the internet happened.

Yes, the internet had been around for a while in 1995, but it wasn't a thing that just anyone could have access to. America Online changed all that. Pretty soon it became a thing to race home from school and go into a chatroom with a bunch of random people to talk about . . . nothing. And that was how we entertained ourselves—*for hours*. What a world, where you could chat with someone who lived in Lancaster, Pennsylvania, about how Soundgarden rules!

As it turns out, though, I wasn't the only person to pick up on this. Another conlanger I'd later meet at the First Language Creation Conference, Matt Haupt, asked exactly the same question, and devoted a blog post to deconstructing that scene specifically. And *we* weren't the only ones. The Ubese language has its own entry on the Wookieepedia (yes, that's a thing) where contributors have written up an entire backstory for the language that is, first of all, not a full language, and, ultimately, poorly constructed and not worthy of serious consideration.

So let me bring back David Benioff and Dan Weiss's question to me on the night of the *Game of Thrones* premiere. If the actors speaking Dothraki or High Valyrian or Castithan or whatever make a mistake, who would know but the creator? Who would care? The truth is probably one in a thousand people will notice, and of those who do, maybe a quarter will care. In the 1980s that amounts to nothing. In the new millennium, though, one quarter of 0.001 percent can constitute a significant minority on Twitter. Or on Tumblr. Or Facebook. Or Reddit. Or on whatever other social media service is currently taking the internet by storm. To take a recent (at the time of writing) example, there was *Frozen* fan fiction and fan art circulating the internet *before the movie had even premiered*—and when it did premiere, it took a matter of hours for everyone to learn that Kristoff's boots weren't properly fastened, and that this was a big deal as it was disrespectful to the Sami people and their culture.

One of the most significant things about our new interconnected world is that the internet can amplify a minority voice exponentially. Yes, few people, comparatively speaking, will care if an actor makes a mistake with their conlang lines. But thanks to the internet, those few people will find each other, and when they do, they'll be capable of making a *big* noise. Every single aspect of every single production on the big and small screen is analyzed and reanalyzed the world over—and in real time. Every level of every production is being held to a higher standard, and audiences are growing savvier by the day. Language—created or otherwise—is no exception. In order to meet the heightened expectations of audiences everywhere, we have to raise the bar for languages created for any purpose. After all, if we don't, we'll hear about it.

Though it might seem like language creation is a recent phenomenon, with the success of shows like *Game of Thrones* and films like *Avatar*, the conscious construction of language is probably as old as language itself. The earliest record we have of a consciously constructed language is Hildegard von Bingen's *Lingua Ignota* (Latin for "unknown language"), which was developed some time in the twelfth century CE. The abbess's creation wasn't a language proper, but rather a vocabulary list of just over a thousand words (most of them nouns). Hildegard developed this "language" for use in song, dropping Lingua Ignota words into Latin sentences for, presumably, a specific kind of religio-aesthetic effect. The words, for the most part, look quite a bit different from either German or Latin, and feature an overrepresentation of the letter *z* (cf. *Aigonz* "God," *sunchzil* "shoemaker," *pasiz* "leprosy")—and she wasn't shy about creating words for concepts that were . . . less than holy (e.g. *amzglizia* "male pudendum," *fragizlanz* "female pudendum," *zirzer* "anus," *maluizia* "prostitute"—the full list is fascinating).

The inspiration for Hildegard's creation came, she believed, directly from God. The same is true for other projects found before the sixteenth century, such as Balaibalan, created in Turkey sometime in the fifteenth century. The impetus for the creation of these languages was always external and supernatural. As far as we know, no one had yet created a language for any other purpose.

Around the sixteenth century, a new type of language began to emerge: the philosophical language. These languages were born of philosophers and scientists who saw problems with our languages (in particular, the arbitrary association between form and meaning), and sought to correct them. Of these types of languages, John

Wilkins' philosophical language is likely the most famous example (though Ro from the twentieth century is a significant improvement on the concept). Using an example reproduced by Jorge Luis Borges, in Wilkins' language, if *de* is the word for an element, then *deb* is the first or primary among the elements (i.e. fire), and *deba* is a part of the first of all the elements (i.e. a flame). Cave Beck had a different take on a potential universal philosophical language in 1657 which made use of numbers. Taking his favorite example, *3*, which has to do with the concept of abatement, *p3* is a man who abates; *pf3* is a woman who abates; *r3* is abatement; *x3* is the act of abating, and so forth. Another favorite: if *q317* is bold, then *qq317* is bolder and *qqq317* is boldest, but there it stops. I think he really missed out here, as it would be incredible to describe a mighty warrior as *qqqqqqqqqqqqqqqqqqqqqqqqqq317* (it just makes sense).

Generally, the goal of philosophical experiments such as these was to perfect language for the purposes of science. If language can obscure intention, on account of metaphor, idioms, and vagueness, then a precise language would be of vital and obvious value to the entire scientific community. As it happened, though, none of the philosophical languages from this era ever caught on, albeit not on account of a lack of effort on the part of their creators.

The entire character of the created languages discussion changed forever in the nineteenth century, though, with the advent of the concept of the international auxiliary language (IAL). Philosophical languages were intended to be precise, but not necessarily easy to learn or use (indeed, using languages featuring categorization systems such as those employed by Beck and Wilkins proved quite cumbersome). An IAL, by contrast, is created to be as simple to learn and use as possible, so that it can be learned and used by large numbers of people across the world—those who would otherwise share no common language.

Though at the time of printing there have been easily more than a thousand IALs produced, the two earliest successes were Volapük (1879) and Esperanto (1887). Volapük, created by German priest Johann Martin Schleyer, was the first IAL to gain major notoriety. Schleyer derived its vocabulary from English, German, and French, and intended for the words to be both recognizable and easy to pronounce. He was marginally successful in this regard, with, for example, the name of the language itself coming from two English words: *vol* from "world" and *pük* from "speak." As the language gained a following, there were some who wanted to change the language (e.g. simplifying some of the tenses, getting rid of the vowels *ä*, *ü* and *ö*, adding *r*, etc.). Schleyer resisted any attempt to change the language, and insisted on maintaining complete control over its character and use. Splinter groups rose up creating knockoff versions of Volapük, and before long, the language had practically no following.

Part of its downfall, though, was no doubt due to the ascension of newcomer Esperanto, created by Ludwik Lejzer Zamenhof. In contrast to Schleyer's methods in presenting Volapük, Zamenhof published his initial grammar of Esperanto under a pseudonym (Doktoro Esperanto—whence the name of the language), and laid no claims on the language's use or distribution. He eschewed copyright, and said that the language was his gift to the world. As a consequence, when splinter groups arose, it was the community itself, rather than Zamenhof, that decided what to do. This led to a major schism, with the majority of Esperantists adhering to Zamenhof's original conception of the language, and a minority splitting off and forming the Ido language: a modification of Esperanto. Both languages continue to enjoy success to this day, though Esperanto takes the lion's share.

The success of Esperanto, in particular, gave rise to innumerable attempts at a simpler or more international auxiliary language. General enthusiasm for the widespread use of an IAL was quelled primarily by the world wars, but interest in their construction has, if anything, increased over time, with new ones popping up online almost every month. None have achieved the success that Esperanto has, and it seems unlikely that any will ever do so—let alone achieve the goal of all IALs, which is to become the world's default auxiliary language.

The next wave of language creation began in the twentieth century, and is known as the artistic language (or artlang) movement. Though early works of fantasy or satire would often feature bits of supposedly fictional languages (cf. Jonathan Swift, James Cabell,

Lord Dunsany, E. R. Eddison), none of these snippets were languages in the proper sense—they enjoy no existence outside the books they're found in, and are largely haphazard or circumstantial in construction. The same is true of the work of Edgar Rice Burroughs, though in his works there's a bit more linguistic material throughout. The first widely known author to use a more or less fully constructed language was J. R. R. Tolkien, who set the bar very high.

Unlike other authors before him—or most who would claim him as an inspiration afterward—Tolkien was a language creator before he penned his major works. In a way, the languages themselves served as the progenitors to the tales. He understood that language itself is inseparable from the culture that produces it (or "mythology," as he put it), and he felt that if the languages he was creating had no place to breathe, they wouldn't have any kind of vitality. Arda became the place where his languages could live, and so his legendarium was born.

In addition to being the first person on record to create a full language for a fictional context, Tolkien also did something no other language creator had done to that point: he created a language *family*. Quenya and Sindarin, his two most famous languages, descend from a common ancestor, Quendian, and themselves have languages that have descended from them, and other languages to which they are related. This is precisely how natural languages evolve in our world, and would naturally be appropriate for a fictional setting that has an alternate history with any kind of time depth similar to ours on Earth. The concept, though, was a novel one, and not fully appreciated in Tolkien's time, as his works of fiction overshadowed his contributions to the history of conlanging.

There were other notable artistic conlang achievements in the twentieth century (for example M. A. R. Barker's creations for the *Empire of the Petal Throne* role-playing game, or Christian Vander's Kobaïan, used in song lyrics by his band Magma—even Vladimir Nabokov created a conlang sketch for his masterwork *Pale Fire*), but none attracted the attention that Tolkien's work did. It was only a matter of time before the phenomenon moved to film and television. Early films and shows would often use ad hoc invented vocabulary for fictional foreign nations (cf. early episodes of *Danger Man*), or for languages the filmmakers didn't want to bother to reproduce faithfully (cf. *Thoroughly Modern Millie*). A handful of films used actual Esperanto, with the most prominent (or infamous) example being the film *Incubus*, starring William Shatner. According to fluent Esperanto speakers who've seen it, the Esperanto is atrocious. Otherwise there was no noteworthy conlang work in a film or show before 1974's *Land of the Lost*, which featured an invented language its creator called Paku (often referred to as Pakuni). Paku was created by UCLA linguist Victoria Fromkin, who was hired specifically for this purpose. Though a few dedicated fans have attempted to take down what little they can hear of the language in the show, the producers clearly didn't think it was in their best interest to publicize the language the way conlangs attached to modern franchises are publicized, which is a pity. The creation of the Paku language was an important event in the history of conlanging, for unless there are other instances that haven't yet come to light, this was the first time in history that an individual had been hired to create a language.

The idea of hiring out for a language was repeated a few times in the late twentieth century—most notably with Klingon, which was fleshed out by Marc Okrand for *Star Trek III: The Search for Spock*, but other notable examples exist, like Matt Pearson's Thhtmaa language for NBC's *Dark Skies*—but the wave really started to grow with the advent of the internet.

The first gathering of language creators—either virtual or in person—occurred on July 29, 1991. That's the date of the first ever message sent to the Conlang Listserv: an online listserv dedicated to those who created languages. The original members of the listserv met on Usenet, and decided to create their own listserv just for language inventors. When they created it, the listserv needed a name, so they took the first syllable of "constructed" and the first syllable of "language" and created "conlang." Thus the word "conlang" was born. At the time, there were a number of competing terms for an invented language—planned language, model language, artificial language, created language, ideal language—but conlang was the one that eventually won out, and which now has made its way into the *Oxford English Dictionary*. The portmanteau strategy proved useful for coining words for other types of conlangs, and so new terms began to spring up: artlang, loglang, engelang, auxlang, altlang, lostlang, jokelang . . . At this point, -*lang* could probably be considered a fairly productive derivational suffix.

The constructed languages listserv was originally run from the Boston University physics department by a fellow named John Ross, before it was moved to the Datalogisk Institut in Denmark, where it stayed for a bit. When it could no longer be housed there, though, David Durand, one of the original members, used his alumni connections from Brown University to get the list a permanent home there, where it remains to this day.

Though the original list members probably didn't realize it at the time, the founding of the Conlang Listserv (hereafter Conlang) was a momentous occurrence in the history of language creation. Aside from contentious gatherings devoted to how to improve a specific auxiliary language, there had never before in history been a place where those who created languages would discuss strategies for doing so. For the first time language creators could compare their work to something other than Tolkien's languages or Esperanto and its many imitators.

Of course, like any community, Conlang had its rocky moments. While many Conlang members were interested primarily in sharing their own work and learning from others who would share theirs, a sizable contingent were advocates of one of a number of IALs: Esperanto, Novial, Volapük, or creations of their own. Arguments would often break out over which was the best language, and which should be supported as the one language that all the world should speak. As a result of the constant bickering, in 1996 a separate listserv was created—the Auxlang Listserv—and advocacy of *any* language was banned from Conlang. Instead, discussion on Conlang would be specifically devoted to sharing non–auxiliary language work, and discussing strategies related specifically to language creation.

This proved to be a real turning point for the craft, as Conlang began to accrue more and more members and develop its own traditions thereafter. In the summer of 1999, Irina Rempt, creator of Valdyan, initiated the first conlang relay. In a conlang relay, the first participant writes a text in their conlang, and then passes on the text, grammatical notes, and a lexicon to the next participant. This next participant has forty-eight hours to use those materials to decode the text and then must translate it themselves into their own conlang, passing the text on with translation materials, and so forth, until all participants have had their turn with the text (called the "torch"). The resulting texts are often ridiculous, which is part of the fun. Here, for example, is the first line of the original text of the thirteenth conlang relay, which was composed by Henrik Theiling in his a posteriori language Da Mätz se Basa:

An ein Muin äna Monat Wöpf kan ana da Drot s ano Bant fona Bos bänti s Urt da lei se Zän is sä ze.

And here's its translation:

One morning in December I could watch the following scene across the street from a bus stop:

Now here's the rest of the text translated:

A boy, obviously on his way to school, stood in front of a garden wall. He had an enormous red tomcat on his shoulder and this animal balanced skillfully while the boy tried hard to shake him off. With increasing panic he watched the bus stop knowing the bus would be due any second now . . . The cat was quite undisturbed. Once, he put a paw on the wall, but seemingly it felt too cold, so he quickly retreated to the boy's backpack. The moment when he was comfortably sitting, having tucked up his legs, the school bus arrived.

I suppose the cat spent quite an interesting day.

Now here's the first line of the final translation of this same text into Minza by Herman Miller:

Vyø jenzelu kaikat, seła køvu nintel vonyli rukumen røǧisit.

Here's the first line translated:

> Before the sun came out, a messenger woman was walking along bringing messages in a cart.

Now here's the rest of the text translated:

> She paused briefly as the cart arrived near the path which led to the market place, but then she disturbed an animal, which growled at her. The messenger woman held up a branch of a tree, and approached near the cougar.
>
> Wanting to avoid danger, the messenger woman was anxious about the cougar, so she stopped far from him, but tried to obtain his trust. She gave a portion of food to the playful cougar. She thought he would approach the cart, but the shameful cougar wanted more food! It began to rain, the woman holding the branch, so she wanted to stay far away from the cougar.
>
> With the branch of a tree, she protected herself quite well from the cougar. From there the messenger woman reached the end of the path with her cart. After that day when she set out, the growl of the cougar has made more women and more men nervous.

The stories are absurd, but the practice is useful. Members of Conlang have found dozens of ways to test out their languages over the years, improving them as they go along. For example, translating the "Babel Text" (Genesis 11:1–9) became a standard stress test for a new conlang, thanks to the website Langmaker.com, created by Jeffrey Henning, which hosted various conlangs' translations of the Babel Text.

Conlang continued to grow and expand, until soon splinter communities began to emerge—including communities that held discussions in languages other than English (e.g. Ideolengua, the first Spanish-language conlang community). The various communities attracted some of the best language creators on the planet, and also produced a new generation of conlangers, of which I was one, whose conlanging heroes weren't Tolkien or Zamenhof or Okrand, but other conlangers like Sally Caves, Sylvia Sotomayor, and Matt

Pearson—names widely known and respected within the conlanging community, but virtually unknown without. To date, the best languages ever created were not created for television series or movies, but were created just for the joy of it—languages like Sally Caves' Teonaht, Doug Ball's Skerre, Sylvia Sotomayor's Kēlen, Matt Pearson's Okuna (formerly Tokana), Andrew Smith's Brithenig, John Quijada's Ithkuil, Carsten Becker's Ayeri, and David Bell's ámman îar, to name a few among hundreds.

A key feature of some of the best languages I've seen in that time—including all those listed here—is that they changed crucially as a result of contact with the community. This is the natural result of community in the most abstract sense. Consider: What artist never looks at any paintings but their own? What musician never listens to any music but the music they create? Yet this was precisely the state of conlanging prior to 1991. Some will have heard of Esperanto or Tolkien or Klingon, but a majority believed that they were the first person *ever* to create a language. For example, I believed I was the first one ever to create a language for purposes other than international communication—and that was in 2000. Part of this was due to a general lack of awareness, but part is also due to the nature of the activity.

Hobbies are what they are. People do things because they find them fun. Some hobbies can eventually lead to something bigger (painting, writing, sculpting, sports, etc.). Conlanging is a hobby that, even as late as 2009, no one in the conlanging community believed would amount to anything real. Part of this comes from older conlangers' personal histories. Parents who found their children creating languages would consider the practice so bizarre that they believed it to be indicative of some sort of mental disorder. Esperantists and other auxlang advocates considered the practice counterproductive and silly. Linguists would, at turns, either dismiss or deride the practice (one of the earliest works by a linguist that discusses conlanging in any depth is Marina Yaguello's 1984 work *Les Fous du Langage*, or *Lunatic Lovers of Language*, which is precisely as insightful as it sounds). On Conlang, members took to talking about their language creation using the same terms homosexuals would to talk about their homosexuality. Revealing to one's parents, friends, or colleagues that one conlangs is still referred to as "coming out."

The truth, of course, is that language creation is just a thing (and I mean that in *the* most prosaic sense). Conlanging is an activity that harms neither the conlanger nor the world around them. If anything, there's an intrinsic benefit in engaging with linguistic material—created or otherwise—as it exercises the parts of the brain that use language, and gives conlangers a bit more of an open mind when they encounter languages other than those they speak natively. Even so, a lifetime of negative feedback has left its mark on the community, which has been tolerant of praise, but allergic to criticism, constructive or otherwise.

This lack of judgment was a key feature of the early Conlang community. Reactions to a piece of art are subjective, of course, but just as with any activity that requires any amount of skill or ingenuity, certain elements of language creation can be measured objectively. The community has routinely rejected any calls for objective measurement of any kind—or any criticism other than positive feedback. The thinking was that if this was a place where a conlanger could actually be themself, it should be a zone free of judgment. In many ways, this has helped to foster growth, but it's also hindered the development of the craft.

What I would advocate is a goal-driven approach to conlang evaluation. That is, when one creates a language, one creates it for a number of reasons. Those reasons will determine the character of the language and the nature of what would amount to acceptable criticism. For example, if one creates a language for personal use and for no other reason, then the only acceptable criticism will come from the creator alone; all other criticism is immaterial. That shouldn't be true of a language created for television or film. The constraints will differ, as paid language creators have to bow to the whims of producers, directors, and writers, and generally don't have as much time to develop their work as a conlanger working for themself, but within those constraints, criticism is appropriate— and healthy for the community. If a language has been developed for a fictional race of people in an otherwise realistic setting, the language should likewise be as realistic as possible. Does such a language appear to be naturalistic in all respects? If not, how could it be improved—how might it appear more authentic? These are good questions to ask, and good examples to learn from.

Which brings us to today—and the conlangers of today. Up until, say, around 2004, I could confidently say that if there was anyone online who had even dabbled in language creation, I had heard of them and of their language, and could list a couple of key traits of that language. The community was tight-knit, and even though it had branched off a bit, everyone still was able to keep tabs on everyone else, for the most part. In 2015, this is beyond impossible. Not only is it impossible to know every language creator, it's not even possible to know every language creation community. There are conlangers active on Tumblr, Twitter, and Facebook who have no connection to any of the original communities—and they're drawing inspiration from languages that didn't exist even five years ago. And while this is great, the newest conlangers lack any means of evaluation or instruction. They know the word "conlang," but have never heard of the Conlang Listserv. They know Na'vi, but have never heard of Moten. They've never had to defend their work as not being a serious attempt to create a new universal language—the first accusation most artlang creators faced when presenting their new language on the web back in the nineties. They're a new breed, and share none of the same assumptions that the early Conlang crowd did. This means they don't have the hangups older conlangers do, but also that they lack the history—and, most important, the knowledge—accrued over years of steady interaction.

When I get an email from someone who's eager to create their own language and wants to know where to begin, I have a tough time explaining what it is they should do. I think my conlang education was good, for what it was, but what exactly did it entail? I joined the Conlang Listserv and spent a decade there sharing my work, learning from others, and learning more about language. Should everyone have to do the same? Where is the collected wisdom of the early conlang community? Why is it not written down somewhere that if you're creating a naturalistic ergative language, it will most likely be split ergative, and that those splits will happen in one of a small number of likely places in the grammar? This is something that every conlanger knows or eventually learns, but the information is only passed via word of mouth—it's like we're living in the 1300s, but we also have the internet and indoor plumbing!

This work is a sincere attempt to give new conlangers a place to start by detailing what things I take into account when creating a language. It won't answer every question (no single book could hope to hold every scrap of information one needs to know to create a good language), but it should allow new conlangers to get a sense of the craft, and avoid having to reinvent every wheel that the conlang community as a whole has created and perfected over the last quarter century. My aim is to help conlangers avoid expending mental energy on some of the nuts and bolts of language creation so they can focus on the more important question: What do I want to say with this new language that I can't say in my native language—or any other language that currently exists?

Before I get into the meat of the text, let me discuss some top-level terminology that will apply to the work as a whole. Many battles have been won and lost on the internet when it comes to conlang terminology, but we've reached a point where there is broad agreement about certain terms, so I'd like to set them down here in print in order to add some stability to the debate. Here are some terms you'll need to know going through every section of the book (other terminology relevant to specific chapters will be discussed in those chapters):

- **Conlang:** The term *conlang* is short for "constructed language," and is the consensus term for a created language. It was coined some time before the Conlang Listserv was founded in 1991, and has increased in use as the primary English term for a created language since then. Any language that has been *consciously* created by one or more individuals in its fullest form is a conlang, so long as either the intent or the result of the creation process is a fully functional linguistic system. This includes Esperanto, Quenya, Dothraki, Lojban, and Lingua Ignota, but doesn't include modern revitalization projects like Modern Hawaiian, Modern Cornish, and Modern Hebrew—nor does it include creole languages like Tok Pisin, Bislama, or Saramaccan.

- **Natlang:** A natlang is a natural language (both terms are in regular use), which is any of the languages that happen to exist in the world and evolved naturally. This includes any spoken language, creole or otherwise (Spanish, Ainu, Moro, Estonian, Kituba . . .), as well as signed languages (ASL, FSL, BSL, TSL, etc.). It also includes revitalization projects like Modern Hawaiian and Modern Hebrew, and dead languages like Latin and Akkadian. The point of emphasis is the nature of the origin of the system. Languages that began their existence by an act of conscious creation will share important features in common with other created languages that they won't share with natural languages. Consequently, even though Esperanto is now spoken natively by speakers all over the world, it's still important to understand that it began as a created language, and that, as a result, there's a reason it looks the way it does.

- **Fictional Language:** A fictional language is a language that's supposed to exist in a given fictional context. For example, in the *Star Wars* scene I referred to above, Leia is supposed to be speaking the Ubese language to Jabba the Hutt. Similarly, the Dothraki language I created for *Game of Thrones* was created to be a real language in the *Song of Ice and Fire* fictional universe. Although in the real world Ubese is a sketch and Dothraki is a fully developed conlang, both are supposed to be real in their respective fictional contexts.

- **Real Language:** A real language is one that actually exists, regardless of its status. Conlangs and natural languages are both real languages, because they actually exist in our world—or exist to the fullest extent that a language *can* exist. (After all, languages aren't objects: they're ideas, or patterns of behavior. If all English speakers remain silent for a few minutes the world over, the language still exists.)

- **Fake Language:** Like Ubese, a fake language is one that's meant to give the impression of a real language in some context without actually being a real language. For example, I could tell you that I went to Finland and saw a sign that read *Kioriluvinen tääriällinä hänäskä*, which means "Leave your skis outside," and unless you knew I've never been to Finland, you might think, "Yeah, that's Finnish, I guess." Of course, it's entirely made up. It's based on nothing but my knowledge of the phonology and orthography of Finnish. Consequently, it's fake language—or fake language material. A conlang is *not* a fake language. It may not be large, but that just means it's not finished yet. Do not call a conlang a fake language. Those who do only make themselves look foolish.

- **Code:** I'll also include here "cipher" and "language game." All of these are systems that are created to hide meaning from those who don't know the system—like the message about drinking Ovaltine in *A Christmas Story* (oh—spoiler alert). A key feature of all codes and ciphers is that they must *crucially* depend on another language in order to work. Take Pig Latin (e.g. *ake-tay ig-pay atin-lay*). No one will "get" Pig Latin if it's based on a system no one knows (e.g. *iss-ray azdozgit-may ifthuliar-kay*). The point is to have an in-group and an out-group, with the in-group understanding the trick that will help them turn the cipher back into the original language. Consequently, none of these things are conlangs. Pig Latin, for example, is nothing more than a bizarre, uncooperative way of speaking English.

- **Jargon:** Once every couple of years a news report will emerge about a company where they speak their own "language." What all of these reports end up pointing out is that any community of individuals will come up with a subset of vocabulary particular to their environment and experiences, and outsiders won't know this vocabulary. This is why those who've seen *Office Space* will know the term "TPS report," and those who haven't won't—or how a Hester is a term for returning a successful roll (or "through") in Gentlemen's Roll, a game my friends and I invented (patent pending). Crucially, no matter how many terms are invented, the language that they're used in is English. I can say something like, "We thoroughfared seven bolsters before the LFC structural last middleseven," and everyone can see that it's still English. No one will know what an LFC structural is, but it's clearly some sort of event. You have to be able to speak English in order for any of this to work, though, so vocabulary subsets like these are not actually separate languages.

- **Dialect:** An instantiation of a language is a dialect. Every human on Earth speaks a dialect of their own language. Your particular version of your language is called your idiolect (for example, I pronounce "both" with an "l" [i.e. "bolth"], and always have. Why? Because I do. Deal with it). A dialect isn't a "type" of language—that is, it's not as if some people will speak the English language, and others will speak a dialect of English. *Everyone* who speaks English speaks a dialect of English. That some dialects have higher prestige than others is an unfortunate by-product of social inequality and history. In the eyes of linguists, all dialects are equal, in that they all achieve the functional requirements of linguistic interaction.

- **Artlang:** Short for "artistic language," this is a conlang created for aesthetic, fictional, or otherwise artistic purposes. Pete Bleackley's Khangaþyagon is an example of an artlang.

- **Auxlang:** Short for "auxiliary language," this is a conlang created for international communication (or sometimes for communication among a specific subset of the populace, as with Jan van Steenbergen's pan-Slavic auxlang Slovianski).

- **Engelang:** Short for "engineered language," this is a conlang created to achieve some specific type of linguistic effect (e.g. to create a language without verbs, as with Sylvia Sotomayor's Kēlen, or to create a language that uses LIFO grammar, as with Jeffrey Henning's Fith).

- **Conlanger:** Someone who creates a language—especially someone who engages in language creation regularly.

- **Linguist:** An individual employed by an academic linguistics or philology department who engages in the scientific study of language. (Important: This is *not* a synonym for "conlanger.")

- **A Priori:** An a priori conlang is one whose grammar and vocabulary are not based on existing languages. Sondiv, which I created for the CW's *Star-Crossed*, is an example of an a priori conlang.

- **A Posteriori:** An a posteriori conlang is one whose grammar and vocabulary are drawn from an existing source. Esperanto is an example of an a posteriori conlang.

- **Translation:** Translation is the practice of rendering the content of a clause from one language into a different one. Here, for example, is a sentence of Castithan translated into English:

°ᗩ᙮ᘯᕀ ᓬᕑ ᓬᙯᑫᕼ ᕁᕘ ᕽᑊᓬᕑ ᘔᕒᓯᕼ°

The boy appreciated the flower.

Translation does not take into account anything about the clause's original language: it simply renders the meaning in a different one.

- **Transcription:** Transcription takes the text of one language and puts it into a form that's readable by a person who speaks a language that uses a different orthography—or into a neutral orthography. For example, here's the same Castithan sentence from above first transcribed in a romanization system that can be more or less understood by English speakers, and then in the International Phonetic Alphabet, used by linguists and dictionaries throughout the world:

°ᗩ᙮ᘯᕀ ᓬᕑ ᓬᙯᑫᕼ ᕁᕘ ᕽᑊᓬᕑ ᘔᕒᓯᕼ°

Fahazwa re rutsaye'ke zwore giopsa.
ˈfa.ha.zwa.ɾe ˈru.tsa.je.ke ˈzwo.ɾe ˈgi.o.psa

Transcription may take into account some of the conventions of the original language's writing system or its phonology, but it is *not* a translation. It's simply a method of rendering the same text in a different writing system.

- **Gloss:** A gloss (also referred to as an interlinear) gives the reader an idea what each word in a clause means, and/or what role it plays in the sentence. Combining actual language data with a transcription, translation, and gloss is crucial in determining not only what data in another language means, but *how* it means what it means. Below are two different ways of glossing the same sentence of Castithan used above (the latter with more detailed information than the former):

Boy flower appreciated.
Boy SBJ flower LOC good remain-PST.

A gloss often provides a reader with more information about a given sentence, but is less comprehensible than a full translation. In presenting language data, using both a gloss and a translation is standard practice.

Again, as more terminology is needed, it will be introduced. Otherwise, as the Dothraki would say, *dothralates*: Let's ride!

CHAPTER I

Sounds

INTRODUCTION

When I was hired to create Dothraki for *Game of Thrones*, I didn't get many notes from the producers. Really there were only two things they wanted from the Dothraki language: (1) They wanted it to incorporate all the words George R. R. Martin had created in his books, and (2) they wanted it to sound harsh.

Harsh.

What does that mean when it comes to a language? Jason Momoa has described Dothraki as sounding like German. Many have described it as sounding like Arabic; a few like Russian. Most English speakers I've run into agree, though, that it sounds harsh. Why?

One tack might be to compare the languages that Dothraki is compared to. What sounds do they have in common? Quite a few, actually. Arabic, Russian, and German have all of these sounds in common: *b, s, z, sh, k, l, m, n, a, i* . . . Even more than that. Does having an *m* in a language make it sound harsh? Probably not. Almost every language on the planet has an *m* sound. In fact, a lot of languages feature those sounds listed above—including English—so perhaps we need to try something different. What sounds do Arabic, Russian, and German have in common that English lacks? Turns out it's only one sound, and its phonetic transcription is [x]. You'll often see it spelled *kh* and referred to as a "throaty" sound like the *ch* in German *Bach*. And, indeed, that does seem like a pretty "harsh" sound to an English speaker. It's so . . . clearing-your-throat-sound-y. That must be it! The presence of that sound makes a language harsh.

But hang on. You know what other languages have that sound (or if not that sound exactly, something very, very close to that sound)? Spanish and French. It's true. The *j* in the Spanish name *Javier* is pronounced pretty much exactly like the *ch* in German *Bach*. And the French *r* comes out as an even throatier version of this sound in words like *trente*, "thirty," and *produit*, "product." Do you know *any* English speaker who's ever described either French or Spanish as "harsh" or "throaty" or "guttural"?

Clearly there's more at work here than the presence or absence of a sound or two. In addition to the history of cultural stereotyping, which certainly plays a role, it's the comparison of entire sound systems that produces a phonaesthetic character in the mind of the listener: the sounds present, the way they're combined, the intonational phrasing, and the rate of speech—plus a number of sociological factors. All of this is compared with the sound systems present in the mind of a speaker. So German may sound harsh to an American English speaker, but might not to a Dutch speaker from the Netherlands.

Even if the judgments are subjective, a conlanger can use the expectations of their users/hearers to achieve a particular phonaesthetic effect. In this chapter, I'll demonstrate how I've done that with some of my languages, and what's involved.

For the most part, I will be focusing on how to construct naturalistic sound systems or **phonologies**, which is what I've spent the bulk of my conlanging career doing. At the end, though, I will touch on sign language phonology and what one might do if one were to construct an alien sound system. As a general note, when a conlanger begins to create a language, they can start anywhere. I like to start with the sounds, though, so that's where we'll begin.

PHONETICS

All spoken languages on Earth use a small subset of the possible sounds a human can produce. For example, an English word like *lava* is pretty understandable: you've got an *l* sound, a nice open *a* vowel, a *v* sound, and then a kind of reduced *a* sound. Even though languages will use different sounds, it wouldn't be surprising to find that type of word in any given language. It would be odd to find a word like *laŝa* in a language. How do you pronounce *laŝa*? Pretty much like *lava*, except instead of putting a *v* sound in between the *a* vowels, you clap your hands together once. So *l-a-CLAP!-a*. No natural language on Earth does this, except in songs or language games (remember that dog Bingo?). There's no reason why a language couldn't do this (it'd be fairly simple to incorporate it into a language. Try replacing the sound *f* with a clap in English. Takes practice, but you can do it), it's simply the case that natural spoken languages don't.

Instead, oral languages utilize sounds made with the mouth, throat, tongue, nose, and lungs. In this section I'll introduce you to those sounds, with examples from both natlangs and conlangs. First, though, I want to talk a bit about transcription.

In English, we use a number of sounds to convey meaning. Sometimes, though, the same sound will be pronounced differently, even if we're completely unaware of it. Try this test out yourself. Put your hand right in front of your mouth and pronounce the word *tall*. Do it a few times. You should feel a nice puff of air on your palm. Now try pronouncing the word *stall*. Focus on the *t*. Notice anything different? Try saying the pair *tall/stall* a few times. You should notice that that puff of air you feel when you pronounce *tall* is totally absent when you pronounce *stall*. And, in fact, even though we would call both of those *t* in English, the sounds are different. The *t* in *stall* is a regular *t* which we would transcribe this way: [t]. The *t* in *tall*, though, is an aspirated *t*, and we would transcribe it like this: [tʰ]. That tiny little superscript ʰ tells you that the sound is pronounced with an accompanying puff of air. When we write English, we don't bother noting the difference because English speakers don't distinguish the sounds. In phonetics, though, we do make a note of the difference, since even though it doesn't produce a meaningful distinction in English, it does in some languages.

Here, for example, are two different words of the Hindi language spoken in India (ignore the funny tail on the *t*; we'll get to that):

टीक [ʈik] "teak"

ठीक [tʰik] "okay"

These two words differ only in one respect: the [ʈ] for the Hindi word for "okay" is aspirated (i.e. [tʰ]) and [ʈ] for the Hindi word for "teak" is not. So even though the distinction between [t] and [tʰ] isn't meaningful in English, such distinctions can be meaningful in other languages. This is probably why the two versions of *t* are spelled differently in Hindi (ट vs. ठ), but they aren't in English.

The spelling you see above in between brackets is what's known as **phonetic transcription**. Any time in this book that you see words in between brackets [ ], it means that, more or less, this is *exactly* how the word is pronounced, and that the word will be written in the **International Phonetic Alphabet (IPA)**. The IPA is a special alphabet used by linguists to transcribe any and all sounds made with the human vocal tract, regardless of native spelling systems. Phonetic transcription of this type contrasts with **phonemic transcription**, which gives you the most crucial phonetic information of a word but leaves out some of the details. Below, for example, is the English word *tall* in phonemic and phonetic transcription:

/tɑl/

[tʰɑɬ]

Notice that the phonemic transcription (which is always given between forward slashes) leaves off the aspiration marker ʰ. This is because it's considered to be a predictable pronunciation detail. The same isn't true of the aspiration in Hindi, which is not predictable. Here's the same transcription for the Hindi word for "okay":

/tʰik/

[tʰik]

They're the same, because the aspiration is a crucial factor in determining the meaning of the word in Hindi.

When I sit down to create a new language, I start with the phonetic level of detail. That is, I draw from *all* possible human sounds before narrowing it down and deciding which ones will be important for distinguishing meaning. I'll now take you on a tour of some of the plethora of sounds humans can make with their mouths.

ORAL PHYSIOLOGY

Before we can talk about sounds, we have to talk a bit about what humans use to produce oral sounds. Below is what someone would look like if you sliced them in half from the top of their skull to their shoulders (perhaps with a sharpened hat, à la Kung Lao from *Mortal Kombat*).

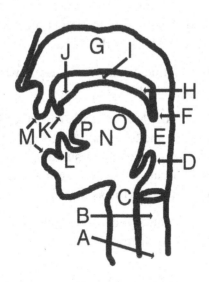

Each of those spots labeled above is referenced in the production of speech sounds. In order to produce a speech sound, in addition to making use of an airstream mechanism, there is an **active articulator** and a **passive articulator**. The active articulator is the part of the mouth that moves to form a constriction. The passive articulator is the part of the mouth that the active articulator either touches or gets near to in order to produce the sound.

Below is a correspondence set of all the points in the mouth with the adjectival form of the word appearing in parentheses next to each noun (where necessary, further explication is given after the adjectival form):

A. Lungs (air coming from the lungs is referred to as *pulmonic*)

B. Larynx (laryngeal)

C. Glottis (glottal): At the bottom of the windpipe, the glottis is the space between the vocal folds.

D. Epiglottis (epiglottal): This is a little flap that closes when we swallow in order to ensure that food goes into the stomach and not the lungs.

E. Pharynx (pharyngeal): This is essentially the back of the throat.

F. Uvula (uvular): This is the little punching bag–like thing that hangs down at the back of the throat.

G. Nasal Cavity (sounds that feature air flowing through the nasal cavity are called *nasal*)

H. Velum (velar): The velum raises (i.e. closes) to block the passage between the nose and lungs, and lowers (i.e. opens) to allow air to flow from the nose to the lungs and vice versa. When we breathe through our noses, the velum is lowered. (Note: Also referred to sometimes as the *soft palate*.)

I. Hard Palate (palatal): Directly in front of the velum, this is often referred to as the roof of the mouth.

J. Alveolar Ridge (sounds produced using the alveolar ridge as a passive articulator are referred to as *alveolar*): The little bump directly behind your two front teeth.

K. Upper Teeth (sounds produced using the upper teeth as a passive articulator and the tongue as an active articulator are referred to as *dental*; sounds produced using the upper teeth as a passive articulator and the lower lip as an active articulator are referred to as *labiodental*)

L. Lower Teeth (dentolabial)

M. Lips (sounds involving the lips in some way are referred to as *labial*; sounds crucially involving both lips are referred to as *bilabial*)

N. Tongue (lingual)

O. Tongue blade (laminal): This is defined as the part of the tongue behind the tip.

P. Tongue tip (apical)

This may seem like a lot of terms to keep track of, but honestly, velar (soft palate from which the uvula hangs), alveolar (bump behind the two front teeth), labial (lips), and palatal (roof of the mouth) are the words you'll end up using the most. Feel free to bookmark this page, but I promise you by the time you get to page 90, you'll have this down (unless you decide to skip directly to page 90; that's cheating, and I guarantee nothing to a cheater).

CONSONANTS

All sounds are produced either by having air pass out of the lungs and through the mouth, or by utilizing some sort of alternate air source that we can manipulate. Without force of some kind, no noise is produced (aside from the teeny tiny noises produced by having your organs move about). A **consonant** is a sound that puts some sort of obstruction in the way of the airflow, thereby changing the current and producing a different sound. Depending on how the current is affected, one can produce different types of sounds. The major divisions are listed below:

- **Oral Stops:** An oral stop is produced when airflow through the mouth is interrupted completely (i.e. stopped), and the velum is raised, allowing no air to pass through the nose.

- **Fricative:** A fricative is produced when a tight constriction is formed somewhere in the mouth. Forcing the air through this tight constriction produces turbulent airflow which we interpret as different types of sounds.

- **Affricate:** A sound that begins as an oral stop but is released as a fricative.

- **Nasal Stops:** A nasal stop is produced when airflow through the mouth is interrupted completely, but the velum is lowered, thus allowing air to pass through the nose.

- **Approximant:** An approximant occurs when the active articulator (the tongue or lips) approaches a position, but never forms a tight enough constriction to produce a fricative, resulting in a "liquid"-like sound. (Note: These sounds are also called glides.)

- **Flap/Tap:** Referred to using either word, a flap or tap occurs when an active articulator is catapulted against a passive articulator.

- **Trill:** A trill is when the root of an active articulator remains rigid, allowing the non-fixed portion of the articulator to flap back and forth aggressively in the airstream.

- **Lateral:** A lateral is an L-like sound that allows air to pass around the sides of the tongue.

Below is a chart of *some* of the major consonants found in the world's languages:

	Labial	Dental	Alveolar	Retroflex	Palatal	Velar	Uvular	Glottal
Oral Stop	p, b	t̪, d̪	t, d	ʈ, ɖ	c, ɟ	k, g	q, ɢ	ʔ
Fricative	f, v	θ, ð	s, z	ʂ, ʐ	ç, ʝ	x, ɣ	χ, ʁ	h, ɦ
Affricate	pf, bv	t̪θ, d̪ð	ts, dz	ʈʂ, ɖʐ	cç, ɟʝ	kx, gɣ	qχ, ɢʁ	
Nasal Stop	m	n̪	n	ɳ	ɲ	ŋ	N	
Glide	ʋ		ɹ	ɻ	j	w		
Flap/Tap			ɾ	ɽ				
Trill	ʙ		r				R	
Lateral		l̪	l	ɭ	ʎ	L		

Since this is the first time we've seen it, let me tell you why most of these cells have two members. Speech sounds feature what in linguistics we call **voicing**. Sounds may be either **voiceless** (sometimes called **unvoiced**) or **voiced**. In each of the pairs above, the voiced sound appears on the right. A quick lexical example to show us the difference between the two are the English words *staple* and *stable*. These two words differ in only one respect, and that's the voicing feature of the second stop in that word. In *staple*, we have a voiceless [p], whereas in *stable* we have a voiced [b].

If you can't pinpoint the precise difference between these two, I'd like you to perform another throat experiment. I'd like you to place your hand against your throat right in the middle just above where the Adam's apple is (this protrusion, known as the laryngeal prominence, is present in all humans; it's just larger in males). Now what I want you to do is hiss like a snake, making an [s] sound: *sssssssssss*. You should feel nothing interesting happening in your throat. While still semi-strangling yourself, I want you to do the same thing, except this time alternate between an *s* sound and a *z* sound. Something like:

sssssssszzzzzzzzzsssssssssszzzzzzzzzzsssss

If you did the above, you should notice a considerable difference. For the *s* sound, your throat should have been relatively still. During z, though, you should have noticed a remarkable vibration. This is because z is a voiced sound. In order to produce a voiced sound, the vocal folds vibrate as air passes through the glottis. When the vocal folds vibrate in tandem with the production of a speech sound, that speech sound is referred to as voiced.

Now, the chart above is a lot to digest, I know, but it's there primarily for reference. The nice thing about the IPA if you're an English speaker is that it was devised primarily by English speakers, so the letter forms should look *fairly* close to their basic English counterparts. To get you into the consonant sounds of the IPA, I'll go over the sounds of English—especially as it will require two symbols that are not present above—and then discuss sounds not found in English.

First we'll begin with the stops of English. English has these six stops:

Labial:	[p] as in *lap* [læp]	[b] as in *lab* [læb]
Alveolar:	[t] as in *sat* [sæt]	[d] as in *sad* [sæd]
Velar:	[k] as in *rack* [ɹæk]	[g] as in *rag* [ɹæg]

I want you to notice that no matter how the word is spelled, the phonetic transcription remains consistent. Even though there's a spurious c in *rack*, there's only a [k] in the transcription. IPA is used to transcribe the sound of a word, regardless of its spelling. This is important to keep in mind when examining English, whose orthography was devised by a team of misanthropic, megalomaniacal cryptographers who distrusted and despised one another, and so sought to hide the meanings they were tasked with encoding by employing crude, arcane spellings that no one can explain. (*"Ha, ha! I shall spell 'could' with an ell! They will be powerless to stop me!"*)

Before moving on to the sounds not found in English, take a look at the glottal column. Notice anything odd? [ʔ] looks pretty lonely up there, doesn't he? (And he also looks a bit like a question mark, making that last sentence look . . . clownish.) That sound is referred to as a glottal stop, and we've actually got it in English. When we say "uh-oh!" in that kind of exaggerated, mawkish way we use with children who appreciate it less and less with each passing year, we actually pronounce a glottal stop. A broad transcription of the phrase might be something like [ʌʔo]. That little catch in your throat in between the "uh" and the "oh" is a glottal stop. You'll hear it in Cockney pronunciations of words like "bottle," or in a native pronunciation of "Hawai'i." It's a good sound used in a lot of languages, but the reason there's no voiced version is that it's produced by smacking the vocal folds together. The vocal folds are what need to be vibrating in order to produce voicing. Consequently, a voiced glottal stop is impossible.

The remaining stop sounds are found in other languages. For example, the appropriate pronunciation of Spanish *t* and *d* in the words *toro* and *mande* are dental (with the tongue tip against the top teeth), rather than alveolar, as with English *t* and *d*. Retroflex [ʈ] and [ɖ], as found in Hindi, are pronounced with the tongue tip bent backward, as if you were trying to swallow the tip of your tongue. The palatal stops can be found in Hungarian, and the uvular stop [q] can be found in Dothraki and High Valyrian from *Game of Thrones*.

Fricatives are among the most diverse consonantal sounds that exist. Here are the fricatives of English:

Labial:	[f] as in *fun* [fʌn]	[v] as in *victory* [vɪktɚi]
Dental:	[θ] as in *thigh* [θaj]	[ð] as in *this* [ðɪs]
Alveolar:	[s] as in *sound* [sawnd]	[z] as in *zoo* [zuː]
Post-Alveolar:	[ʃ] as in *sheep* [ʃip]	[ʒ] as in *genre* [ʒɑnɹə]
Glottal:	[h] as in *hot* [hɑt]	

A couple of notes on these. Notice that English actually does distinguish the sounds [θ] and [ð]; it just doesn't do a very good job of it. We spell both *th*, and it's up to the speaker to realize that the pronunciations of *th* in *this* and *thin* are totally different ([ð] and [θ], respectively).

Second, you'll notice that the post-alveolar symbols [ʃ] and [ʒ] don't appear on the chart above. This is because the fricatives are the only major sounds that are produced at that point of articulation. We happen to have them in English (they also exist in French and Portuguese), and the sounds are quite common, so it's important to know their symbols: [ʃ] for *sh* and [ʒ] for the voiced version like the *s* in *vision*. They're contrasted in the pair of English words *Confucian* [kʰəɱfjuʃɨn], as in a follower of Confucius, and *confusion* [kʰəɱfjuʒɨn] (thanks to Kim Darnell for pointing this pair out to me!).

In between the post-alveolar [ʃ] and glottal [h], there are a whole host of fricatives that enjoy wide use in many non-English languages. These are the so-called throaty or guttural sounds produced with the back of the tongue. There's actually nothing uncommon or ugly about them. To truly appreciate them, one has to hear them in the original languages. Below I've given you some examples of some "guttural" fricatives in a few natural languages:

Azerbaijani:	*xoş* [xoʃ] "pleasant"	~	*ağac* [aɣadʒ] "tree"
Arabic:	خبز [χubz] "bread"	~	غربي [ʁurbi] "west"
Arabic:	حبيب [ħabiːb] "beloved"	~	عين [ʕain] "eye"

The latter two fricatives don't appear on the chart above. They're pharyngeal fricatives, which are rare, but not vanishingly so. The voiceless pharyngeal fricative [ħ] is like a heavy, forceful *h* sound (we produce it when fogging up a mirror), and the voiced pharyngeal fricative/approximant [ʕ] sounds—and feels—very much like choking. It's a really fun sound to practice!

Affricates are a combination of a stop and a fricative. It might seem odd to call such a combination a single sound until you realize that the two most prominent affricates in English are rather often thought of as single sounds:

Post-Alveolar: [tʃ] as in *cheap* [tʃip]   [dʒ] as in *job* [dʒab]

Most English speakers would have no problem thinking of the *ch* and *j* sounds as single sounds, and yet they don't sound the same running forward as they do backward (in fact, the word *mushed* [mʌʃt] will sound almost identical to the word *chum* [tʃʌm] if you record it and play it backward—and vice versa). That's what an affricate is: a combination of a stop and fricative that speakers treat like single sounds. In English, the post-alveolar [tʃ] and [dʒ] are the only true affricates, but many languages have others. For example, the *ts* in the Japanese word *tsunami* is an affricate, as is the *pf* in the German word for "horse," *Pferd*. For other affricates, simply combine a stop with a fricative of the same voicing in the same place of articulation, as in the chart above.

The remaining consonants are much more restricted when it comes to where they are produced in the mouth. Nasal stops, for example, can only be produced at the uvula or forward. The reason is that a nasal consonant is identical to a voiced oral stop, except that the velum is lowered, allowing air to pass through the nose. Consequently, anything farther back than a uvular nasal is impossible, as the tongue would be blocking air from passing through the mouth *or* the nose.

Nasal stops are quite common in the world's languages, but most languages have two or three of them only. In English, we have three types of nasal stops that distinguish meaning:

Labial:	[m] as in *sum* [sʌm]
Alveolar:	[n] as in *sun* [sʌn]
Velar:	[ŋ] as in *sung* [sʌŋ]

Notice that these only contrast at the end of a word. In some languages, like Vietnamese or Moro, spoken in Sudan and South Sudan, words can begin with all three of the nasals and others. Compare this pair of words from Moro:

Palatal:	[ɲ] as in *nyera* [ɲɛɾa] "girls"
Velar:	[ŋ] as in *ngera* [ŋera] "girl"

When creating a language, it's important not to get hemmed in by the phonological patterns of one's own language. There's a *lot* we can do with the sounds we can make with our mouths!

The remaining sounds all tend to get clumped together under the catchall term "approximant." The first set are the glides. A glide is basically the consonantal version of a vowel. In English, we have three glides, as shown below:

Alveolar:	[ɹ] as in *red* [ɹɛd]
Palatal:	[j] as in *yet* [jɛt]
Labio-Velar:	[w] as in *wet* [wɛt]

Each of these is very closely associated with a vowel: [ɹ] with [ɚ]; [j] with [i]; and [w] with [u]. Consider these pairs of words:

purr [pʰɚ] ~ *piranha* [pʰɚˈɹɑ.nə]

me [mi] ~ *meow* [miˈjaw]

who [hu] ~ *whoever* [huˈwɛ.vɚ]

The first set you can pronounce and hold indefinitely. Then notice what happens with the second. The second set starts out as the first set does, but then the constriction in the mouth becomes tighter, and what was a vowel suddenly becomes a consonant. That's what a glide is, and in the world's languages they're notoriously tricksy, in that they sometimes show up as consonants and sometimes as vowels. For a beginner, it's best just to treat them like stable consonants. As you get more advanced, though, glides can do a lot of fun things.

Taps (or flaps) and trills are all *R*-like sounds. For example, the IPA symbol [r] is the trilled *r* in Spanish *rojo*, "red," or the trilled double *rr* in Spanish *perro*, "dog." A single instance of that Spanish *r* in between vowels is a flap, as in Spanish *pero*, "but." We actually have this flap sound in English as the pronunciation of the first *t* in words like *pitiful* [pʰɪɾəfəɫ], *gratitude* [ɡɹæɾɪtʰud], and *catatonic* [kʰæɾətʰɑnɪk]. Despite that fact, the trilled [r] has a reputation of being a difficult sound to pronounce. With practice, though, anyone can master it.

There are two other trills found in the world's languages: the bilabial trill [ʙ] and the uvular trill [ʀ]. The latter is found as a variant of *r* in many languages, including German and French. The bilabial trill is quite rare, but it's a fun sound. It's the sound that horses make when they blow a whole bunch of air out of their mouths and their lips flap together like window shades.

The last category is lateral approximants. These are the *L*-sounds. Most languages have just one *L*-sound, and it's usually [l]. Some, though, have other variants, like the palatal [ʎ] which is close to the *lli* in English *million*. Not featured on the chart are the voiceless and voiced lateral fricatives [ɬ] and [ɮ]. These sounds are somewhat rare, but [ɬ] is found in Welsh. It sounds very much like an [h] and an [l] pronounced at the same time. It's the sound at the beginning of the name *Lloyd*, if pronounced as a Welsh name. Funny story. The [ɬ] sound was so bizarre to English speakers that they mistook the sound for [fl]. This is what gave birth to the new name *Floyd*.

This, of course, isn't even half of the total consonants found in the world's languages. **Nonpulmonic** consonants use an airstream mechanism other than the lungs. There are three main types of nonpulmonic consonants found in the world's languages: **implosives**, **ejectives,** and **clicks**. Each is characterized by a different airstream mechanism. Briefly, implosives are produced by lowering the glottis, causing air to rush *into* the mouth in order to produce a stop sound. Ejectives, on the other hand, are simply oral stops produced while holding one's breath, which causes the glottis itself to propel air out of the mouth. Clicks are produced by making two closures in the mouth: one at the velum or uvula, and another somewhere in front of that. Sucking air into that enclosure causes an explosive popping sound when the anterior closure is released.

For those creating their own languages, if you want to use any of the three of these types of consonants in your conlang, it is *strongly advised* that you investigate how these sounds work in natural languages. As a general bit of advice for each of the three:

- The bilabial implosive [ɓ] is the most common implosive. Implosives become rarer as you move away from the lips and toward the glottis. Sample language: Hausa (West Africa).

- The velar ejective [k'] is the most common ejective. Ejectives become rarer as you move away from the uvula toward the lips. Sample language: Hausa (West Africa).

- Click consonants occur in bunches. No language has just one click. Rather, they have clicks in at least three different places of articulation, and with at least three different voicings (e.g. nasal, voiced, palatalized, aspirated, etc.). So far, clicks have *only* been found at the beginning of a syllable. Sample language: !Xóõ (Botswana).

VOWELS

Wherever you are (especially if you're in a library, bookstore, or at work), open your mouth and scream. *Loud.*

SCREAM!!!

That's a vowel.

A **vowel** sound is produced when air is allowed to pass out of the lungs totally unimpeded. We can move our tongues and lips around and even lower our velums and wiggle our epiglottises to alter the sound of the vowel, but so long as air is allowed to pass out of the lungs in an unimpeded stream, the resulting sound is a vowel. Vowels are among the most fluid sounds we have. They're *desperately* hard to pin down. This is why the *i* in *burrito* is pronounced differently in English and Spanish, *even though they're the exact same sound*. It's easy to move your tongue *just* a little bit and change the overall character of a vowel. It's also the hardest thing to approximate. Those who are able to do other accents well or who can make themselves sound like a native when speaking another language are incredible at imitating other vowel sounds. Consonants are a cakewalk with no admission fee compared to vowels.

Unlike consonants, which need to be dealt with based on their manner of articulation, we're going to go ahead and look at all the vowels at once. Below is a chart of all the major vowels found in the world's languages (where vowels appear in pairs, the vowel on the right features rounded lips):

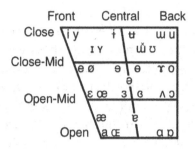

The first question you'll probably have after seeing that chart is why is there an oddly shaped quadrilateral behind the vowel symbols. The reason has to do with how vowels are described by linguists. All vowels are defined by three basic measures: **backness** (whether the tongue body is closer to or farther away from the pharynx); **height** (whether the tongue body is closer to the roof of the mouth or closer to the bottom of the mouth); and **rounding** (whether the lips are rounded or not when pronouncing a vowel). The symbols are placed where they are to mirror the position of the tongue body. Consequently, the tongue body is quite high and forward in pronouncing a vowel like [i], but quite low and back when pronouncing a vowel like [ɑ]. You may also notice that your mouth is far more open for the vowel [ɑ] than it is for [i]. **Openness** is another way of describing vowel height. In other words, rather than noting that the tongue body is low in the mouth for [ɑ], you'd say the jaw is open. For our purposes, these two systems shall be treated as identical.

You can actually hear the effect of height and backness by doing two clever tricks that my phonetics professor John Ohala taught me. To hear the effect of height, what you should do is mouth, in order, the vowels in *meet* [i], *mate* [e], *met* [ɛ] and *Matt* [æ]. Don't actually pronounce them. While doing this, take your thumb and forefinger and flick the skin underneath your back jaw. This will produce a hollow popping sound (something like clapping your palm over an open bottle). As you move from the higher vowel to the lower vowel, the tone of that hollow popping sound will actually get higher. You can repeat the example with *moot* [u], *moat* [o] and *mot* [mɑt] and hear the same result.

For backness, you can whisper the vowels and hear a difference.

When whispering (no vocal fold vibration at all), you can't affect the tone of your speech. The inherent tone of each vowel *decreases* the farther back in the mouth the tongue body goes. So if you whisper the vowels for *meet, mate, met, Matt, mot, moat,* and *moot* in that order, the pitch will get progressively lower. Neat, huh?

The last feature is lip rounding, which doesn't really need a trick, as it's pretty easy to tell when your lips are rounded and when they aren't. You should notice that your lips round quite a bit when pronouncing *moo* [muː], but unround completely when pronouncing *me* [miː]. That's fairly standard. Now try to do the opposite. Keep your lips *completely* unrounded and pronounce *moo*. If you succeed, you should be pronouncing [muɯ] (and sounding like a stereotypical Southern Californian in the process). Now try *me* with your lips *completely* rounded. If you succeed, you'll be pronouncing [myː]. It may sound like a strange sound, but it's found in French, German, and Turkish—and also English, in certain circumstances.

You know how at sporting events it's not uncommon to chant the name of the home team in one fashion or another? Think about the teams you know that have a main [i] vowel. One that always comes to mind for me is the Miami Heat. When fans chant "Let's go Heat!," more often than not the name of the team comes out [hyt] rather than [hit]. The reason is that the lip rounding makes the sound more resonant: it lengthens the tube that is our vocal tract, so to speak, and allows the speaker to give more volume to what they're saying. This is also why players with [u] in their name are much more likely to have their name chanted.

With this information in hand, you should be able to pronounce *any* vowel. It also should become clear how these vowel symbols are really just buoys on the vast ocean of vocalic possibility. I bet right now without even trying you can produce five or six different sounds that would qualify as [i] but which are all slightly different. The way a specific language works is there's an entire range of sounds that qualify as a particular sound, and so long as you're somewhere in that range, you're fine. If you cross the boundary, though, you'll either be pronouncing a different vowel or a strange sound that will ring false in the ear of a native speaker.

Since English has a goodly number of vowels, let's go over them so you can note the differences and use these as reference. I'm assuming a Standard American pronunciation (so not even my pronunciation). If you need a reference for some of these words, think of a stuffy male news anchor pronouncing them, and that should be a good enough frame of reference:

Front Vowels	Back Vowels
bead /bid/	*booed* /bud/
bid /bɪd/	*hood* /hʊd/
bayed /bed/	*bode* /bod/
bed /bɛd/	*baud* /bɔd/
bad /bæd/	*bod* /bɑd/

With that inventory in mind, all the other vowels can basically be described in reference to English. For example, [y], [ʏ], [ø], [œ] and [ɒ] are simply the vowels [i], [ɪ], [e], [ɛ], and [ɑ] pronounced with fully rounded lips. The vowels [ɯ], [ɨ], [ɤ], and [ʌ] on the other hand, are just like [u], [ʊ], [o], and [ɔ], pronounced with fully *un*rounded lips. The vowel [a] is like [æ], but lower.

Moving to central vowels, one that pops up a lot in language after language is schwa: [ə]. It's the reduced vowel at the end of the word *sofa* [sofə]. If you completely relax your jaw and produce the laziest sound in the world, you'll be producing [ə]. As for the other central vowels, do you know the song "Better Man" by Pearl Jam? (No judgment if not; they've done better.) See if you can find it on YouTube. Listen to the part of the chorus where Eddie Vedder sings "Can't find a better man." Hear how his voices changes—how it kind of sounds huskier? This is something you heard a lot in the nineties (Scott Weiland did it; Shakira does it a lot; Dave Matthews did it [or Dave, as his true fans call him]). What Eddie Vedder is actually doing is centralizing all the front vowels. His typical pronunciation of "can't find a better" is something I'd transcribe as [kʰɘːmfɘːnəbɜɾə]. Naturally, he doesn't *always* sing this way. Every so often he simply feels the need to kick it into overdrive, and so he centralizes all the vowels. It's a noticeably different sound. As for why, the only thing I can come up with is that it obscures a lot of the vocalic variety of English (there are fewer distinctions for central vowels than for front vowels), and makes it easier to hold a tone. It's also why *baby* comes out *babay* a lot of times ([e] is lower than [i], which means your mouth is open wider). Anyway, if you're trying to nail central vowels, remember Eddie Vedder (but hopefully for "Corduroy," "Yellow Ledbetter," "Black," "Guaranteed," "Oceans," and "I Got Id" rather than "Better Man").

Now that we have all the vowels down, I'd like to discuss some properties of vowels that certain languages will make use of beyond vowel quality. The first is **vowel length**. Compare the vowel in the English word *bat* to the vowel in the English word *bad*. Yes, the stops at the end will be different, but pay attention to the length of the vowel. Notice how the *a* vowel of *bad* takes more time to pronounce than the *a* sound in *bat*. This is because vowels are naturally lengthened before voiced consonants in English—and, in narrow vocalic transcription, we'd transcribe those two words [bæt] and [bæːd], respectively. You can try this experiment with any vowel pair in English, and the distinction should hold true: *bit/bid, rot/rod, neat/ need, loot/lewd, mate/made*, etc. The mark we use to indicate a long vowel is a kind of modified colon that looks like this: [ː]. You place that mark after a vowel to indicate that it's long. You can also use one little triangle after a vowel [ˑ] to indicate that a vowel is *slightly* longer than a short vowel.

Unlike English, though, which uses vowel length phonetically, many languages use vowel length to distinguish meaning. Among natural languages, Hawaiian, Arabic, Japanese, Hungarian, Finnish, and Latin distinguish long and short vowels. Among conlangs created for television and film, High Valyrian from HBO's *Game of Thrones*, Shiväisith from Marvel's *Thor: The Dark World*, and Lishepus from Syfy's *Dominion* contrast long and short vowels. Here's an example from High Valyrian:

kelin [kelin] "I stop"

kēlin [keːlin] "herd of cats"

Another common use of vowels is the **diphthong**. A diphthong is a vowel that starts out as one vowel but finishes as another.

Consequently, it doesn't sound the same going forward and backward—kind of like affricates. For example, try slowing down your pronunciation of the word *lie*. Notice where your tongue is when you start the vowel of that word and where it ends up. At the beginning, you should be pronouncing a vowel very much like [a], and at the end it should sound a lot like [i]. Despite that fact, we treat this as a single sound (English speakers will think of this as a "long *i*"). That's what a diphthong is: a dynamic vowel that is treated as a single vowel. So, for example, the *i* in *light* [lajt] is a diphthong, as is the *ow* in *how* [haw], but the *ea* in *react* [riækt] is just two vowels occurring next to each other.

Also, as a note, vowels are, by default, voiced. Certain languages, though, have made use of voiceless (or whispered) vowels. For example, in Japanese, the high vowels [i] and [ɯ] tend to be voiceless in between voiceless consonants. This is why names like *Daisuke* appear to be pronounced [daiske]. In fact, a name like that will be pronounced [daisɰke], with the vowel being whispered in between the two consonants.

Finally, a common feature of vowel systems is nasality. We've already discussed nasal consonants, so you understand how nasality works. Now apply those same principles to vowels. Try pronouncing a nice [ɑ] vowel with your velum lowered. This will mean that air will primarily be passing out of your lungs but also will pass out through your nose. If you do this successfully, you'll be pronouncing [ɑ̃], which is precisely how you pronounce French *an* (one of the words for "year" in French). Nasalization can be applied to any vowel, but most languages that employ nasal vowels only allow a subset of nasal vowels. French, for example, has eleven oral vowels (or regular vowels), but only three nasal vowels. This is usual, but not necessary. It's perfectly possible to pronounce any vowel as oral or nasal: just pronounce the vowel with a lowered velum. (See one of the Gbe languages of West Africa for an example of a language that has the same number of oral and nasal vowels.)

It takes practice to be able to produce, distinguish, and remember the various sounds we've discussed thus far. Please feel free to use this section as a reference guide that you can refer to in future sections, as we'll be relying on your understanding of the phonetic principles of language as we move through the book.

PHONOLOGY

The phonology of a language is an abstract layer of understanding that treats actual sounds (**phones**) as subsets of other sounds (**phonemes**). The phonology of English is the reason we think of the *t* in *stall* as identical to the *t* in *tall*, even though the former is [t] and the latter [tʰ], and there exist languages that treat them differently. We consider both sounds to be realizations of the phoneme /t/ (recall that phonemic transcription is written between forward slashes).

Throughout the rest of this section we'll be discussing phonology and phonological phenomena. This is where things get interesting.

SOUND SYSTEMS

You've seen the myriad speech sounds available to the human mouth. Being a speaker of a human language, you also should have noted that your language doesn't utilize *every possible* speech sound. This is true of every language on the planet. How a language chooses sounds is a bit of a mystery (the history is lost to antiquity), but it's up to the conlanger to choose the sounds for their language. The result will be the conlang's **sound system**. In creating a naturalistic language, there are a number of principles that will help to guide a conlanger in doing so, and this section will detail those principles.

First, take a look at the phonology of *any* language. For example, let's look at the consonantal inventory of Tukang Besi, an Austronesian language spoken in Indonesia whose reference grammar was written by superlinguist and martial arts expert Mark Donohue (he is literally both of those things).

Manner	Bilabial	Dental/Alveolar	Velar	Glottal
Oral Stop	p, b*, ^{m}p, ^{m}b	t, d*, ^{n}t, ^{n}d	k, g, ^{ŋ}k, ^{ŋ}g	ʔ
Implosive	ɓ	ɗ		
Nasal Stop	m	n	ŋ	
Fricative	β	s, ^{n}s, z*		h
Trill		r		
Lateral		l		

Note that sounds marked with an asterisk appear only in loanwords, and everything other than [r], [s], and [n] in the **Dental/Alveolar** column is dental. What can we say about this? First, it's worth noting that [b] and [d] aren't native, and that there are only two implosives: [ɓ] and [ɗ]. And the one place where there isn't an implosive (the **Velar** column), there is a native [g]. Other than that, notice how balanced everything looks. There are basically four native stops in each major place of articulation: voiceless, voiced (either implosive or regular), and both prenasalized and plain. There's one r sound, one l sound, a couple glottals, and then a sibilant (or strident) fricative [s] and a weaker voiced one [β]. This looks natural. The following, however, would strike me as bizarre:

Manner	Bilabial	Dental/Alveolar	Velar	Glottal
Oral Stop	^{m}p	t, d, ^{n}t, ^{n}d	k, g, ^{ŋ}k, ^{ŋ}g	ʔ
Implosive		ɗ		
Nasal Stop	m		ŋ	
Fricative	β	s, ^{n}s, z	x, ɣ, x^{w}, ɣ^{w}, x^{j}, ɣ^{j}	h, ɦ
Trill		r		
Lateral			ɭ̆	

This is basically the same phonological inventory with a couple changes. Notice that there's now exactly one bilabial stop, and it's a prenasalized voiceless bilabial stop [^{m}p]. There's also only one implosive, and it's dental. There is no dental or alveolar [n], for apparently no reason; there's a full series of plain, labialized, *and* palatalized velar fricatives (there are no other labialized or palatalized consonants); and there's only one *L*-sound, and it's a *voiceless* velar lateral. This should strike you as exceedingly unnatural. That is, even though all of these are sounds human beings can produce (and without too much difficulty, I might add), I would *never* expect a language to exist that had precisely this phonological inventory. The reason behind the nonoccurrence of sound systems like this one is a principle that I call **acoustic economy.**

Acoustic economy is, simply, the idea that languages will conspire to take maximal advantage of the sounds available to human beings. They will do so *not* because certain sounds are more difficult to *pronounce* than others, but because certain distinctions are more difficult to *hear* than others. Let me illustrate what I mean by this.

In English, we distinguish *t* from *k* from *p* well enough (e.g. *kick* vs. *tick* vs. *pick*). Consider the word *September*, though. Would you expect there to exist an entirely separate word that was spelled *Sektember* (or maybe *Sectember*. Yeah, that looks more Englishy)? This would be a word totally unrelated to *September*, mind. It's certainly something English *could* do, of course, but the place where the *p* occurs in *September* is, for a plethora of reasons, a really poor environment to distinguish those otherwise easily distinguished sounds. Again, it's easy enough to pronounce *Sectember* (in fact, that *is* how my late stepfather used to pronounce *September*), but you have to think about it from the listener's perspective. In noisy environments, with a word like this pronounced lazily on occasion, having to distinguish *September* and *Sectember* consistently wouldn't work.

Now if you can pull back and imagine a language evolving over thousands of years, and there being billions of word pairs like this, and billions of interactions among billions of different speakers, you should be able to begin to understand the role that acoustics plays both in the organization and reorganization of sound systems, and in historical sound change (which we'll discuss in detail later on). A user of a language reproduces the language in the way that they believe it's supposed to be used, and that's based on what they hear—and also what they read, if the language has a written form. Consequently if a certain distinction is routinely difficult to perceive, it can eventually collapse. This is what happened in English with many vowels before *r*. The words *fur, stir,* and *her* didn't all used to rhyme.

In general, the principle of acoustic economy expects languages to maximize the phonological space available, so that words are audibly distinct. If they're difficult to distinguish, the distinctions tend to collapse, ironed out by evolution. Competing with the idea of acoustic economy, though, is something I call the principle of **brand identity**. In marketing, the goal is to make sure that every piece of information related to a brand has the characteristics of its brand identity on it (logos, color schemes, slogans, fonts and type-faces, etc.). You should be able to look at anything associated with a particular brand and tell it's from that brand. In language, the same principle applies, albeit a little differently.

Looking at sound systems, there are certain phonemes that have a rarer distribution crosslinguistically than others. For example, voiced aspirated stops are fairly rare. In Hindi, though, you get a voiced aspi-rated stop at every single possible place of articulation, as shown below—and words that use them are *everywhere* in the language!

भाट [bʰaːʈ] "bard"

धोबी [d̪ʰobiː] "washerman"

ढाल [ɖʰaːl] "shield"

झंकार [dʒʰaŋkaːɾ] "chime"

घंटा [gʰaɳʈaː] "hour"

This is a phenomenon you'll see in language after language. It may be difficult to distinguish [t] from [tˤ] or [o] from [õ], for exam-ple, but if the language is going to do it, it will do it a *lot*. This actu-ally helps to preserve the distinction. That is, if there is a *class* of pharyngealized sounds, or palatalized sounds, or glottalized sounds, or what have you, speakers and listeners get constant interaction with the phenomenon. If one is able to distinguish a nasalized vowel from an oral vowel, then it's not a problem to distinguish a *particular* nasalized vowel from its oral counterpart. This is what I mean by brand identity. A language will take advantage of its unique sounds and make them a hallmark of the language. From English, consider our rarer sounds: [θ, ð, ɹ]. The sound [ð] isn't in a lot of words, but it does find itself in a lot of *really* high frequency words: *the* [ðə], *this* [ðɪs], *that* [ðæt], *then* [ðɛn], *though* [ðow], etc. The sound [θ] is common enough, and is used in the *-th* ending in words like *width, warmth, depth,* and in the ending for ordinal numbers like *fifth, eighth, twentieth,* etc. And you can't get through a sentence without using an *r.* It's everywhere!

In building the sound system for a naturalistic language, then, I keep these two principles in mind. For those building their own language, one question might emerge that I can address—namely, how big or small does one's sound system have to be?

On the high end, my suggestion is not to worry about the number of consonants or vowels. Instead, the question should be: Does my system make sense? For example, the !Xóõ language of Botswana has more than a hundred consonants (the majority of them clicks), but the distribution of consonants is still quite principled. The same is true of all natural languages.

Now, if you go in the *other* direction, that question is quite interesting.

The natural language with the fewest number of consonants is a language of Papua New Guinea called Rotokas. Depending on the dialect and the analysis, Rotokas is analyzed as having either six or nine consonants—and that's it. They're basically /p, t, k, b, d, g/ (don't let the spelling of the name of the language fool you—its orthography uses the Roman alphabet and has some funky spelling rules). It has ten vowels (five qualities, long and short), so there's plenty of syllabic possibilities (which is probably the real question that needs to be answered), but it looks like the answer to the question of how many consonants does a language *have* to have is six. You might be able to go smaller, but doing so would raise an eyebrow or two.

As for vowels, there are a group of languages all found in the Caucasus Mountains that are famous for having, depending on the analysis, exactly two vowels. Some argue there are three; some argue there are more than that. Nevertheless, a two-vowel analysis has been made for a number of languages in this region—in particular, Ubykh and Kabardian, though Abkhaz and Adyghe are often thrown in. What are the two vowels? It may surprise you: /a/ and /ə/. Each vowel ends up being realized in a lot of different ways depending on the consonants surrounding it, but since the realizations are consistent, the vowels are analyzed as being just /a/ and /ə/, while each of these languages has an *extremely* large consonantal inventory.

Most languages have between four and six vowel qualities (not counting long vowels as separate), and between twenty and thirty consonants. English has an average number of consonants and an above average number of vowels. A language like Spanish is much more ordinary, with between eighteen and twenty consonants, depending on the dialect, and five vowels. That should give you an idea of what the usual bounds are for natural languages. So long as you're aware of them, you can make a conscious decision to have your language fall within expected norms, or be an outlier.

In addition to the foregoing, here are some quick tips for those sitting down in front of a blank sheet of paper and creating their first sound system:

- Your system *will* be revised. Feel free to try things out to see how they work.

- Look at a variety of different languages' sound systems for inspiration, or just to get a better idea of what kind of variety there is. Wikipedia is great for this. Search for "[language name] phonology" (or if it's a lesser-known language, "[language name] language") and jump to the phonology section. Most pages have nice big charts to look at.

- Remember that sounds come in groups—especially **obstruents** (stops, fricatives, and affricates). Don't go to add a palatal *sound*: go to add a palatal *series*.

- **Sonorants** (vowels, laterals, trills, flaps, approximants, and nasals) tend to be voiced and tend not to have voiceless counterparts. Treat this as a default which can be circumvented if so desired.

- Bilabial obstruents are more likely to be voiced; velar/uvular obstruents are more likely to be voiceless. In between, distinguishing voicing is quite likely. This isn't a rule, but a tendency.

- Implosives grow increasingly less common starting from the lips and moving inward; ejectives grow increasingly less common starting from the velum and moving in either direction (i.e. outward or inward).

- **Sibilants** (s-like and sh-like sounds) are acoustically strong; nonsibilant fricatives are acoustically weak. It's not uncommon for a language to have one sibilant and one nonsibilant—and also not uncommon for nonsibilants to be confused for each other (e.g. [f] for [θ], [h] for [ɸ], etc.).

- If a language has an opposite rounding vowel (i.e. front rounded or back unrounded), it will *almost* always have the regular version of the vowel as well. So if a language has [y], it will also have [i]. This isn't a rule, but a tendency.

- Low vowels, whether front or back, are most commonly unrounded. You will find [ɒ] in plenty of languages (it's the *o* in Alan Rickman's pronunciation of *Harry Potter*), but [ɑ] is much more common.

- *Always* sound things out. It will help you to understand the sound and its acoustic effect better.

Of course, selecting the sounds one wants to use isn't the extent of creating a phonology. Indeed, that's just the beginning!

PHONOTACTICS

Take an English word like *strong*. It's a nice, sturdy English word. A phonetic transcription of it would be [stɹɑŋ]. The sounds that comprise that word are, without a doubt, English sounds. Consequently, one should be able to take those sounds and create a new word—say, a word like [tŋsɹɑ]. That makes a nice plausible English word, right?

Channeling a young Jennifer Connelly: Of *course* it doesn't! (Any *Labyrinth* fans out there? Those crickets I'm hearing?)

The reason it doesn't is that the **phonotactics** of English simply do not permit a word like [tŋsɹɑ] to exist. If it had to exist, we'd probably end up pronouncing it [tʰʌŋzɹɑ]. In other words, we'd modify the word so that it obeyed the phonotactics of English. That's what the phonotactics are there for. They're a set of rules that tell the speaker of a language which types of combinations of sounds form coherent words, and which don't. This allows us to identify a given language and ignore everything that doesn't sound like the language we're listening for.

Once the sound system of a language has been set up, the next important step is deciding how the phonotactics of the language will work. In addition to the sounds present in the language, the phonotactic patterns present in a language are one of the three key factors in determining its phonaesthetic character (this will be discussed in detail later). If phonotactics are ignored, more often than not the phonotactic patterns of a conlanger's native language are borrowed into their conlang, resulting in a conlang that behaves, for an English speaker, much more like English than the conlanger was intending.

The first step in creating a phonotactic system for a conlang is determining what constitutes a **syllable**. A syllable is a prosodic unit of measurement used to divide words into smaller parts. A syllable itself can be divided into two main parts: an **onset** and a **rhyme**. Onsets are optional in many languages, but rhymes are not. The rhyme can also be subdivided into two parts: the **nucleus** and **coda**. In a stereotypical syllable (something like the English word *dog* [dɑg]), the onset is a consonant ([d]), and the rhyme is the rest of the syllable ([ɑg]). Within the rhyme, the vowel is the nucleus ([ɑ]) and the last consonant is the coda ([g]). Syllables are often diagrammed like this:

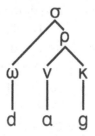

The symbols above come from Greek and are as follows: σ = syllable; ω = onset; ρ = rhyme; v = nucleus; κ = coda. One of the most important parts in setting up the phonotactics of a conlang is determining which syllables are allowed. For example, all languages allow onsets, but some, like Arabic, require them. Many languages allow **closed syllables**—i.e. syllables with a coda—but not all of them do (Hawaiian requires **open syllables**, syllables without a coda). *All* languages have rules about what sounds are allowed in the onset, nucleus, and coda positions.

In addition to syllabic restrictions, there are also word boundary and word-internal restrictions. In discussing these restrictions, I'll need to introduce a new bit of transcription. A period [.] is used to separate syllables. In future, all phonetic transcriptions will be broken down syllabically. Going back to boundary restrictions, in English the sound [ŋ] isn't allowed to begin a word, but it may begin a syllable. So while there will never be a word of English that begins with [ŋ] (one of the reasons why English speakers have such a hard time with the last name Nguyen), the word *strongest* is best syllabified [stɹɑ.ŋəst].

Since I transcribed the word, though, this is a good time to talk about **ambisyllabicity**. Certain sounds in certain languages often turn out to be neither a coda nor an onset—or they're both. For example, [ŋ] ordinarily isn't an onset, so in *strongest*, one almost wants to say that it's both coda *and* onset. This happens a lot with [ɹ], where in a word like *baron*, it's hard to say if it should be [bɛ.ɹən] or [bɛɹ.ən], because the [ɹ] is clearly having some sort of appreciable effect on the vowel the way a [t] or [s] wouldn't. This is generally a fairly advanced concept, but I would like to use it to introduce **geminates**. A geminate is to a consonant what a long vowel is to a vowel. Compare the [s] sound when pronouncing *Miss Ally* versus *Miss Sally*. The [s] sound should be quite a bit longer in the second. In effect, that is what a geminate is: a long consonant. Any consonant can be a geminate. Certain languages treat geminates as the incidental co-occurrence of the same sound (as in English), but others treat geminates as longer versions of a single consonant—i.e. a consonant that is required to occupy both the coda of the previous syllable *and* the onset of a following syllable.

Many languages will place extra selectional restrictions on onsets and codas. For example, Japanese only allows [n] as a coda. In Dothraki, a largely permissive language when it comes to consonants and consonant clusters, the consonants [g], [q], and [w] can't end a word, but may end a word-internal syllable. Thus, a word like *leqse* "rat" is transcribed [leq.se]. A verb like *haqat*, "to be tired," though, which *should* be *haq* [haq] in the past tense, turns out to be *haqe* [ha.qe], because word-final [q] isn't permitted. The addition of the [e] in Dothraki is what is known as a **repair strategy**. All languages have different types of repair strategies to ensure that their phonotactic rules aren't violated. Consider all these words which came to English (ultimately) from Greek: *psychologist, pterodactyl, pneumonia, gnomic*. All of those words were pronounced with an initial [p] or [g] in Greek. In English, we simply can't begin a word with consonant clusters like these. Our repair strategy was to pretend those initial consonants simply didn't exist.

Other languages employ different strategies. For example, though it's fine for a word to begin with [st] or [sp] or [sn] in English, it's impossible in Spanish. No syllable in Spanish can begin with a fricative followed by a stop of any kind. Thus, when a Spanish speaker goes to a Starbucks, the way they'll pronounce it is [es.ṭar.boks].

The strategy employed in both situations is to preserve the canonical syllable structure of each language. Part of defining the syllable structure is defining which consonant clusters are allowed. While English is more permissive in this regard than Spanish, it's not as permissive as, say, Russian, where the Russian equivalent of *psychologist* leaves the [p] from Greek intact: психолог [psi.xɔ.lək].

In order to avoid having to pair every single consonant in one's inventory with every single other consonant, one generally uses classes of sounds (e.g. oral stops can be followed by approximants). How to decide which clusters will work and which won't, though? Let me introduce the **sonority hierarchy**. The sonority hierarchy defines classes of sounds based on how likely they are to serve as the nucleus of a syllable. Going from least likely to be a nucleus to most, this is the sonority hierarchy:

Oral Stop > Affricate > Fricative > Nasal > Approximant > Vowel

As you can see, vowels are most likely to be the nucleus of a syllable and stops are the least likely, which should be fairly intuitive. That is, if you have a basic syllable [pa], it's pretty safe to say that, no matter what your language, [p] will be the onset and [a] will be the nucleus. It's almost unimaginable to conceive of it any other way.

Having said this, the sonority hierarchy is more like a maxim than a law. Consider that if you obey the above hierarchy precisely as written and you had to arrange three consonants—[t], [s], and [a]—into a coda-less syllable, the optimal order would be [tsa]. In English, we know that won't work, and that the nonoptimal order [sta] would be preferred. Hungarian, on the other hand, is perfectly fine with [tsa], and wouldn't be okay with [sta]. This is part of what defines both languages.

That's about how I make use of the sonority hierarchy in designing a sound system. It's not a law that dictates how sounds should be arranged, but a guideline that can be used to help one define *one's own* sound system. In English, for example, it's not especially noteworthy that approximants like [ɹ] and [l] can follow stops and fricatives. It is worth noting, though, that [s] (and occasionally [ʃ]) can precede stops and nasals. Notice how English does that, though. Off the top of your head, you should be able to think of dozens of words that begin with [sn], [sm], [st], [sp], and [sk]. You should also be able to come up with a lot that begin with [spɹ], [stɹ], [skɹ], and [spl]. How about [skl]? There's *sclerosis*, but can you come up with any others? And how about [stl]? There are *none*. Think about how odd that is, given the classes of sounds. What's wrong with [tl]—or [dl], for that matter? Other languages do it. One of my favorite Irathient words is ᘂᗠᘍᗋ [tla.nəs], which means "short visit." In English, however, it's forbidden.

By making use of and reference to the sonority hierarchy, it's possible to identify what clusters and combinations are outlawed or allowed in a conlang that would be surprising or out of the ordinary. For example, Sanskrit allows the consonants [r] and [l] to serve as the nucleus of a syllable. Some languages are even more permissive than that. Here, for example, is a word from Georgian, with my best attempt at syllabification afterward: გვფრცქვნი [gv.prts.kvni] "you peel us" (I'm sure there's a context where this sentence would make sense). Pretty much anything that has even the *slightest* bit of continuity can serve as the nucleus of a syllable, if you want it bad enough. Consider *pssst!* in English. It's not a word in the conventional sense, but it has clear meaning ("Hey! Pay attention to me, but don't make it look like you are!"), and is quite clearly [pṣ] with no vowel. In English, this isn't wordlike enough to get word status, but why couldn't it in a different language? And, indeed, words like this can and do occur in many languages around the world.

Before leaving the sonority hierarchy, it's worth noting that if you run the sonority hierarchy in reverse . . .

Vowel > Approximant > Nasal > Fricative > Affricate > Oral Stop

. . . it gives you the end of a syllable. The thing to remember about codas, though, is that they're simultaneously *less* permissive and *more* permissive than onsets. For example, Ancient Greek allowed codas of [n], [r], and [s] *and that's it.* Such a thing is far from uncommon. But look at English. Compared with a language like Spanish, we allow tons of onset types, but, my stars, the things we can end a word with! Bask in some of these truly, *truly* awful codas:

strengths [stɹɛŋθs]

worlds [wɚldz]

sixths [sɪksθs]

fifths [fɪfθs]

crafts [kʰɹæfts]

If there's anything to take away from this, it's two linguistic tendencies. The first is that languages in general tend to place a lot more restrictions on codas than onsets. The second is that certain languages will pile up coda consonants—apparently because they think the word is done with and no one will notice or care.

For a conlang, though, all of this must be worked out and stated explicitly. As a language creator, doing so helps to craft words that look and feel like they all came from the same language, and it helps to prevent one's native language intuitions from constraining the phonology.

ALLOPHONY

Discussing allophony is really the first step toward understanding the systematicity of language. To explain it, let me take a fun topic like werewolves and ruin it by turning it into math.

The idea behind the most common version of the werewolf is simple. Some individual (we'll call him Tony) is a regular human being, but when there's a full moon in the sky, Tony becomes a werewolf: a wolflike man. Tony as Tony and Tony as the werewolf are never in the same place at the same time, because they're one and the same person. Furthermore, assuming that Tony acquired his wolfish second skin via some sort of bite that he received late in life, we can say that Tony is *basically* human (i.e. he started out human, most of the time he's human, and he thinks of himself as a human being with a bizarre ability). Furthermore, Tony doesn't become a *wolf*: he becomes a wolf*man*. So he's still basically human. If we wanted to describe Tony's two states, then, we might describe them this way:

Tony as a Human = [+human, -wolf]

Tony as a Werewolf = [+human, +wolf]

Humans are naturally [-wolf] (that we know of), so really [+human] is all you need to describe Tony. After all, we would also assume he's naturally [-bird], [-car], [-credenza], [-butter], etc. If you had to describe Tony using a set of equations, then, you might do so in the following way:

1. /Tony/ > [+wolf] / _sky[+full moon]

Translation: Tony becomes [+wolf] in the context of a sky that is [+full moon].

2. /Tony/ > [Tony] / elsewhere

Translation: Tony remains regular Tony in all other contexts.

Here, the forward slashes make reference to a kind of meta-Tony that manifests himself in one of two ways. The greater than sign > is used as an arrow to indicate that some change occurs in Tony. In equation (1), Tony acquires the feature [+wolf]; in equation (2), there is no change, so he comes out as natural Tony. After this comes a forward slash / after which appears the environment that effects the change. In equation (1), the underscore _ stands for Tony, who is "occurring" (or existing) before a sky that has a full moon (in this case, it is [+full moon]). In equation (2), the environment is "else-where," which indicates that every other possible environment will cause Tony to remain Tony.

If you can understand the alternation between Tony and his werewolf form, you can understand allophony.

Allophony describes the *regular* distribution of sounds in a language. Some sounds rarely change, or change very little (like [g] in English), but others change quite a bit. When the change is regular and predictable, we call each instantiation of the sound an **allophone** of one **phoneme**. Using our example above, Tony, the individual consciousness, would be a phoneme, and both human Tony and werewolf Tony would be allophones of the individual Tony. To use a relatively simple example from English, let's talk about aspiration. Here's one way you could write up the aspiration rule of English:

$$/p, t, k/ > [p^h, t^h, k^h] / \#\_$$

$$/p, t, k/ > [p, t, k] / \text{ elsewhere}$$

In other words, /p, t, k/ become aspirated at the beginning of a word (the little hashtag # mark is used for a word boundary, so #_ means when the sound in question occurs with nothing before it), and they remain themselves otherwise. The actual details are a little more complex than this, but that's the gist of it.

Now, as an English speaker you should have the sense that there is no important difference between [p] and [pʰ]. The *p* in *peak* feels like the same sound as the *p* in *speak*; you wouldn't want to say they were different, even though they are. This is why we can refer to the phoneme as /p/ without too much trouble. Other languages experience changes just like this with their phonemes that we would perceive as rather different. For example, in Hawaiian, the phoneme /w/ surfaces as [v] when it occurs after [i] or [e]; as [w] when it occurs after [o] or [u]; and is in free variation between [w] and [v] after [a]. Basically [v] and [w] are treated as realizations of the same sound. In English, the two are quite different (consider *why* and *vie*), of course, but it's the language that determines which distinctions are going to be relevant and which aren't.

Instrumental in determining which sounds are relevant in a language is the presence or absence of **minimal pairs**. A minimal pair is a pair of words that have different meanings and *exactly one* phonetic difference. Compare the two English words mentioned above:

why [waj]

vie [vaj]

We know these are two different words with two different meanings. They also have *exactly one* phonetic difference: the first word begins with [w] and the second with [v]. Thus, we know that [w] and [v] are separate phonemes in English, and that English speakers think of these sounds as totally different. If English speakers thought the sounds were basically the same, we'd always be wondering if someone was saying *vie* or *why* (or *wet* or *vet*, or *wick* or *Vick*, etc.). German speakers have a lot of trouble distinguishing these sounds, though. In German, the sounds [v] and [w] are treated as basically the same, and the phonetic distinction is never used to distinguish words. Consequently, you can't find a minimal pair in German with [v] and [w] the way you can in English, which means that [v] and [w] are not separate phonemes.

It can be difficult to distinguish between **synchronic** (or current) allophonic variation and **diachronic** (historical) sound changes, so common allophonic variation will be looked at in detail in the section on Phonological Evolution in Chapter III. For now, let's move on to the role intonation plays in a language's sound system.

INTONATION

If the phonological structure of a language is the body, intonation is the blood. Intonation is why a language written down on paper looks stale, while a language spoken aloud is music. Intonation is what will take a conlang from being a construct to being a *language*.

Intonation is also *the* most difficult element of language to represent graphically.

Before getting into it, let me give you a couple English examples that will help to demonstrate what intonation is. Consider the word *subject* in the following sentences:

Linguistics is my favorite subject.

Please don't subject me to another boring lecture on linguistics.

Notice the difference between the two instances of *subject*? What an English speaker does is alter the intonation of their voice to produce the two different meanings. In effect, that's all intonation is: the principled modulation of the pitch of one's voice for semantic or pragmatic reasons. Sometimes, as above, it's used to distinguish meaning. Other times it's used to convey extra information not encoded in the words. For example, say my friend Kyn invites Jon and me to Harbor House to eat food late at night like we were still in our twenties, and he says the following:

I'm moving to Tallahassee.

Either Jon or I is liable to respond thus:

TALL-a-HASS-ee?!

Without resorting to using any other type of machinery, if you're an English speaker, you *should* recognize this intonation pattern. It's what I've taken to calling the WTF intonation. The way it works is the word has to end in a dramatic high to low pitch contour. We do fun stuff with it depending on the number of syllables the word we're expressing dismay over has. Consider:

BO-ored?! (1 syllable)

AN-na?! (2 syllables)

ba-NA-na?! (3 syllables)

ME-nin-GI-tis?! (4 syllables)

bur-KI-na FA-so?! (5 syllables)

HOW i MET your MO-ther?! (6 syllables)

But notice what happens when the intonational pattern doesn't play nice with the natural stress pattern of the word!

a-DU-ult?! (2 syllables)

ME-ri-da?! (3 syllables)

co-MU-ni-ty?! (4 syllables)

Ahh, I love language . . . Looking back at the monosyllabic example, notice that in order to make the pattern work, we lengthen the vowel to accommodate the pitch contour. Neat, huh? Then in the ill-fitting examples above, we select the pattern the word should fit (1, 2, and 3 syllables, respectively), and the remaining syllable is kind of lumped on to the end (the beginning for the first example, and the end for the next two).

Intonation ends up being drastically important to language, but since we have absolutely no good way to transcribe it—and since many conlangs are rarely spoken—it often falls by the wayside for a lot of conlangers. In the coming sections I'll point up a few fun things that can be done with intonation.

PRAGMATIC INTONATION

I opened this section on intonation with an example of a very specific intonational pattern of English. All languages have specific patterns like that, but here I'd like to talk about some more general tendencies.

Before getting to examples, there is one general note that you should always keep in mind when it comes to oral language: Human beings have a *finite* amount of breath. Anything that a language does that requires breath will be easier to do at the beginning of an utterance.

One area where it's easy to spot distinctive intonational patterns in a language is in questions. There are two types of basic questions: yes/no questions and WH-questions (there are also "I wonder" questions, but we'll leave those aside for the moment). A **yes/no question** is a question that calls for an answer of "yes" or "no." A **WH-question** is a question that typically, in English, has a word that begins with "wh." These are questions that have *who, where, when, why, what, what kind, which, how,* and/or *how much.* Their intonational patterns are typically different. Consider the following three-way example from English (in this case, this is my English, so your mileage may vary):

1. *David Bowie is a genius.*

2. *Is David Bowie a genius?*

3. *What is David Bowie?*

In sentence 1, the pitch starts out high and kind of gradually lowers as the sentence progresses. In sentence 2, the pitch rises throughout the sentence, rising to its highest point on the last syllable. In sentence 3, the pitch starts high and remains high until the end, where it drops off sharply. (Also, the answers to 2 and 3 respectively are "yes" and "a genius.") This is fairly standard for American English, but not all languages will show the same intonational patterns. Here, for example, is how you'd translate those sentences into Irathient:

1. *ᘒᗧᑔᑋᕴᕴᕩᕮᕂᕮᕮᕮᕴᑗᕮᕮᕴᕴᒐᕴ*

Gyaba Deivid Bəwi. [ɹa.ba de.vid bə.wi]

2. ᗧᑔᑋᕴᕴᕩᕮᕂᕮᕮᕮᕴᑗᕮᕮᕴᕴᒐ

Gyaba Deivid Bəwi? [ɹa.ba de.vid bə.wi]

3. ᕩᕮᕂᕮᕮᕮᕴᑗᕮᕮᕴᕴᒐᒐᑉᑊᒐ

Deivid Bəwi hazə? [de.vid bə.wi ha.zə]

The pitch contours are markedly different, so I've recorded myself saying them and included images of the pitch tracks below:

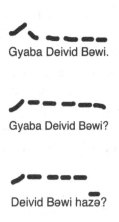

Gyaba Deivid Bəwi.

Gyaba Deivid Bəwi?

Deivid Bəwi hazə?

As you can see, each intonational phrase has a part where it rises and a part where it falls. For statements in Irathient, the sharp fall is the first unstressed syllable after the focus (in this case, *gyaba*, "genius"). In yes/no questions, there is a rise, then the pitch stays high and lightly falls off at the end of the phrase. In WH-questions, the pitch rises very high and stays there until the unstressed portion of the final word (in this case, the last syllable), and then it drops *sharply*. As you can see, these are markedly different from English—and other languages have different patterns still. Even with the same language, patterns can differ. For example, some varieties of British English typically denote yes/no questions with a *falling* intonation at the end of the phrase—the exact opposite of American English.

Although questions are the most obvious place where intonation has a role to play in language, it is utilized in other constructions, as well. Consider the intonational patterns of the underlined elements in the following English sentences:

- <u>Him</u> I like.

- I like <u>Iron Maiden</u>, <u>Dream Theater</u>, <u>Sonata Arctica</u>, and <u>the Decemberists</u>.

- You're going <u>home?!</u>

- No, I'm going to the <u>store.</u>

- My sister, <u>whom you all know as Natalie</u>, loves mushrooms.

Each of these constructions has a special intonation associated with it. There's also the simple contrastive intonation we can use with any word in an English sentence, as shown below:

- I ate the <u>apple.</u> (Not the banana!)

- <u>I</u> ate the apple. (It was me, not my sister!)

- I <u>ate</u> the apple. (I didn't throw it away!)

- I ate <u>the</u> apple. (The one you begged me not to!)

Again, while different languages will use different intonational patterns for different purposes, they all do something. And while there may be some universal tendencies (e.g. rising intonation with yes/no questions), I'd go so far as to say that the patterns are *entirely* language-specific, and that there are no universal characteristics for intonation crosslinguistically, outside this one point: Changing the intonation of something marks it in some way. If it's usual to speak with a general fall, then marking something with a rising intonation will make it more noticeable, and vice versa. How a language will treat the fact that an item is more noteworthy than usual is language-specific.

The IPA doesn't have any outstanding conventions for marking intonation in a phrase. It has two symbols: [↗], which means the pitch basically goes up, and [↘], which means the pitch basically goes down. They can be combined to form rising and falling intonational patterns. For me, this simply isn't enough to capture the nature of intonation in a language, so I find using these things to be more trouble than it's worth. When I'm working on shows like *Defiance*, I don't even describe intonation patterns in the materials that go to the actors. Instead, I do two things. First, I break down every phrase syllabically and use all caps to indicate "high" tone and all lowercase to indicate "low" tone. Second, I record the line. The combination of those two things is usually good enough to get the right impression across.

If you're creating a language on your own and you're the only speaker, intonation is usually not high on the list of features to focus on, but intonational flavoring is well worth it (read: crucial) when it comes to making an authentic language.

STRESS

Stress is a property of certain languages whereby some combination of pitch, vowel length, and/or volume is used to lend acoustic prominence to a particular syllable. Stress is usually a property of words, but in some languages (like French) it's a property of phrases or clauses. Stress can be **lexical** (meaning that it's different for every word and has to be memorized) or **fixed** (meaning that stress can be predicted by a number of language-specific principles). The best way to understand stress is to see how it works. Here are some

English words stressed on the last or **ultimate** syllable, with stress marked using the IPA symbol for **primary stress** [ˈ]:

alone [əˈlon]

portmanteau [pɔɹt.mænˈtʰow]

understand [ʌn.dɚˈstænd]

Here are some English words stressed on the second-to-last or penultimate syllable:

sofa [ˈso.fə]

illicit [ɪˈlɪ.sət]

Mississippi [mɪ.səˈsɪ.pi]

Here are some English words stressed on the third-to-last or antepenultimate syllable:

mechanize [ˈmɛ.kə.najz]

infantilize [ɪnˈfæn.tə.lajz]

un-American [ʌ.nəˈmɛ.ɹə.kʰɪn]

In the last two sets you'll see also that *sofa* and *mechanize* are stressed on the first or **initial** syllable. Given the general pattern of English, though, it's more likely that the stress is assigned from the right edge, so it makes more sense to say the stress in *mechanize* is antepenultimate, rather than initial. For example, if you add more syllables, it's easy to see the shift in stress, as with *mechanization*.

The mark [ˈ] indicates primary stress. In addition to this, there is also **secondary stress**, which is marked with [ˌ]. However it's realized in a particular language, secondary stress will be indicated in some lesser way than primary stress, but will have some sort of marking that will distinguish it from an unstressed syllable. Secondary stresses *tend* to radiate out from a syllable with primary stress, skipping every other syllable. For example, looking at *un-American* again, secondary stresses appear on the first and last syllables: [ˌʌ.nəˈmɛ.ɹəˌkɪn]. If you like the theory that [ʌ] only appears in stressed syllables, syllables with secondary stress count, which is what licenses [ʌ] in the first syllable, but not the second.

There are a couple of ways to design a good stress system depending on what kind of stress system you'd like to have. If you want to design a lexical stress system (i.e. stress placement is idiomatic and must be memorized), the only good way to do it is to evolve the system. The reason English has such a random stress system is because our words have lost a *lot* of sounds over the centuries, and we've borrowed a lot of words whose stresses we also borrow (sometimes). There were regular stress rules for English at one point, but with the way the language has evolved, it just threw up its hands and said "whatever." English pretty much just sits around all day unwindulaxing on the couch in PJs watching reruns of *Chuck* (in other words, English is a lot like me). This is why English words are stressed all over the place: they derive from a *ton* of different regular patterns. To produce something like English, you have to emulate that history. You could also just decide randomly what syllables are going to have which stress, but the result will be artificial and unimpressive.

Fixed stress systems are a lot of fun. Certain stress systems in the world are very simple. In Finnish, for example, stress is always on the first syllable, and the first syllable is often special in some way. If you look at Finnish, you'll notice a lot of the time the first syllable has either a long vowel, a diphthong, or a coda consonant. That's not an accident. Finnish *loves* its initial stress system—so much so that certain dialects will actually geminate a following consonant if the first syllable is light and the next syllable is heavy. If anything, in Finnish placement of secondary stress is more interesting than placement of primary stress.

Aside from Finnish and languages like it, most languages have a series of complex rules to determine where primary stress is placed. For example, in Arabic, primary stress goes to the rightmost heavy syllable in the root (with the caveat that word-final case vowels have been dropped in many instances). If there are no heavy syllables, it goes to the antepenultimate syllable. Here are some examples:

سيارة /saj.jaː.ra/ [saj.ˈjaː.ra] "car"

قلم /qa.lam/ [ˈqɑ.lam] "pen" (*lost word-final case vowel*)

كتب /ka.ta.ba/ [ˈka.ta.ba] "he wrote"

كتاب /ki.taːb/ [ki.ˈtaːb] "book"

زيتون /zai.tuːn/ [ze.ˈtuːn] "olive"

طفولة /tˤa.fuː.la/ [tˤɑ.ˈfuː.la] "childhood"

Most of the time it's fairly predictable. But aside from simply saying what happens, how does this stuff actually *work*? How do Arabic speakers intuitively know what syllable to stress?

The best way I've seen to analyze fixed stress systems is with a linguistic framework called Optimality Theory (OT). Eric Baković was my OT instructor at UCSD, and though I'm not convinced that the framework is applicable to all areas of phonology, I think it works astonishingly well for fixed stress systems and level tone systems (more on those in the next section). There isn't time to do a full introduction to OT here, but if you're interested in seeing just what you can do with stress in a language, I recommend looking into it.

The main idea behind OT is that there are competing forces at work in any language, and what we produce orally is the *least bad* version of the language based on the various competing principles in our heads. So, with an Arabic word like /saj.jaː.ra/ that could be stressed on any one of those three syllables, the version with penultimate stress, [saj.ˈjaː.ra], is the least bad—or optimal—candidate. Why? Because Arabic likes to have the stress as close to the right edge as possible, but also likes heavy syllables to be stressed. Stressing those heavy syllables, though, is more important than getting the stress as far right as possible, so [saj.ˈjaː.ra] is better than the impossible *[saj.jaː.ˈra] (we use an asterisk * to indicate that a form is ungrammatical or unattested).

In order to create a system using competing candidates, one needs the appropriate set of tools. Below is a list of theoretical constructs that are particularly helpful in constructing fixed stress systems:

- **Foot:** A foot is a prosodic unit that many languages find useful in evaluating stress. A standard foot is composed of two light syllables, though it may have more. For example, *sofa* is a foot in English, and we write it in parentheses: (so.fə). *Mississippi* has two feet: (mɪ.sə)(sɪ.pi).

- **Trochee:** A trochee is a foot that has stress on the first syllable. For example, ('so.fə) is a trochee in English.

- **Iamb:** An iamb is a foot that has stress on the ultimate syllable. For example, *ago* (ə.'gow) is an iamb in English.

- **Dactyl:** A dactyl is a foot that has three syllables and initial stress. For example, *Canada* ('kʰæ.nə.ɾə) could be analyzed as a dactyl in English.

- **Anapest:** An anapest is a foot that has three syllables and final stress. For example, *Illinois* (ɪ.lə.'nɔj) could be analyzed as an anapest in English.

- **Amphibrach:** An amphibrach is a foot that has three syllables and penultimate stress. For example, *Nevada* (nə.'væ.ɾə) could be analyzed as an amphibrach in English.

- **Mora:** A mora is a timing unit that can be useful in building stress systems. An open syllable with a short vowel is equal to one mora. An open syllable with a long vowel is equal to two mora. A closed syllable with a short vowel is also equal to two mora. Basically, each vowel unit is one mora, and each coda consonant is one mora. Some languages don't count moras beyond two, but some do. It's up to the conlanger to decide what works for a given conlang.

All right, I know this probably seems like a bunch of gobbledygook unless you're familiar with poetics, but here's what this buys you. Let's make up some words (it doesn't matter what they mean here, just that they have different shapes):

ka.la	hem.bek	sa.va.lon	bi.se.lu.li
pu.lim	a.ri.la	ir.gu.des	am.pe.ro.gu
tam.ba	bon.du.le	o.wek.tu	a.ten.do.run

That's enough for now. Where are these words stressed? If it's lexical stress, it's wherever the dictionary says they are. If it's a superregular system like Finnish, it's always the same syllable. If it isn't, this is where all our parameters come into play.

For example, let's say that in this language . . .

1. A foot may consist of two syllables at most.

2. Extra syllables are not footed.

3. Feet are built from the right edge to the left.

4. Feet are iambic.

5. Main stress is on the right-most foot; secondary stress is placed on others.

Here's our list again with stresses marked:

(ka.ˈla)	(hem.ˈbek)	sa.(va.ˈlon)	(bi.ˌse.)(lu.ˈli)
(pu.ˈlim)	a.(ri.ˈla)	ir.(gu.ˈdes)	(am.ˌpe.)(ro.ˈgu)
(tam.ˈba)	bon.(du.ˈle)	o.(wek.ˈtu)	(a.ˌten.)(do.ˈrun)

The result is that main stress is always on the last syllable and secondary stress on the antepenultimate syllable *except* in trisyllabic words. If you had a phonological rule that was sensitive to stress (like the [ʌ]/[ə] alternation we've seen in English), trisyllabic forms would behave differently from tetrasyllabic forms.

Now let's change one thing. Let's say instead of main stress being on the *right*-most foot it's on the *left*-most foot. Here's what happens:

(ka.ˈla)	(hem.ˈbek)	sa.(va.ˈlon)	(bi.ˈse.)(lu.ˌli)
(pu.ˈlim)	a.(ri.ˈla)	ir.(gu.ˈdes)	(am.ˈpe.)(ro.ˌgu)
(tam.ˈba)	bon.(du.ˈle)	o.(wek.ˈtu)	(a.ˈten.)(do.ˌrun)

And look at that! Everything is pretty much the same except that suddenly when you get to tetrasyllabic words, primary stress falls on the antepenultimate syllable. And all we did was make one *tiny* adjustment. Try taking some of the features listed above and making them *drastically* different. You'll end up with a whole host of crazy stress patterns!

As with most linguistic frameworks, OT overgenerates, but for conlanging, that turns out to be a good thing, as it gives the conlanger more options. If operated correctly, though, any system generated with an OT framework should be *theoretically possible*, even if it doesn't exist in the real world.

Allophonic rules that are sensitive to stress tend to work hand in hand with stress-placement rules, unless the effect is purely phonetic. So, for example, vowels becoming long in stressed syllables, vowels reducing or disappearing in unstressed syllables, geminating a following consonant to make a stressed syllable heavy—all of these types of changes occur because the point of stress is to make the stressed syllable prominent in some way. A conlanger can use these rules to their advantage in designing a system with the right sound.

TONE

You've probably heard a thing or two about tone languages. You've probably heard languages such as Thai and Vietnamese described as "musical," "singsong," and "exotic" (all of this is the by-product of cultural stereotyping). It may also be the case that you've never heard of the tone languages of Africa—or America. In this section, I'll give you the basics on tone, and give you an idea where to start if you want to create a tonal language.

First, **tone** in linguistics is the uniform association of pitch with phonological material used to distinguish meaning (either semantic or grammatical). The most famous example comes from Chinese, where four words with roughly the same phonetic representation— [ma]—have four different tones, and, consequently, four different meanings:

媽 *mā* [ma˥] or [ma55] "mother"

麻 *má* [ma˧˥] or [ma35] "hemp"

馬 *mǎ* [ma˨˩˦] or [ma214] "horse"

罵 *mà* [ma˥˩] or [ma51] "scold"

There's also a fifth *ma* that gets its tone from context only. The four words above use the IPA characters associated with tone. The characters have a vertical line as a standard with a left-pointing bar that indicates the approximate level of the tone, with low being low and high being high. The characters are (in order of lowest to highest): [˩], [˨], [˧], [˦], [˥]. They can be put in order to indicate contours or vowel duration. These characters are often replaced with numbers, using 1 through 5 going from lowest to highest. Personally, I prefer the number system, so I'll be using it throughout the rest of the book.

The first important thing to know about tone is that it is *not* the same as a musical scale. A note of G is a specific sound that can be further specified if you indicate the octave. Tone level in a tone language, though, is relative. If a word like [ma55] has a high tone associated with it, the tone will *always* be higher than a word with a dipping [214] tone in the same utterance, but it will *not* always be the same exact pitch. Such a thing requires perfect pitch, which not all people have. Furthermore, it's unnecessary. Maintaining relative tone levels throughout a discourse is enough to distinguish meaning, and that's what's important for a language.

Second, regarding the number of tones, natural languages can run as high as nine, and as few as two. If there are two tones, they're always high and low. Languages with more than three tones will have a contour tone of some kind. Languages that are claimed to have more than nine tones usually can't produce minimal pairs with all examples (e.g. some tones will occur only with certain codas while others occur only without codas), so their status is debatable. It is theoretically possible for a human to distinguish each pitch that an ear can hear, but languages never come close to exploiting the physical limitations of humans. This is something that can be explored for engelangs which aren't attempting to be naturalistic (or even user-friendly), but such a language would prove prohibitively challenging to use and understand.

Tone languages themselves seem to come in two varieties: contour tone languages and level or register tone languages. I'll address each type briefly.

CONTOUR TONE LANGUAGES

Though I'll be introducing them here, I will start off with this caveat. If you're a conlanger intending to create a contour tone language, it *must* be evolved. Based on what we know about the evolution of contour tone languages, there's no way to do it faithfully without having a full history behind it. The same isn't necessarily true of register tone languages.

With that out of the way, a **contour tone language** is a language that typically assigns a specific tone to a specific syllable, and that tone is fixed. Contour tone languages usually have at least four tones, and sometimes as many as nine. For a contour tone language, the word "tone" itself will often apply to a tone melody, rather than an actual pitch level. Most (but not all) contour tone languages in the world can be found in Southeast Asia. We've already seen the tones of Mandarin. Here's an example from Thai:

นา [naː33] "paddy field"

ทมห [naː21] "nickname (i.e. this is someone in particular's nickname)"

หน้า [naː51] "face"

ป้า [naː45] "maternal aunt"

หนา [naː14] "thick"

Contour tone languages typically name the tones that are present in the language, and it's known that a particular word has a particular tone. This is actually quite different from register tone languages, where tones may change for grammatical purposes, or when affixes are added. It's also not uncommon for contour tone languages to have an overabundance of monosyllabic roots and words.

Though each syllable has a fixed tone, there are two exceptions to how tone is realized. Some words (*especially* function words) have no particular tone and simply adopt a tone from an adjacent word. In addition, the tone of other words that *do* have specific tones will change depending on what words precede or follow them. Both of these phenomena are instantiations of what we call **tone sandhi**. Tone sandhi rules differ from language to language, but they describe what happens when a word with a particular tone comes in contact with another word with a particular tone. Here's an illustrative example from Chinese:

你 *nǐ* [ni214] "you" + 好 *hǎo* [hao214] "good" = 你好 *ní hǎo* [ni35. hao21] "hello"

In Chinese linguistics, this is an example of the change that occurs when two "3" (or dipping) tones come together. The first "3" tone becomes a "2" (rising) tone, and the second "3" tone loses its rising intonation at the end. There's nothing that would force this to happen phonetically: it just does.

If you're interested in creating a contour tone language, it behooves you to examine the tone systems of various natural languages. Essentially, though, the sandhi rules are there for two reasons. The first reason is it makes pronunciation simpler. The second is it occurs as a natural result of compounding (i.e. making one word out of two distinct words). Now we'll move on to register systems.

REGISTER TONE LANGUAGES

Register tone languages have at most four tones, and often have as few as two. They are sometimes called level tone languages, because many such languages are analyzed as having *only* level tones, with all contour tones simply being combinations of the other level tones. Most register tone languages have a high (H) and low (L) level tone, though some will also have a mid tone. Those that have contours usually have only a falling (HL) tone or sometimes also a rising (LH) tone.

In many register tone languages, the low tone is treated as default, with other tones being treated as special. For example, some register languages put restrictions on how many high tones may appear in a root. Others may permit only certain tone contour patterns in a word. A common pattern is to allow only all H tones, all L tones, HL, or LHL. These types of restrictions vary widely from language to language, though, so it's important to take a look at a variety of level tone languages if you're a conlanger interested in producing one.

Here are some examples of words in the register tone language Hausa, spoken in Mali (tone pattern indicated in parentheses at the end and with diacritics; long vowels not marked):

shekára [ʃeːka.raː] "year" (LHL)

shekarú [ʃeːka.ruː] "years" (LLH)

surúká [su.ru.kaː] "mother-in-law" (LHH)

surukúwá [su.ru.ku.waː] "mothers-in-law" (LLHH)

lábabá [la.ɓaːɓaː] "to sneak up on" (HLH)

kwáná [kwaːnaː] "nighttime" (HH)

kwanakí [kwaː.na.kiː] "nighttimes" (LLH)

da [daː] "if" (L)

dâ [daː] "previously" (HL)

I included a couple singular and plural pairs so you can see how the tones will shift around depending on the grammatical status of a word. This is far from uncommon. Take a look at these forms:

tábbatá [tab.ba.taː] "to confirm" (HLH)

tabbatáccé [tab.ba.tat.tʃeː] "confirmed (singular adjective)" (LLHH)

tabbatattú [tab.ba.tat.tuː] "confirmed (plural adjective)" (LLLH)

tábbátár [tab.ba.tar] "to confirm (used with auxiliary)" (HHH)

The tones are moving about, but it's clear that all of these word forms are coming from the same root. This isn't something you'd see in a contour tone language. In effect, the difference between a contour tone language and a register tone language is the same as the difference between a lexical stress language and a fixed stress language. And, just as OT can be good for designing fixed stress systems, so can OT be good for designing register tone systems. When I was creating my register tone language Njaama, I kept the following questions in mind:

1. **Inherent Tone:** Will certain words have inherent tone? Which tones will be inherent: Just high? High and low?

2. **Inherent Tone Melodies:** Will tones or tone melodies be inherent? If the latter, which melodies? H, HL, LH, L, or more?

3. **Default Tone:** What's the default tone? What happens to syllables that don't have tone?

4. **Repair Strategies**: What happens when an affix with an inherent tone is added to a word and the result is an infelicitous melody? For example, say an H tone suffix is added to a word with an HL melody and the HLH melody is disallowed. What happens?

5. **Contour**: What happens when two tones are assigned to one syllable? What contour tones are allowed? If one is disallowed, what happens when that melody occurs on a single syllable?

How these questions are answered will determine the character of the register tone language. Also, it's important to note that tone assignment can be sensitive to the tones of surrounding words. For example, the Hausa copula takes the opposite tone of whatever it follows:

Sárkí ne. [saɽ.kiː neː] "It is a chief."

Yáro né. [jaː.roː neː] "It is a boy."

In Njaama, subject and object pronouns are distinguished by a change in tone (*tekaané* means "saw" below):

⊰Ⳡ ^Λⵁⳑⵁ⊦ⵁ °ⳑⵁⵘ

Wa (L) *tekaané yáá* (H). [wa te.kaː.ne jaː] "I saw you."

⊰ⳑⵁⵘ ^Λⵁⳑⵁ⊦ⵁ °Ⳡⵁⵘ

Yaa (L) *tekaané wá* (H). [jaː te.kaː.ne wa] "You saw me."

It really depends on the language what the tone will or won't do. Looking at a plethora of level tone languages can be confusing, so it's ideal to take a look at one, figure out exactly how it works, and then move on to another. Everything that's been discussed in this section is a possibility, though. In my opinion, register tone languages are among the most interesting languages I've seen, and I'd love to see more register tone conlangs.

SIGN LANGUAGE ARTICULATION

Advance warning: This subject requires *its own book*. I'm going to try to fit as much as I can into a couple pages.

First, a **sign language** or **manual language** is one that uses the hands as its primary articulators. Sign languages also use facial expressions, eyebrow location, and other parts of the body in articulation. Sign languages have been in existence for as long as humans have had language and deafness has existed. Sign languages are full systems and are complete languages; they are *not* the same as the gesturing that occurs in spoken language or "body language." Sign languages have the same expressive power as any spoken language— and, indeed, can do some incredible things that spoken languages cannot. The sign languages that exist in the world today are not based on spoken languages or in any way subordinate to them. This means that American Deaf signers who can read English are bilingual. Sign languages have their own histories that are independent from the histories of spoken languages. For example, modern French Sign Language (FSL) and modern American Sign Language (ASL) both have a common ancestor in Old French Sign Language (OFSL). British Sign Language (BSL) is unrelated to either. Sign languages are not used exclusively by deaf individuals. Many children of Deaf adults (CODAs) are fluent signers, as are other hearing individuals who have Deaf family members. Also, in American Deaf culture, *deaf* with a lowercase *d* refers to the inability to hear; *Deaf* with an uppercase *D* refers to the ability to sign.

That's basically the first few weeks of a Deaf culture class in one paragraph. Now on to the languages themselves.

After I signed on to be David Perlmutter's TA in his Deaf Culture course at UCSD, I found it disappointing, but not at all surprising, that no one had created a constructed sign language (CSL). The history of Deaf signing always lies somewhere below the surface of common knowledge. The lack of languages, though, wasn't so much due to lack of interest, but due to a lack of ways to represent them. Video remains the best way to record and transmit a sign language when face-to-face communication is impossible, but it's not (yet) convenient. This led me to create the Sign Language IPA (SLIPA), which was an attempt to encode the phonological structure of signed languages in ASCII.

Though the analogue isn't perfect, sign languages can be described in roughly the same way as spoken languages if you assume the following:

Places (P) = Consonants

Movements (M) = Vowels

Handshape (HS) = Tone

Independent Hand Movement (IHM) = Secondary Articulations

In order to describe signs, then, I came up with this framework (think of the following as a syllable):

p[HS]Mp[HS]

Places are always written in lowercase; movements are always written in uppercase; handshapes are always written in uppercase and contained within brackets. Syllables are described as either starting or ending at a place via some manner of movement. A word can also be a place by itself if it has a secondary articulation.

To use a simple example, the word for "king" in ASL is as follows: The signer makes a [K] handshape (the ring and pinky fingers are tucked into the hand; the middle finger bends forward; the index finger is extended straight up; the thumb touches the middle finger) then touches their left shoulder (s_h). After that they pull their hand to their right hip (bl) in a low arc (E^G), as if they're describing the path of a sash. To write that sign, you'd do the following (describing it from the signer's perspective):

s_h[K]E^Gbl

It looks like something you'd see in a spam e-mail, but it does the trick. SLIPA isn't the only transcription system that exists, but it's the only one that will work with ASCII.

Now for what sign languages can do. First, they're very much like spoken languages, in that they describe the world using nouns and verbs and place them in a particular order. Just like spoken languages, which rely on linear order, sign languages feature phenomena like affixation. For example, the ASL words for "teacher" and "student" each involve the signs for "teach" and "learn," respectively, followed by a sign where one takes one's flat hands and moves them from the shoulders down to the belt area. Thus, "teacher" is a combination of "teach" and an agentive suffix, and "student" is a combination of "learn" and an agentive suffix.

Sign languages can also make use of their medium in ways that natural languages would never do. In ASL, for example, the sign for "week" requires the signer to make a [1] shape with their hand (like an English speaker holding up a number 1) and wipe it from left to right across the palm of their left hand. That's the basic sign for "week." Since handshape is used to indicate numbers, though, you can change the shape of your hand to indicate more than one week. I'm not sure how well it would work for numbers past ten, but it's a simple thing to change the handshape and sign, in one motion, "two weeks," "three weeks," "seven weeks," etc. Furthermore, since the region behind a signer is generally associated with the past and the region in front generally associated with the future, a signer can then pull their dominant hand backward at the end of a sign to mean "ago," and push it ahead to mean "in the future." Thus, this single sign can be used to indicate between one and at least ten weeks—and either in the past or the future, if the signer so chooses.

The equivalent of this in spoken language would be inflection. It would be as if you could say not only *week* and *weeks* in English, but *weekso* for "two weeks," *weekt* for "three weeks," *tweek* for "three weeks ago," *fweek* for "four weeks in the future," etc. This is something that a spoken language would *never* do because it's needlessly complex. Since in ASL you *already* have to use a handshape in the production of the sign, though, why not change the handshape to add more information? Sign languages routinely take advantage of the medium of sign in ways just like this to make distinctions spoken languages never would. One of my favorite examples is the sign for "understand." To form it, you face your hand toward you, raise it to your head, and then raise your index finger (kind of like a light going on). If you're really annoyed at someone who's explaining the same dumb thing to you for the fifty billionth time, though, you can go ahead and raise your middle finger instead as a way of saying, "Yeah. I get it, dude."

This section on sign language is roughly like summarizing *War and Peace* in a haiku. If you're a conlanger *at all* interested in producing a CSL, I strongly recommend you do a little investigating to see what sign languages can do so you can decide what you want to do with yours.

ALIEN SOUND SYSTEMS

Humans can do some pretty amazing things with their mouths, hands, and bodies, but everything we can possibly do is still quite human. What if there was a being that didn't have our unique physiology? How might they communicate?

At base, for language to work (as we understand it), one creature has to produce some sort of perceivable series of tokens, and another creature has to be able to perceive and decode those tokens correctly. As humans, we're able to understand and work with our five senses, so an alien language would probably need to make use of at least one of those senses, unless you're able to think up a distinct type of sense (thought doesn't count). In order to determine what makes sense, you'll first have to come up with an alien.

A lot of the aliens in television and film are humanoid, and differ from humans in ways that really have nothing to do with language. While Klingons have an extra set of lungs and forehead ridges, they still have one set of vocal folds, a vocal tract shaped like human vocal tracts, a tongue, an alveolar ridge, and ears. As aliens, they're simply not *linguistically* alien enough to warrant anything other than a spoken human language—and the same goes for the aliens on *Alien Nation, Star-Crossed, Stargate, Roswell,* and most of the aliens in the *Star Wars* and *Defiance* universes.

If we're focusing on speech and sound, in order to actually need different speech sounds, the aliens will need to have different vocal anatomy. How might one create a different vocal tract?

Now I'm no biologist, so I can't answer questions about what's plausible, but I do know how speech sounds work, so I can give you an idea. First, recall that our anatomy was not *designed* for language. It *allows* for it, sure, but our vocal tract is really for eating and breathing. The same will likely be true of aliens. (It would be a bizarre evolutionary trend to push *specifically* for speech, since language would already have to exist. These beings would need to have language but not be able to use it, so that those that *could* use it had a distinct, evolutionary advantage. It seems implausible, at the very least.) Since humans are the only creatures on Earth that can use their vocal tract to speak fluidly, it makes sense to take an in-depth look at it.

Other animals can produce speech sounds, of course. None of them can produce all the speech sounds humans use in language. Part of that is due to the facility of our tongue; part of it is due to the shape of the roof of the mouth; part of it is due to what we can do with our lips. A large part, though, is due to the acoustic properties of the sounds we can produce with our mouths. If the human vocal tract is modeled as a tube, this is what the tube's standing wave's first three resonant frequencies would look like:

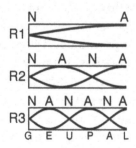

Key (Top and Left): N = node, A = antinode, R = resonant frequency

Key (Bottom): G = glottis, E = epiglottis/pharynx, U = uvula, P = palate, A = alveolar ridge, L = lips

Let me explain what you're seeing here. A sound wave travels from the lungs and out toward the world. When it hits the mouth, some of it escapes, but the rest bounces off the lips and heads back toward the glottis, but with opposite polarity. This can produce a standing wave in ideal conditions. The first wave (R1) of sound has the longest wavelength, and its first overtone (R2) has half the wavelength of the original, the second (R3) has a third the wavelength, the third (R4) a quarter, etc. For speech, the first three resonances are most relevant. Where the amplitudes of the positive and negative wave are equal, that's called a node (N). Where the amplitudes are at their min and max, that's called an antinode (A). The average male vocal tract is seventeen centimeters long.

Now here's the key takeaway. If you look at where the nodes and antinodes lie for R3, they're all at key points in the vocal tract. There's a reason that a uvular stop sounds different from a velar stop, even though the surface is roughly the same. It's the combination of all these factors that allows us to produce sounds that are acoustically distinct.

To design a different set of sounds, one has to design a different vocal tract—and perhaps a different set of ears. For example, while harmonics beyond the third can play a role in speech perception, it's really just the first three that are most relevant for language. If beings had better ears, they might be able to make better use of harmonics beyond the third. The vocal tract, though, is the one that will require the most work. For example, two alveolar ridges in the mouth would add a passive articulator, but whether or not it would sound appreciably different depends on the length of the vocal tract, and whether or not that second ridge is at a node or antinode. Different holes in the tract (like a second nose with a passageway that led to a spot just below the pharynx) will mean that there will be different types of nasal-like sounds available. Depending on how well the tips could be controlled, a forked tongue might not be able to produce any stop consonants unless done with the tongue body. Also, imagine if a being had no tongue—or teeth—but two lips and two toothless alveolar ridges, one above and one below. What types of sounds might they be able to make?

If you've got plenty of resources, you can actually *design* a working vocal tract and simulate what it would sound like if there were a being with a nonhuman vocal tract. This is probably beyond the realm of practicality for most people (or even productions), but it exists as a possibility.

Moving beyond sound, what if there were an alien that didn't have a mouth at all? What if it had one gigantic eyeball and forty-nine tentacles, seven of which were shorter and used as armlike appendages? This is the question Denis Moskowitz asked, and the language he created, Rikchik, is his answer. Rikchik is the language used by rikchiks, which look like this:

Since the seven tentacles rikchiks use to sign are the same, Denis created a language where words aren't spelled out with the signed equivalent of phonemes; rather, words are combinations of a fixed set of shapes. Each word in Rikchik has four elements:

1. Four tentacles form the shape of a semantic category. These four tentacles are in the middle of the signing space.

2. One tentacle in the lower left-hand corner makes a shape that corresponds to the class of a word. This combines with the semantic shape to form a **lexeme** or word.

3. On the top of the signing space one tentacle tells you what role the word plays in the sentence (whether it's a subject or object, etc.).

4. The last tentacle, on the lower right, indicates how many of the previous signs it "collects" (i.e. how many of the previous signs go together with the current sign).

In order to be able to convey the language, Denis had to create his own transcription system, so that a word looks like this:

The four lines in the middle are the four word tentacles that indicate that the word has something to do with crystal. The small circle indicates that this word doesn't collect any others (it's just a word on its own), and the swoosh at the top indicates that this word is a quality word (meaning that it defines the quality of whatever collects it). The last symbol, the Tetris-like shape in the lower left, indicates that the type of word it is is a modifier, so basically an adjective. Literally it would be "crystal-like," but the actual definition is "sweet," since rikchiks eat crystals as a kind of treat.

The "phonology" of Rikchik is defined by the shapes those seven tentacles can bend themselves into. While the glyph above is approximately what you will see, those are only the *ends* of the tentacles; the rest of them are connected to the body. The limitations, though, aren't breath or tongue elasticity, but tentacle elasticity (how much they can bend and into what shapes). The language that Denis has built isn't the only *possible* language that could be built using the physiology of the rikchiks; it's just the one he built.

Once you move on to things like smell, taste, and touch, the question becomes what kind of language a conlanger wants to build. For example, if you consider the number of speech sounds the human mouth can make, it's easy to construct languages that build words from sounds. If the number of possible sounds becomes too restrictive—or the time to produce them becomes too long— you may have to move away from words built up of arbitrary parts to a classification system like Rikchik uses. That, then, takes you beyond the realm of phonology, and into the realm of morphology and semantics.

The key point to remember in building a *truly* alien sound system (or sign system or smell system) is that there is no road map. Instead, the conlanger carves their own path using the basic principles we know about sound production, sound perception, object recognition, motor control, and physics. If you want to create a language for beings that can consciously change the color patterns on their wings, you need to become an expert in chromatophores. Once you know the science, then you can apply your knowledge of language to the being you've created and build on top of it.

Case Study

THE SOUND OF DOTHRAKI

I'm often asked what inspired me to create Dothraki, but I always find the question a little odd. The process I used for Dothraki—my first professional language—was different from any I had used before, because Dothraki was *not* my creation; the people did *not* spring from my imagination. It wasn't as if I was inspired to create a particular type of language that ended up being Dothraki. Rather, it was as if I had been given a very small part of a puzzle that had been put together, and it was up to me not only to determine what the picture was, but also to create the rest of the pieces and then put them all together.

The bit that I started with was a set of Dothraki words and names from the first three books of *A Song of Ice and Fire*. This is a list of all those words (with George R. R. Martin's spellings):

khal	khaleesi	khalasar	dosh	rhae	Iggo	Ogo
khaleen	arakh	khas	hranna	mhar	Zollo	Temmo
rakh	haj	rhaesh	andahli	rhaggat	Bharbo	ko
dothrae	mr'anha	khalakka	vaes	dothrak	Pono	Rhogoro
Dothraki	hrakkar	Drogo	Haggo	Cohollo	maegi	qiya
Qotho	Jhogo	Quaro	Rhaego	Rakharo	qoy	shierak
Fogo	Jommo	Irri	Jhiqui	haesh	rakhi	Moro
tolorro	jaqqa	rhan	Mago	Aggo	Jhaqo	ai

Unless I've missed any, that's a total of fifty-six words, twenty-four of which are proper names. Ignoring grammar, the first job I had to do was figure out how to deal with the spelling. I knew going in that Martin didn't care how fans pronounced the words and names in his books (though he does have a couple of pet peeves—like pronouncing *Jaime* [dʒem]). Those of us who were applying for the Dothraki job didn't have George R. R. Martin as a resource while creating our proposals, but it also didn't seem appropriate to rely on him as a direct resource. Since he didn't put out a pronunciation guide for his books, it was up to the fans to determine how things "ought" to be pronounced. My job, then, was to figure out how fans would most likely pronounce all the words on the list above. Figuring that the bulk of fans would be English speakers—and that the executive producers, Dave and Dan, were American—I decided to go with how I thought the words would be pronounced by an American English speaker.

That was the first constraint. The next was to filter that through the desire for this to be a foreign- and "harsh"-sounding language. That meant that, among other things, non-English consonants were *not* out of play. Here I was guided by the spelling. When George R. R. Martin uses spellings that are distinctly non-English, I felt that licensed the use of non-English sounds or clusters.

Finally, I was determined to treat the spelling as canon. I didn't want to change the spellings unless it was simply to regularize them for the sake of consistency (so, for example, what was spelled *Cohollo* became *Kohollo*, since *c* is only used in the digraph *ch*). This would be the rough equivalent of changing a British spelling of *colour* to an American spelling of *color*, or vice versa. Otherwise, if two words were spelled differently, then they would be pronounced differently.

With those constraints in mind, I noticed two things:

1. The vowel *u* never occurs as a vowel; it only occurs in the cluster *qu*.

2. The consonants *p* and *b* are never used.

The only exception to the first point was in certain editions of *A Clash of Kings*, where *Vaes Tolorro* was misspelled *Vaes Tolorru*. This, though, was clearly a misprint. As for the second, if you take a careful look at the table above, you'll notice that there are two key exceptions: *Pono* and *Bharbo*—the latter Drogo's father. I missed these two names entirely when crafting my proposal. This would have consequences later on.

After these realizations, I started to make some decisions about the pronunciation of the various letterforms in the extant vocabulary:

- Vowels would have their cardinal pronunciations.

- Most consonants would be pronounced just like they looked—or, at least, to an English speaker. This meant that *j* would be pronounced [dʒ] and *y* would be pronounced [j]. Q, however, would be pronounced [q], when occurring on its own.

- *Qu* would be reinterpreted as a sequence of [k] and [w], and would be respelled *kw* (though I also allowed the sequence [qw]).

- The spellings *th*, *sh*, *kh,* and *jh* would be pronounced [θ], [ʃ], [x], and [ʒ], respectively, and the latter would be respelled *zh*. Other instances of *h* would be pronounced separately as [h], no matter where it appeared in the word.

- All vowels would be pronounced separately, even when they occurred next to another vowel. This was inspired by a phenomenon I like in Spanish, where in a word like *creer*, there are two distinct vowel sounds: [kɾe.ˈer]. This also meant I wouldn't have to figure out a unique pronunciation for the *ae* digraphs which are ubiquitous in Martin's works. They'd just be treated as *a* followed by *e*.

- *R* would work almost identically to *r* in Spanish. Phonetically, it would be a trilled [r] at the beginning or end of a word, and elsewhere it would be [ɾ]—unless it was doubled, in which case it would be [r].

- In order for the language to sound maximally different, all coronal consonants ([t], [d], [n], [l]) would be dental (pronounced with the tongue tip against the top teeth). If pronounced accurately, it would give the language a recognizably foreign sound.

- There would be no [u], [p], or [b]. I rationalized this by finding no instances of these sounds in the extant words (though this was a mistake!). My motivation for doing so was to give the language a unique sound (addition by subtraction, as it were). Plus, I dislike [p], [b], and [u]. I find them to be ugly sounds.

Having done this, I was able to put together the following phonetic inventory:

	Labial	Dental	Alveolar	Palatal	Velar	Uvular	Glottal
Stop		t, d			k, g	q	
Affricate				dʒ			
Fricative	f, v	θ	s, z	ʃ, ʒ	x		h
Nasal	m	n	n	ɲ	ŋ	N	
Glide				j	w		
Lateral		l					
Tap/Trill			ɾ, r				

	Front	Back
High	i	
Mid	e	o
Low		a

Most of the nasal consonants would simply be allophones of the phoneme /n/ occurring in specific contexts (i.e. [N] before [q], [ŋ] before [x], [k], and [g], etc.). Looking at the table I saw a couple of gaps, but the only one I decided to fill was adding [tʃ] to the palatal column to pair with [dʒ], which would be spelled *ch*. That's the only sound I added to Dothraki that wasn't present in the books, based on how I interpreted the spelling of the extant vocabulary.

For the most part, I think I did a pretty good job of matching fan expectations for the sound of Dothraki, though there are two deviations worth noting. First is George R. R. Martin's pronunciation of the word *Dothraki*. He *consistently* pronounces it [do.ˈθɹæ.kaj]. This pronunciation is still, to me, unfathomable. I'm glad I didn't know about his pronunciation before I did my work, and I think I did right by the fans by going with what I believe is the "usual" *doth-ROCK-ee* pronunciation.

One place where this didn't work, though, was with the word *khaleesi*. Obviously if you look at that word, as an English speaker, you're going to pronounce it [kʰə.ˈli.si]—the way it's currently pronounced by everyone—but in determining pronunciation, I had to adhere to my rule that George's spellings were sacrosanct. By that rule, the word should be four syllables long, and the two *e*'s should be pronounced separately. This means its proper pronunciation is [ˈxa.le.e.si]. Now, the change from [x] to [kʰ] is to be expected (this is what we do with Greek borrowings into English, after all). If the word were *really* pronounced [ˈxa.le.e.si], though, then English speakers hearing it and turning it into an English word would naturally pronounce it either [ˈkʰa.lə.si] or [kʰə.ˈle.si] (the latter as if it were spelled "kha-lacy"). Since Dothraki is a spoken language, not a written language, the pronunciation [kʰə.ˈli.si] should be impossible. It'd be like pronouncing *fiancé* [fi.ˈɑn.si]; it just wouldn't happen. Since we use the spelling system we do in the *real* world, though, English speakers will of course pronounce *khaleesi* [kʰə.ˈli.si]. This is the one place I wish I would have made an exception. In order to reflect the real-world pronunciation, I should have changed the Dothraki spelling to *khalisi* and been done with it. Alas, it wasn't to be, so the gaffe will live on, to my shame.

After determining the spelling system, the goal was to produce words that looked like the extant vocabulary. For example, if you know that *band* is a word in English, and it has the structure CVCC, you should expect for there to be other words like it, and there are: *cart, ford, lamp, sand, wind, bolt*, etc. Part of what will give a language its character is having a bunch of words that look like they obviously fit together. That's what I did with Dothraki:

Book Word(s)	Pattern	Created Words
khal, haj, dosh	CVC	rek, qov, nith, maj, jin, has, fir, dim, chath, sash, tor
hranna	C(C)V(C)CV	shilla, mhotha, qwizha, rhiko, vroza, krista, hrelki
rhaesh	C(C)VV(C)	rhoa, noah, leik, khaor, daen, fiez, koal, mai, neak
Aggo, jaqqa	(C)VC:V	lorra, ricchi, ville, yalli, zajja, zhille, naffa, khirra, gillo
tolorro, Cohollo	CVCVCCV	zhokakkwa, najahhey, movekkha, Kovarro, inavva

The next step was to ensure that a lot of high frequency words would have a kind of "harsh" or "foreign" sound. The first step was to design the stress system to ensure that the rhythm would differ from that of English. In English, for example, it's rare for a word to be stressed on the last syllable, unless the word is borrowed, or a verb. In Dothraki, all words that end in a consonant are stressed on the last syllable. Referring to our discussion of stress systems, a Dothraki word looks at the right edge of the word to determine its stress. If the word ends in a consonant, the last syllable is stressed. If it ends in a vowel, it looks to the penultimate syllable. If that syllable is heavy, it's stressed. Otherwise the first syllable is stressed. This would mean that several key words wouldn't be stressed right (for example, *Dothraki* and *khaleesi* should both be stressed on the first syllable), but since they would be borrowings when spoken in English, that wasn't a big deal. What was more important was ensuring that the dialogue had that characteristic Dothraki rhythm.

So given a normal Dothraki sentence like this . . .

> *Lajak oga haz oqet ha khalaan.*
> [la.ˈdʒak ˈo.ga haz o.ˈqet ha xa.la.ˈan]

"The warrior is slaughtering that sheep for the khal."

. . . the stresses of the first, fourth, and final words would be in the opposite place one would expect them to be if these were native English words.

The final step in making sure that the Dothraki-ness of Dothraki came through was to make sure some of the "harsh" sounds were used in high-frequency terms. Remember how I talked about brand identity? This is where it becomes important. What are the sounds that were characteristic of Dothraki? In my mind, it's the doubled vowels, the voiceless velar fricative [x], geminate consonants, the trilled [r], the uvular [q], and the forceful [h], which often comes out as [ɦ]. Since the audience of *Game of Thrones* would be hearing the language through the lines, I had some control over what Dothraki words they heard. I used that to my advantage.

First, I didn't have to work very hard with [x]. Spelled *kh*, that sound is used in the words *khal, khaleesi,* and *arakh,* which are used frequently. Just to make sure I got as much mileage out of that sound as I could, though, I made the form of one of my objective derivational suffixes *-(i)kh*. This means that words ending in [x] are *extremely* common in Dothraki: *achrakh* "smell," *mechikh* "roast quail," *nesikh* "knowledge," *sewafikh* "wine," etc.

The sound [r] was already going to be common enough, but I created two productive suffixes that end in *r*. One was derived from George R. R. Martin's word *khalasar*. This became a collective suffix that is used somewhat frequently: *astosor* "story," *gimisir* "commoners," *jereser* "market," *lajasar* "army," etc. I also created a new affix ending in *r* that forms abstract nominals, and *that* strategy is simply ubiquitous in Dothraki. It's the strategy that turns *davra* "good" into *athdavrazar* "excellent," and *jahak* "braid" into *athjahakar* "pride."

I used a similar strategy with geminates, where turning a verb from a regular verb into a causative verb involves geminating the first consonant (e.g. *layafat* "to be happy" becomes *allayafat* "to please"), and also with double vowels (two grammatical suffixes attached to nouns are *-aan* and *-oon*), but with [q] and [h], I did something different. Neither sound really lends itself well to morphology, so instead I simply targeted words that either were high frequency or that I knew were going to be used in a script, and made sure to use [h] and/or [q]. For example, one of my favorite words, *mahrazh,* "man," and the word for "horse," *hrazef,* make prominent use of [h] in a position where English wouldn't use it. A high frequency word that I knew would be used periodically is the word *qora,* which is the Dothraki word for both "hand" and "arm." I also lucked out with the phrase "blood of my blood," since one of the defined words from George R. R. Martin's list was *qoy,* "blood."

After this, though, it was all in the hands of the actors. Those actors who really put a lot of effort into it and took it seriously were the ones who were really able to sell it as a living, breathing language. Jason Momoa was a gift. Not even in my wildest dreams could I have imagined a better Drogo or a better ambassador for this language. Up to that point, he was the hulkiest, beefiest, dreamiest mountain of a human being ever to speak a created language, and he was speaking *my* language. Try calling *him* a nerd and see how far you get! Both his and Amrita Acharia's performances sit near and dear to my heart.

Even though the process for Dothraki was a little different since I wasn't creating a language from scratch, the principles I employed can be profitably reproduced in an original conlang. The phonetic inventory is just the starting point. The phonotactics, the stress system, and the common word endings are going to be what are most noticeable to the listener, since that's what they'll be hearing the most. A conlanger can use that to their advantage. By controlling those aspects of the language, they'll be defining its character, and that's what will give it a sound that is unmistakable and all its own.

CHAPTER II

Words

INTRODUCTION

When I was an undergraduate, an English professor of mine named Nikolai Popov turned me on to a book by William Butler Yeats called *A Vision*. He described it as one of the strangest books ever written, and, having now read it, I must admit he was right. As a graduate student I picked up a book purporting to analyze the work, hoping to gain some insight. In the introduction, the author wrote that he couldn't begin to analyze a work like *A Vision* without first defining what a *book* was.

After reading that, I rolled my eyes and put the book back. I can't *stand* stuff like that: simple questions that winkingly suggest they're not as "simple" as they seem.

So it's not without some irony and crow-eating that I now pose to you this question: What is a word?

It's an odd question, because we all know what a word is, even if we've never had to define the concept explicitly. A word is what's printed on paper or a screen that has blank space around it. Yet if one is to start examining claims like the number of words some such language has (English has a million words, say "sources"), one needs criteria.

Let's go about it systematically. Is *cat* a word? You bet. No question. How about *cats*? Of course, it *is* a word, but it shouldn't count as a separate word, right? If it did, you'd have to take all the nouns in English and double them to get a real word count. So even though *cats* is a word, we have to believe it's not a separate word from *cat*, since it's just the plural version of that word.

So what about *person* versus *people*? In one sense, *people* is just the plural of *person*. But you could also say something like *The Dothraki are a warlike people*. There it's clear *people* is being used slightly differently. Consequently, we'll have to assign wordhood to at least one sense of "people."

And certainly the same logic that treats *cat* and *cats* as versions of the same word would also treat, say, *sleep* and *slept* as versions of the same word. *Slept* is just the past tense of *sleep*, and shouldn't really count as a separate word. But what about *excite*, the verb, versus *excited*? The two are obviously related, and in certain circumstances, *excited* is the past tense of *excite*, but it's also an adjective that, while related, is still different enough that it feels like it's a separate word. So we'll count that.

How about a *bank* where you keep your money and the *bank* of a river? Incidental homonyms. Obviously separate words. But what about a *plate* that you eat off and a tectonic *plate*? They're likely related, but they refer to very different things. You might say the latter is a secondary definition of the former, but is it different enough to count as a different word? And how about an *email* versus the verb *email*? Clearly related, but they belong to different grammatical realms.

And what about all the new product names that keep entering our language? I'd say *kleenex* is enough of a word that it doesn't even need to be capitalized anymore—and the same with *xerox*—but are we there yet with *google*? Can you still *TiVo* something if you don't have TiVo, or do you have to say you're *DVRing* it?

Also, is *one* a word? Sure. *Two*? Of course. *Twenty-three*? Yes . . . But if that's the case, doesn't English then have an infinite number of words . . . ?

And that's just English. English is easy. Take a look at some of these words from the Siglitun variety of Inuktitut:

tuktu "caribou"

tuktuaraaluk "little caribou"

tuktuaraalualuk
"pitiful old little caribou"

tuktuaraalualutqiun
"spare pitiful old little caribou"

tuktuaraalualutqiunnguaq
"spare pitiful old little toy caribou"

tuktuaraalualutqiunngualiqiyi
"peddler of spare pitiful old little toy caribous"

I could keep going. I haven't even used any of the verbal suffixes. If I were to add -*liaqtuaq* to the end of that last word, for example, I'd produce a word that meant "He went hunting peddlers of spare pitiful old little toy caribous." Now you might say to yourself, "But that's an entire sentence!" In English, it is. In Inuktitut, it's a word. In fact, if you take any piece of discourse in a language like Inuktitut, the majority of the words will be used exactly once. In English, by contrast, most words are used multiple times (consider we have words like *the, a, is, and, but*, etc.).

So where does that leave us on the definition of *word*?

The answer, of course, is that what a word is is dependent both on the language one is examining and on the culture surrounding that language. Consider how evidence for wordhood may differ coming from a language with a writing system versus one without. In creating a language, it's up to the conlanger to decide not only what counts as a word, but how words themselves will be used— how grammatical features like tense, number, and aspect will be reified. In linguistics, this is what's known as **morphology**, and it's where all the action is.

KEY CONCEPTS

Before we get into it, let me introduce some key concepts. First, morphology is divided into two separate but related phenomena: **inflectional morphology** and **derivational morphology**.

Inflectional morphology has to do with changes to a word that don't affect its grammatical category (i.e. whether it's a noun or verb or an adjective). An example of inflectional morphology would be noun pluralization. It doesn't affect the base meaning of the noun, and doesn't change its categorical status in any important way: it just tells you that there's more than one of the noun. Derivational morphology is the opposite. When you change a word like *graphic* (a noun) to *graphical* (an adjective), you've *derived* the second word from the first. We'll be looking at inflectional and derivational morphology separately in this section.

As we examine morphology, though, we're going to see a couple of word changing strategies again and again. Here's the vocabulary you're going to need to be able to discuss them:

- **Affix:** This is a cover term for any type of phonological string that's been added to a base word resulting in a new, modified word. Prefixes, suffixes, circumfixes, and infixes (defined below) are all types of affixes. Affixes are generally *not* independent words, and must appear attached to a base word.

- **Suffix:** A suffix is an affix that's added to the end of a word. In English, the plural *-s* is an example of a suffix. Schematically, you can say that *cats* comprises a base *cat* and the suffix *-s*.

- **Prefix:** A prefix is an affix that's added to the front of a word. In English, the negative *un-* is an example of a prefix. Schematically, you can say that *unpopular* comprises a base *popular* and the prefix *un-*. Prefixes are crosslinguistically common, but while there are languages that are exclusively suffixing (i.e. languages that have no other type of affix but suffixes), *no* natural language has been found to be exclusively prefixing. Inuktitut, the language shown in the introduction to this chapter, is an example of an exclusively suffixing language.

- **Circumfix:** A circumfix is a combination of a prefix and a suffix. Unlike the word *unbridled*, which has an independent *un-* prefix and a *-d* suffix, a circumfix *requires* both parts to form a full word. A marginal example from English is the word *elongate*. There is no word *longate* or *elong*: you *must* say *elongate*. Schematically, you can say that *elongate* comprises a base *long*, the suffix *–ate*, and the prefix *e-*. Circumfixing is not common, crosslinguistically, but it's not rare. Georgian is a language that has a number of circumfixes. A common Dothraki circumfix is one that forms an abstract noun from a base word. For example, *jahak* is the Dothraki word for "braid"; *athjahakar* is the Dothraki word for "pride." Neither *athjahak* nor *jahakar* is a licit word in Dothraki.

* **Infix:** An infix is an affix that is inserted into the middle of a word. The only marginal examples that exist in English are slang terms like *infreakingcredible*, or the two types of *Simpsons* infixation: Flanders-style (*scrumptious* > *scrumdiddlyumptious*) and Homer-style (*saxophone* > *saxomaphone*). Schematically, you can say that *saxomaphone* comprises a base *saxophone* and the infix *-ma-* (sometimes also written ‹ma›). Though *quite* rare, there are languages that use infixes. Tagalog is one such language, where the focus of a sentence is sometimes determined by a change in infix (it also has other types of affixes). For example, *bumilí* means "to buy," with a focus on the person who's buying something, while *binilí* means "to buy," with a focus on the thing that's purchased. The root is *bilí*. Infixes can often show up as prefixes or suffixes depending on the shape of the word. For example, if *-um-* is added to a word beginning with a vowel in Tagalog, it appears as a prefix. You can see this with the root *isip*, which becomes *umisip*, "to devise," when *-um-* is added. It is my *strong recommendation* that infixes *not* be used in an inflectional or derivational system *unless* the language is being developed from a proto-language. It's extremely difficult to create naturalistic infixation without evolving a system that supports it.

* **Apophony:** This is a cover term that refers to any type of word-internal process that is used to effect a change in a word (either inflectional or derivational). A nice example from English is the irregular plural of *goose*, *geese*. Rather than adding an *-s*, the interior of the word itself changes. There are many different types of apophony: vowel change, initial consonant change, final consonant change, tone change, stress change . . . Sometimes it'll even be a combination of these. There should still be some part of the word

that is identifiable, though, as with the initial [g] and final [s] of *geese* and *goose*. Schematically, there's no specific way to deal with phenomena like this. The description tends to be language-specific.

- **Suppletion:** Suppletion is when two forms that *should* be related are not related at all. A great example from English is *good* and *better*. Take any other small adjective and compare similar forms to see how they're related systematically—for example, *black* and *blacker*, *light* and *lighter*, *short* and *shorter*, etc. There's absolutely no systematic relationship between *good* and *better* aside from the fact that they belong to the same paradigm (i.e. just as *shorter* means "more short," so does *better* mean "more good"). In discussing forms like these, you'd say that *better* is the suppletive comparative form of *good*. Suppletion *only* arises from a language's unique history, so one should be careful in using it in a naturalistic conlang.

- **Reduplication:** Reduplication is when part or all of a word is repeated for morphological reasons. Sometimes reduplicated forms are reduced or changed in some way as part of the process. For instance, words like *lovey-dovey, ooey-gooey, hanky-panky, super-duper*, and *hoity-toity* are all examples of reduplication in English. A separate pattern is the mocking *shm*-reduplication, for example *mall-shmall, game-shmame, dog-shmog*, etc. Just about every language uses reduplication in some form. When an entire word is repeated (e.g. "Is it *big* big, or is it just big?"), that's called full reduplication. Other types of reduplication are called partial reduplication, and the reduplicated portion is often referred to as an affix, depending on where it appears in the word (Doug Ball's Skerre uses a reduplicating prefix to indicate plurality in some nouns, e.g. *keki* "son" ~ *keekeki* "sons").

- **Paradigm:** A paradigm is a set of inflectional forms. For example, *short, shorter*, and *shortest* form a paradigm for the adjective *short*. You'd illustrate it like this:

Positive	Comparative	Superlative
short	shorter	shortest

• **Exponence:** This is a cover term to refer to the reification or instantiation of any inflectional or derivational category. So, for example, in *cats*, the exponence for the plural is *-s*. In *geese*, the exponence is the apophony whereby *oo* becomes *ee*. It's more general than the word "affix," as it can refer to any affix or any other change effected in a word. If a word has no change (e.g. *hit* in the past tense is *hit*), then you'd say the word has no exponence for the category in question (in the case of *hit*, for the past tense).

I'll be making reference to all of these terms in the sections to come, so feel free to bookmark this section. Now let's move on to inflectional morphology!

ALLOMORPHY

Before we delve into the exciting world of grammar (and it *is* exciting. Don't you snicker! You bought this book!), let me touch very briefly on **allomorphy**. Allomorphy is to morphology as allophony is to phonology. The same principles introduced in the allophony section apply to allomorphy. The difference is that while allophony applies to sounds, allomorphy applies to grammatical realizations. Often allomorphy is based on the phonology, so it can be confusing to decide what type of phenomenon you're looking at it. Consider the three main forms of the plural suffix in English:

cats /kæts/ = [s] suffix

dogs /dɑgz/ = [z] suffix

thrushes /θɹʌʃəz/ = [əz] suffix

There are three different suffixes here, but I think English speakers will all agree that it's really the same suffix. The rule is you get the [əz] suffix after /ʃ, ʒ, s, z, tʃ, dʒ/; the [z] suffix after other voiced sounds; and the [s] suffix after other voiceless sounds. Thus, the phonology plays a part in this morphological rule. But this isn't something that you would say about the sounds /s/ and /z/ in English. This is something you'd say about the plural suffix (or the third person singular present tense suffix, as it's identical).

Perhaps a more obvious example of how phonology plays a part in determining grammatical exponence is the comparative -er suffix. Take a look at these pairs:

sad ~ sadder

big ~ bigger

nice ~ nicer

strong ~ stronger

weak ~ weaker

Now compare them to these (note: an asterisk * means the form is ungrammatical):

resplendent ~ *resplendenter

magical ~ *magicaler

hilarious ~ *hilariouser

important ~ *importanter

As English speakers, we know we can't say the forms on the right. Instead we have to say *more resplendent* or *more important*. How do we know whether we can use -er versus when we have to say *more x*? A simple characterization of just these data (this isn't the complete answer) is that you can use -er with adjectives that are one syllable long; otherwise you have to say *more x*. Consequently, the formation of the comparative in English is dependent upon the phonology of the word (how many syllables it has), but its realization is pretty random (i.e. we wouldn't want to say there's any systematic *phonological* relationship between an *-er* suffix and a separate adjective *more*). That's what makes the rule morphological. And sometimes the allomorphy of a given category (say, plural) isn't even really phonological. Consider the following singular/plural pairs:

kid ~ kids

goose ~ geese

child ~ children

fish ~ fish

We understand that all the forms on the right are plural forms, but the pairs don't look anything alike. In this case, they are all realizations of plurality in English; they just take different shapes depending on the noun being pluralized. That is, the forms are irregular and must be memorized, but there's no difference in the *meaning* of these plurals, so *geese* is to *goose* as *kids* is to *kid*. It doesn't matter that the form is weird: it's nothing more than a plural noun.

Most morphological categories exhibit some kind of allomorphy. It's actually pretty rare to find one that always has the same realization. They exist (like *-ing* in English. Doesn't matter what word you add that to; it's always *-ing*), but more often than not the form of a category will change for some word—sometimes based on the phonology, but sometimes not. Keep this in mind as you go through this chapter.

NOMINAL INFLECTION

For season four of *Game of Thrones*, I ran into a bit of a snag. For one particular scene, I was supposed to translate the sentence, "You stand before Daenerys Stormborn, the Unburnt, Queen of Meereen, Queen of the Andals and the Rhoynar and the First Men . . ." So I went about doing that. Notice that in the sentence above, Daenerys Stormborn is the object of the sentence (i.e. she is the one stood before; she's not the one doing the standing). In English all that means is that the name *Daenerys Stormborn* has to come after the word *before*, and that the whole phrase will probably come after the verb. Not so in High Valyrian. Here's what the first part of that sentence looked like when I first did the translation:

Daenero Jelmāzmo naejot iōrā . . .
[ˈdaɛ.ne.ɾo ɟel.ˈmaːz.mo ˈnaɛ.ɟot ˈioː.ɾaː]

Why? Because the High Valyrian word *Daenerys* was the object of the postposition *naejot*, which means "before." Consequently, the final *-ys* in *Daenerys* had to change to an *-o*. That's just the way the grammar of the language works.

So I recorded that and sent it off. A little while later I got an email back from Dave and Dan. They said that they understood that I was just translating, but that the name *really* had to be *Daenerys*, so fans would recognize it. I told them that this was impossible, because of the construction that was being used. I said if we shifted the focus and said instead of "You stand before Daenerys" that "Daenerys sits before you," I could swing it. They said that was fine, and so I changed the translation of the first part to the following:

Daenerys Jelmāzmo aō naejot dēmas . . .
[ˈdaɛ.ne.ɾys ɟel.ˈmaːz.mo ˈaoː ˈnaɛ.ɟot ˈdeː.mas]

I also changed the English line so that the translation was appropriate and sent that all off.

I got another email from Dave and Dan later. They said the actors were confused because the translated lines didn't match the lines in the script. And, indeed, that is what happened. Though *I* had changed the translation (I imagined the subtitle would read "Daenerys Stormborn sits before you" in English), they kept the line as written ("You stand before Daenerys Stormborn"). Dave and Dan said they were fine with the translation, but that the *English* line had to remain the same; it didn't matter if the translation didn't match up exactly—at which point I was like, "*Ohhhhhhhhh . . .*" (and I may have even typed that up in my email response).

It was much ado about nothing, really, but the tiny little linguistic detail that precipitated it all was the suffix on the name *Daenerys*. Dave and Dan—and most folks working on *Game of Thrones*—are native English speakers, and as native English speakers we've come to expect certain things from language. One of those things is that the form of a noun is invariant. Yes, a noun will change when it's pluralized, but otherwise, nouns don't change—and that goes double for names. Here, for example, is my name being used in a bunch of different grammatical contexts:

David loves the cat. (Subject)

The cat loves David. (Object)

The cat often brings her string to David. (Indirect Object)

The cat is a fan of David. (Possessor)

The cat sits on David. (Location)

The cat likes to walk downstairs with David. (Companion)

David! It's four a.m. and the cat is meowing! Go feed her! (Addressee)

As you can see above, the name *David* never once changes its form: it always looks and sounds exactly the same. If this is your linguistic baseline, there's no reason to ever imagine that a language *could* do anything different. But what if *David* were a name in High

Valyrian—say, *Davidys*? Turns out the name would look quite a bit different in those exact same contexts:

Davidys [da.'vi.dys] (Subject)

Davidi [da.'vi.di] (Object)

Davidot [da.'vi.dot] (Indirect Object)

Davido [da.'vi.do] (Possessor)

Davidȳ [da.'vi.dyː] (Location)

Davidomy [da.vi.'do.my] (Companion)

Davidys [da.'vi.dys] (Addressee)

To give you an example of what this would look like in context, let's take the sentence "The cat sits on David" and translate it into High Valyrian, along with its opposite, "David sits on the cat" (note: I don't recommend this). Remember that the only difference in meaning between these two sentences is who's sitting on whom:

Kēli Davidȳ dēmas.	*Davidys kēlī dēmas.*
['keː.li da.'vi.dyː 'deː.mas]	[da.'vi.dys 'keː.liː 'deː.mas]
"The cat sits on David."	"David sits on the cat."

Kēli is the word for "cat" above (and, yes, the name of my cat is Keli. I can do that because *I'm the conlanger* [that sound you just heard was the mic dropping]). Here the main difference between the two sentences is the form the nouns take. In fact, you could put the nouns in the same linear order in both sentences without changing the meaning. So, for example, *Davidȳ kēli dēmas* would still mean "The cat sits on David."

Though High Valyrian and English differ in how they mark their nouns, all languages have some strategy for indicating (or not indicating, as the case may be) three core grammatical categories (though there are others): number, gender, and case. We'll look at each of these in detail below, and then I'll comment on how some other grammatical categories are reified in nouns.

NOMINAL NUMBER

Grammatical number is a good place to start for nouns, as I believe it's the simplest concept to grasp. All grammatical number refers to is how many of a particular noun there are, and how that is marked (or not marked) on the noun. In English, it's fairly simple. An unmodified noun is considered to be singular, and a noun with an -*s* on the end is plural, meaning there's more than one. There are other pluralization strategies, of course, but regarding meaning, that's all there is to it. If we say *cat*, it refers to exactly one feline entity; if we say *cats*, it can refer to two, three, or an infinite number of cats—pretty much any number of cats except for exactly one.

Lots of languages do the same thing, but is that really all there is to nominal number? Not by a long shot! Outside of singular and plural, here are some other nominal numbers attested in natural languages:

- **No Marking**: Some languages make no morphological distinction between singular and plural outside of a couple instances. Nouns in Mandarin Chinese are neither singular nor plural; the only place where plural marking exists obligatorily is in the pronoun system. There, the suffix 们 [men] is added to the pronouns for "I" 我 *wǒ* [wo214], "you" 你 *nǐ* [ni214], and "she/he/it" 他 *tā* [ta55] to form their plurals "we" 我们 *wǒmen* [wo21.men4], "you (plural)" 你们 *nǐmen* [ni21.men4], and "them" 他们 *tāmen* [ta55 .men2]. This suffix can be used with certain other nouns in certain contexts, but this marking is always optional.

- **Dual**: A dual number refers to exactly two of some item. It's fairly common in the world's nominal systems. In Arabic, for example, رجل ['ra.ʒul] is "man" and رجلان [ra.ʒu.'laːn] is "two men" (cf. رجال [ri.'ʒaːl] "men").

- **Trial:** A trial number refers to exactly three of some item. It's *extremely* uncommon in the world's nominal systems. There are no attested systems that encode specific numbers beyond three. In Kamakawi, a language of mine, 秂ᕁ [ɛ 'lɛ.ʔɔ] is "the egret"; 秂ᕁ' | [ɛ 'lɛ.ʔɔ.kə] is "the two egrets"; 秂ᕁ'△ [ɛ 'lɛ.ʔɔ.nɔ] is "the three egrets"; and |ʌᕁ' [u 'lɛ.ʔɔ] is "the egrets."

- **Paucal:** Paucal number refers to a few of some item, but not to a specific number. This is similar to the word "few" or "several" in English. In High Valyrian, the paucal is distinguished from the singular, plural, and collective numbers. For example, *vala* ['va.la] is "man"; *vali* ['va.li] is "men"; *valun* ['va.lun] is "some men," and *valar* ['va.lar] is "all men."

- **Collective:** The collective number refers to a large group of items. Sometimes these items are treated as the sum total of those items, while other times it refers to a large group as a unit. Using High Valyrian again, *valar* is "all men," but *azantyr* [a.'zan.tyr] is "army" (cf. *azantys* [a.'zan.tys], the singular, which means "knight").

- **Singulative:** For languages that routinely mark groups of things or masses, the singulative refers to one of a group of items or a substance whose *most basic form* is plural or masslike. In Arabic, a word like شَجَر ['ʃa.ʒar] refers to trees in general as a mass; by adding a feminine suffix, you get شَجَرة ['ʃa.ʒa.ra], which refers to a single tree. A rough English analogue might be *rice*, which is simpler than *grain of rice*.

- **Distributive:** Distributive number refers to a plural entity that's evenly divided among a group. So, for example, if there are three dogs and each one has a leash, then the three dogs have leashes. If I own three leashes independently of any dogs, then I also have leashes. Some languages, though, would mark the second example as plural, and the first as distributive, since in the first example each dog has *one* leash. In Southern Paiute, distributive number is marked with initial partial reduplication. Compare /puŋ.kuŋ.wɯ.raŋ.wa/ "our horses (that we all own collectively)" to /pum.puŋ.kuŋ.wɯ.raŋ.wa/ "our horses (each of us has one horse)."

Here, the reduplicative prefix is used to indicate that each member has one horse, and ownership is not shared. Distributive number *frequently* co-occurs with possessive morphology.

Those are the categories that one finds in natural languages. Some languages may distinguish different types of paucals or different types of collectives, but that's about it. Obviously in an alien language one could do plenty of things (tetral, quinqual, sextal, etc.), but in natural languages, that's all we find.

Number Applicability

Having explicated all these systems, there are always certain instances where number marking appears to have trouble appearing. It will vary from language to language and lexeme to lexeme, but there are three categories you'll want to pay attention to: **animacy**, **definiteness**, and **mass nouns** versus **count nouns**.

In Dothraki, only animate nouns get plural marking, and this is fairly common for languages that make animacy distinctions of any kind. For example:

mahrazh [maˈhɾaʒ] "man"	~	*mahrazhi* [ˈma.hɾa.ʒi] "men"
negwin [neˈgwin] "stone"	~	*negwin* [neˈgwin] "stones"

It's not the case that the singular is the same as the plural, as with English *deer*: the entire class of inanimate nouns makes no singular/plural distinction whatsoever, despite the existence of the plural category elsewhere in the language.

In many languages that make a distinction between definite and indefinite, an indefinite noun either can't be realized as plural, or changes in some important way in the plural. In English, the presence of the definite article *the* has no bearing on the form of a noun in the singular or plural (e.g. *the cat* vs. *the cats*). The indefinite article *a*, though, can only accompany a singular noun (e.g. *a cat*; never **a cats*). This is not the case with all languages. French, for example, allows indefinite plural nouns:

le livre [lə livʁ] "the book"	~	*les livres* [le livʁ] "the books"
un livre [ɛ̃ livʁ] "a book"	~	*des livres* [de livʁ] "some books"

The translation we usually use for French *des* is "some," but the actual connotation is slightly different (*some* has some peculiar properties in English). The takeaway is that it's actually not surprising for a language to either include or exclude an indefinite plural form.

Finally, many languages make a distinction between *mass* and *count* nouns. Some English mass nouns are *water, blood, grass, mercury,* etc.—things that denote substances. They appear to be singular in form, but they tend to lack plurals, something count nouns do not. Whether or not a noun is a mass noun is language-specific, just as the way that mass nouns are treated in the grammar is language-specific. In English, for example, when mass nouns are forced to be count nouns, they take on a separate connotation. Here are some examples:

water "water (the substance)"	~	*a water* "a glass of water"
grass "grass (the substance)"	~	*a grass* "a type of grass"
fire "fire (the substance)"	~	*a fire* "a specific conflagration"

Some count nouns can be turned into mass nouns by removing the articles, turning them into substance-like nouns:

a stone "a specific stone"	~	*stone* "stone (the substance)"
a bone "a specific bone"	~	*bone* "bone (the substance)"
a diamond "a specific diamond"	~	*diamond* "diamond (the substance)"

Pluralizing a mass noun in English always results in some sort of meaning shift (e.g. "I came to Casablanca for the waters," "The many grasses of North America," etc.). In their bare forms, mass nouns are treated as uncountable, boundless substances. Many idea nouns are treated in just this way (*life, love, happiness, death,* etc.).

GRAMMATICAL GENDER

Grammatical gender gets a bad rap for the wrong reasons. People see examples like this . . .

niño ['ni.ɲɔ] "child" (masculine gender, Spanish)

vache [vaʃ] "cow" (feminine gender, French)

Mädchen ['mɛt.çən] "girl" (neuter gender, German)

. . . and cry, "*Sexism!*" And, listen, I will not say such cries are without merit, but first let me lay out all the relevant facts.

To understand what grammatical gender is, it's important to understand *why* the original grammarians used the term "gender" when referring to the systems one sees in the Indo-European languages (Spanish, French, German, Greek, Russian, Latin, Sanskrit, etc.). The meanings of the words in these various languages tend to obscure the original intent. The idea behind calling these systems gender systems was to point up the fact that nouns in a given language are "born," in essence, with a specific set of morphological properties. These morphological properties place the noun into one of however many genders the language has. In other words, it's just like when the doctor holds up a newborn and says "It's a girl!" based on whatever biological features are present (and the cultural associations the doctor's culture places on those features). That's what happens with words in languages with gender.

So a language like Spanish isn't saying that there's anything particularly feminine about tables or masculine about ceilings: the meanings of the words have nothing to do with it. The language is saying that the noun *mesa* is of a different gender from the noun *techo*, because *all* nouns *must* belong to one or the other gender.

What has confused things is the fact that the languages we commonly encounter in the Western world (i.e. every Indo-European language, and also the unrelated Semitic languages like Arabic and Hebrew) have sex-based gender systems (i.e. they all have a masculine and feminine gender, and some have a neuter). *Not all languages have gender systems based on sex.* A lot do, but it just so happens that the ones Westerners run into the most are pretty much all related to one another, and so, of course, they have the same genders (or none, if they've gotten rid of them, like English has).

Okay, if you've followed all this, then the remaining objection to the term "gender" would be recent discussions of the social construction of gender—that gender isn't based purely on one's biology, and is, in fact, a social construct. A better linguistic term than "gender," then, might be "species" (instead of nominal gender, we'd call it nominal species), but I doubt that linguists will readily adopt the term. It's too entrenched.

Another term used instead of gender is the term **noun class**. Unfortunately, there's been some confusion in the field about the use of the term. Some linguists distinguish between gender and noun class; others say they're synonymous. The term "noun class" tends to be used with Bantu and Australian languages, while "gender" is used with Indo-European and Semitic languages. Personally, I don't care what it's called, I just care what it does. I'll probably use both terms in this section depending on the language. What will be important to look at will be how a specific system works, not the terminology, so if you're able to follow that, you're fine.

The main reason that gender systems exist (or survive, rather) is that they build redundancy into the language. Here's what I mean by that. Take a look at the following Spanish sentences and their English translations:

Los libros son rojos. "The books are red."

Las tarjetas son rojas. "The cards are red."

Let's say you didn't hear any of these sentences very well. How much could you pick up just by the endings? In English, you get two clues that the subjects of the sentences (underlined above) are plural. One is the verb *are*. If the sentence were singular, you'd have to use *is*. If you missed the first noun, by hearing *are*, you'd know the noun was plural. You also get the plural *-s*. If you miss most of the noun, the *-s* tells you the subject is plural.

Now let's look at the Spanish. In Spanish, the word that translates as "the" is marked for plural (basically the -*s* ending); the subject is marked for plural (the -*s* ending again); the verb is conjugated for a third person plural subject (*son*), and the adjective has a plural ending, as well (-*s* again). There are a *ton* of cues that tell you the subject is plural. Even more, though, in the first sentence, the form *los*, the -*o* in *libros*, and the final -*o* in *rojos* tell you the subject is masculine. In the second sentence, the form *las*, the final -*a* in *tarjetas*, and the -*a* in *rojas* all tell you the subject is feminine. So if you're listening to someone say either of these sentences in a noisy environment, the redundancy built into the language will give you multiple opportunities to decode the meaning of the sentence—opportunities you don't have with English.

Though redundancy can be annoying, in language, it makes the message stronger. Grammatical gender exists in order to force the words around it to agree, and the agreement is what increases the number of cues for the listener. Of course, this does mean that the language learner has to *learn* all the genders, and must memorize additional agreement patterns and the gender of every single noun in the language, but, well, life is rough.

When considering employing a gender system, it's important to understand that gender systems wouldn't exist if they weren't reified in some way. For example, we could say that English has a gender system, and assign every single word to a gender (*ship* is feminine, but *boat* is masculine, because why not?), but it wouldn't take, because we don't have adjectival agreement or verbal agreement that's sensitive to gender. The most we have is a distinction made in third person singular pronouns, and that usage is already inconsistent. We have a *long* history of referring to inanimate objects that we admire as *she* (cars, boats, computers, etc.), and if you refer to anything as *he*, it's somehow considered to be cute (like "Don't you talk to him that way!," said of a particularly charming toaster). In order for a gender system to work, the grammar has to make use of it in some crucial way, otherwise it'll just fall by the wayside (looking at you, French).

Finally, gender systems are *mandatory*. If you're creating a language where each noun is a member of one of four genders, but you can remove the suffix to use a genderless form of the noun, it's not a gender system. Rather, it's like what we do in English, where we can make reference to a *male aardvark* or *female aardvark*, but the grammar takes no notice of it. Now let's take a look at some systems.

• Sex-based gender systems assign nouns to either a masculine or feminine gender, with a neuter gender sometimes thrown in for flavor. Sex-based gender systems tend to arise from animal terminology, as it's important for farmers to distinguish between, say, a bull and a cow. Words referring to human beings tend to be slotted into the appropriate genders, as do words for gendered animals, but after that assignment is more often than not based on the sound of the word. This is why *Mädchen*, the German word for "girl," is assigned to the neuter, rather than the female gender. All German words that end in *-chen* are neuter, regardless of their biology. Sex-based gender systems tend to group mass swaths of word types into one or the other gender. Some key word types that regularly get lumped together are as follows:

- Naturally gendered humans
- Nongendered humans
- Animals
- Animate things
- Inanimate things
- Diminutives (small things)
- Augmentatives (big things)
- Instruments/tools
- Vessels
- Places
- Plants

• Animacy-based gender systems make reference either to how active a particular noun is, or how alive it is. Dothraki is typical of many languages that employ such a system. Some classifications are quite obvious:

Animate Nouns	Inanimate Nouns
mahrazh [ma.ˈhɾaʒ] "man"	*negwin* [ne.ˈgwin] "rock"
chiori [ˈtʃi.o.ɾi] "woman"	*hranna* [ˈhɾan.na] "grass"
inavva [i.ˈnav.va] "sister"	*jesh* [dʒeʃ] "ice"

Others are less so. For example, animals tend to be grouped as animate if they're important or dangerous, and inanimate otherwise:

Animate Nouns	Inanimate Nouns
vezh [veʒ] "stallion"	*hrazef* [hɾa.ˈzef] "horse"
hrakkar [hɾak.ˈkaɾ] "lion"	*eshina* [ˈe.ʃi.na] "fish"
kolver [kol.ˈveɾ] "eagle"	*alegra* [ˈa.le.gɾa] "duck"

Nonliving entities tend to be grouped by their interactional properties:

Animate Nouns	Inanimate Nouns
vorsa [ˈvoɾ.sa] "fire"	*eveth* [e.ˈveθ] "water"
chaf [tʃaf] "wind"	*tawak* [ta.ˈwak] "metal"
lei [ˈle.i] "spirit"	*khadokh* [xa.ˈdox] "corpse"

As with sex-based gender systems, phonological similarity will tend to trump semantics in many cases. For example, in Dothraki, all words that end with a collective suffix are treated as animate, such as *hoyalasar* "music," *ikhisir* "ash," and *vovosor* "weaponry."

• Semantic systems are larger than gender or animacy systems and take into account the actual semantics of a language. There will sometimes be crossover with a gender- or animacy-based system. For example, in the Australian language Dyirbal, all nouns are assigned to one of four classes, each taking a different article, presented below:

Class I: *bayi* /ba.ji/ = men and other animate things

Class II: *balan* /ba.lan/ = women and certain stinging things

Class III: *balam* /ba.lam/ = edible plants and trees with edible fruit

Class IV: *bala* /ba.la/ = everything else

As with all other classification systems, some assignments make sense, and some don't. All such systems do have an "other" class, though, which is important. This is the default class that a noun that has no obvious designation gets dumped into. Otherwise, semantic systems usually group nouns into categories like the following: male entities; female entities; human beings; animate entities; inanimate entities; animals; plants; diminutives; augmentatives; groups; instruments/tools; ideas/abstracts; substances; exceptional entities; places; natural phenomena. In a conlang, though, one can always do strange or fun things just because. Here's a classification system I came up with:

- Humans who love lentils
- Useless humans
- Lamps or things that could be confused for lamps
- Objects that cats consider chairs
- Spoons that have been been bent trying to scoop ice cream
- Cats and regular spoons
- Animals that cats believe to be divine (i.e. cats)
- Animals cats hold in disdain (i.e. all other animals)
- Rainbows, gems, unicorns, and other objects depicted on Trapper Keepers
- Celestial phenomena (not stars)
- Stars, birds, cooking pots, and certain types of treasure
- Everything else

Aside from the "everything else" class, this is pretty unrealistic, but not all conlangs need to be realistic.

Reification of Gender

Since gender is basically a random bit of semantic trivia attached to every single noun, it's often (I really want to say *always*, but I'll hedge for safety) attached to some other grammatical category. In other words, you won't find a language where you can say, "That's the gender suffix," and it will do absolutely nothing else. Here are some usual combos you'll see in a language:

1. *Gender + Definiteness*: In French, the only foolproof indication of gender co-occurs with the equivalent of the words "the" and "a."

2. *Gender + Number*: In Swahili, every noun has a prefix that tells you its gender and number, for example, *mgeni* [m.'ge.ni] "stranger" versus *wageni* [wa.'ge.ni] "strangers" (compare *kigeni* [ki.'ge.ni] "strangeness").

3. *Gender + Case*: In Dyirbal, those initial words also tell you the grammatical role of the noun. For Class I, you use *bayi* with the subject of a sentence, but use *bagul* with the indirect object of a sentence (e.g. when someone is given something).

The piece of the noun that's gender is almost never separable from some other crucial part of the word or grammar.

That said, gender systems based at least partially on phonology (like Spanish) are much more likely to survive than those based purely on semantics. Though the sound of a word will change over time, the entire class of words will change with it, so the gender cues should remain stable for the class (or be washed away in a group). Semantic classifications are always up for interpretation, and a system based purely on semantics may not always be successfully passed on to a younger generation.

NOUN CASE

If you've ever taken a Latin class, you probably got all worked up about noun case. But listen. Noun case is *easy*. Verbs are tough. Verbs are a nightmare! Verbs are quite literally the worst thing to ever happen to human beings. Black Plague? I don't know, I'm vaccinated; I like my odds. If I ever actually have to learn the verb system of Japanese, though—and not for fun, I mean, but to actually be *required to learn it*—I will be forever and officially done. *Nothing* that happens with or to a noun in a language—created or otherwise—should be cause for concern. Nouns are the carbs you never want to stop filling up on; verbs are castor oil or . . . *kale*.

Back to nouns, then, **noun case** is a form of a noun that indicates what role the noun plays in the sentence. It's often looked at askance by English speakers because we don't have much of it, but we do have some of it. Take, for example, the word *him*. Try using it in a sentence. Chances are you probably didn't come up with a sentence like this:

Him went to the store to pick up some temporary tattoos for his grandmother.

That doesn't work. Nor does a sentence like this work:

Just give he the remote control so we can get out of here!

You may never have given *he* versus *him* much thought, but you can tell straightaway that these sentences are ungrammatical—and, furthermore, that you'd never, *ever* produce sentences like these even by accident. The reason is that *him* can only be used in specific grammatical contexts, and *he* can only be used in a different set of specific grammatical contexts. The distinction is one of case. That is, *he* and *him* are two versions of the same word: they're simply in two different noun cases.

In English, this applies only to a certain number of pronouns and demonstratives (yes, at the end of this section you will know how to use *who* and *whom*). In some languages, it applies to every single pronoun, noun, and demonstrative in the language—and sometimes adjectives, too. In this section, we'll examine noun case and its many uses. Unfortunately, the discussion must start with an introduction to morphosyntactic alignment.

Morphosyntactic alignment is basically a fancy way of referring to how a language codes who does what to whom. There are many systems present in the world's languages with many slight variations, but we'll only go over the two main ones.

Nominative-Accusative Alignment

Every single Indo-European language, Finno-Ugric language, Semitic language, Japonic language, and Sinitic language is a nominative-accusative language. This means that if you speak English natively and have ever had experience with another language, odds are that language was nominative-accusative. In a nominative-accusative language, you will observe the following phenomenon:

(1) *I am sleeping.*   (3) *He is sleeping.*

(2) *I hugged him.*   (4) *He hugged me.*

In both sentences (1) and (2), *I* is the subject. This means that *I* does the sleeping and does the hugging. Since it is the subject in both sentences, it doesn't change form. In sentence (4), though, *I* is the object, which means that it gets hugged. Consequently, it changes form to *me*.

In English, word order determines who does what to whom most of the time, but we see case distinctions with the pronouns when they occur as objects. In a language like High Valyrian, the form of the noun more than the word order determines who does what to whom. Compare these two sentences:

(5) <u>Vala</u> abre vūjitas. ['va.la 'a.bre 'vuː.ɟi.tas]
    "<u>The man</u> kissed the woman."

(6) <u>Vale</u> abra vūjitas. ['va.le 'a.bra 'vuː.ɟi.tas]
    "The woman kissed <u>the man</u>."

Above, the word order stays the same (man > woman > kissed), but the meanings change thanks to the ending on the nouns *vala* "man" and *abra* "woman." Using just the first word, if *vala* is used, it's the subject of the sentence (the one that does the kissing); if *vale* is used, it's the object (the one that gets kissed). The difference between *vala* and *vale* is roughly the same as the difference between *I* and *me*.

The missing piece of the puzzle is something called **transitivity**. Transitivity refers to a verb's ability to take an object. A verb like *kiss* in English is a **transitive** verb, because it has a subject (one who kisses) and an object (one who is kissed). A verb like *sleep* in English is an **intransitive** verb, because it has a subject (one who sleeps) and no object.

In nominative-accusative languages, both the subject of a transitive verb and the subject of an intransitive verb take the same form. This form is called the **nominative case**. Objects of transitive verbs take a different form, and that form is called the **accusative case**. Knowing this, we can set up a table for some of the English pronouns and High Valyrian nouns we've seen so far:

Meaning	Nominative Case	Accusative Case
I (pronoun)	I	me
He (pronoun)	he	him
Man (High Valyrian)	vala	vale
Woman (High Valyrian)	abra	abre

All of these will work the same way if you plug in different intransitive verbs ("cry," "laugh," "die") and different transitive verbs ("see," "take," "pet"). If you think about some of English's other pronouns, like *we*, *they*, and *her*, you can probably plug them into the table above fairly easily (and then try it with *who* and *whom*! *Mystery solved!*). Other pronouns like *you* and *it*, and every noun of English, on the other hand, will look the same in the nominative and accusative. This is partly why our word order is so strict. If the nouns look the same in the nominative and accusative, you won't know who did what to whom unless you have a verb in the middle of them.

Hopefully this was fairly easy to follow. Now things will get a little tricky.

Ergative-Absolutive Alignment

If you get lost at any point during this short discussion, just remember this: ergative-absolutive languages are the mirror image of nominative-accusative languages.

Taking our four examples from above, *if English were an ergative-absolutive language,* those four sentences would look like this:

(1) *I am sleeping.*   (3) *He is sleeping.*
(2) *Me hugged he.*   (4) *Him hugged I.*

Before you throw this book in the garbage can, know that, yes, there are real languages that work this way. The key to understanding the difference between a language like English and an ergative-absolutive language is that the latter type of language focuses on the differing experiences of the participants in a sentence. That is, in an ergative-absolutive language, the subject of an intransitive verb (in the first and third sentence, the one who *experiences* sleep) and the object of a transitive verb (the one who *experiences* a hug) are marked with the same case. This is called the **absolutive case.** For the remaining role, the subject of a transitive verb (the one who perpetrates an act upon someone else) is marked with a different case. This is called the **ergative case.**

Let me show you an example from a natural language that will help to illustrate. Hindi is a language that displays ergativity in the past tense. Just as I showed you how cases worked with High Valyrian above, here's how the ergative and absolutive cases work in Hindi.

(5) आदमी ने मजदूर देखा. [ˈad.mi.ne mazˈdur ˈde.kʰa] "The man saw a laborer."

(6) मजदूर ने आदमी देखा. [mazˈdur.ne ˈad.mi ˈde.kʰa] "The laborer saw a man."

As with High Valyrian, the verb comes at the end. In Hindi, the ने [ne] suffix indicates the noun it's attached to is the actor—or agent—of the action of the sentence. In the first example, the man (आदमी ने ['ad.mi.ne]) is the agent that enacts the action of seeing, and the one seen is the laborer (मजदूर [maz.'dur]). The situation is reversed in the second sentence.

Now compare the forms of the two nouns in the sentences above to their forms in these sentences:

(7) आदमी सोया. ['ad.mi 'so.ja] "The man slept."

(8) मजदूर सोया. [maz.'dur 'so.ja] "The laborer slept."

Notice that the form for "man" in sentence (7), आदमी ['ad.mi], is identical to the *object* form in "The laborer saw the man" above. So, there you have it. Languages do this. Why? The answer lies in the history of each language, as is usually the case. But the phenomenon hits closer to home than you'd think.

Consider for a moment the suffix -*ee* in English (used in words like *awardee*, *refugee*, etc.). If you had to explain it to someone who didn't know how to use it, how would you do it? The -*ee* suffix is usually associated with someone who *does* something, kind of, but we can do better than that. Let's consider two -*ee* words: *escapee* and *employee*. What is an *escapee*? Someone who escapes. Now what is an *employee*? Someone who employs? No, that's an *employer*. In fact, an *employee* is someone who is *employed*.

Does that pattern remind you of anything? The -*ee* suffix is *precisely* an absolutive suffix. It's not case, of course—it's a derivational suffix—but it remains true that -*ee*, when attached to an intransitive verb, produces a noun referring to the subject of that verb, while it produces a noun referring to the object of the verb when attached to a transitive verb. If you can understand how the -*ee* suffix works in English, you can understand an ergative-absolutive language.

With this info in mind, we can now set up a table much like we did above illustrating ergative and absolutive forms:

Meaning	Absolutive Case	Ergative Case
man (Hindi)	आदमी ['ad.mi]	आदमी ने ['ad.mi.ne]
laborer (Hindi)	मजदूर [maz.'dur]	मजदूर ने [maz.'dur.ne]
present (verb)	*presentee*	*presenter*
employ (verb)	*employee*	*employer*

Most important, if you wanted to use these forms with an intransitive verb (a verb that has no object), you *must* take the forms from the absolutive column. The ergative column is used only with the subjects of transitive verbs.

With these alignment cases out of the way, we can move on to the rest of the many possible cases found in languages. Though they'll be less familiar, they'll be easier to understand and work with.

Indirect Objects

The canonical indirect object is the one to whom something is given when "give" is used as a verb. Here's an example in English with roles marked:

The man (SUBJECT) *gave the dog* (INDIRECT OBJECT) *a treat* (DIRECT OBJECT).

The treat is the thing that gets given, so it's the direct object (the accusative argument, using our new terminology). The man is the one that does the giving, so the dog is just the one who gets it. It's affected *indirectly* by the action of the verb, and since it has no other important role, it's tagged as the indirect object.

Languages differ based on whether or not they treat an indirect object specially. English doesn't. Compare the form of the pronoun *she* in the following contexts (its role will be in parentheses):

I saw her. (DIRECT OBJECT)

I gave her a raise. (INDIRECT OBJECT)

As you can see, the forms are identical. English treats indirect objects the same as direct objects; it just changes the word order. If you imagine a context where it would be appropriate to say *I gave her him*, *her* would be the indirect object, and *him* the direct object. Generally the indirect object is the first noun that follows a **ditransitive verb** (a verb that takes a direct and indirect object). Some languages have a special case reserved just for indirect objects. This case is called the **dative**. Languages such as Latin, Russian, Turkish, and High Valyrian have a dedicated dative case, as does Shiväisith, the language of the Dark Elves in Marvel's *Thor: The Dark World*. Take a look at the sentences below:

ᛕᚡᛚ ᛦᛰᚔᛏᚱᛚ ᛘᛰᛏᚤ ᛋᛰᛰᛖ—	ᛕᚡᛚ ᛦᛰᚔᛏᚱᛚ ᛘᛰᛏᛣ ᛋᛰᛰᛘ—
Kir eelenär läinie geilää.	*Kir eelenär läiniä geilee.*
[kiɾ 'eː.le.næɾ 'læi.nie 'gei.læː]	[kiɾ 'eː.le.næɾ 'læi.niæ 'gei.leː]
"I gave a child to the warrior."	"I gave a warrior to the child."

The words in both sentences are in the exact same order: I gave child warrior. The difference is the ending on "child" (*läinie* vs. *läiniä*) and the ending on "warrior" (*geilää* vs. *geilee*). The versions that end in *-ä* are the dative versions of each noun, and the versions that end in *-e* are the accusative versions. Thus, *läiniä* means that the child is the one who received the gift, and *geilää* means that the warrior is the one who received the gift.

The dative case is one of the more common cases you'll find in the world's languages. Outside of the core alignment cases, the dative is most likely to be the third or fourth case found in a language. Those that lack a dative case (like Dothraki) typically use some other case or strategy to take care of indirect objects. For example, in English, this is actually the most common way to indicate an indirect object:

I gave a scholarship to the student.

Above, *the student* is the indirect object, and it's preposed by *to*, which we understand to indicate the recipient in a giving construction. It's not uncommon to have more than one strategy to indicate an indirect object in a single language.

Possession

When not indicated with a separate pronoun or adjectival construction, possession is handled by one of a couple nominal cases. The most common of these is the genitive. The **genitive case** is attached to the possessor in a possessive construction. Unlike all other cases, possessive cases like the genitive are more commonly associated with nouns than with verbs (i.e. a genitive case will be necessitated by the context of a noun as opposed to what it's doing in the sentence). Here's an example from Latin to help illustrate:

pater puellae	"the girl's father" *or* "the father of the girl"
puella patris	"the father's girl" *or* "the girl of the father"

The underlined words above are in the genitive case, and are the possessors in these possessive phrases. The nonunderlined terms are the possessees, and are in the nominative case. They could be in any case, because the possessees are actually a part of the sentence. A possessor is just background information.

Sometimes possession works a little differently (you can see two examples in the English translations above). Languages are often characterized by whether the possessor comes after or before the possessee. Compare the first Latin example with its High Valyrian equivalent below:

Classical Latin:	*pater puellae*	"the girl's father"
High Valyrian:	*riño kepa*	"the girl's father"

In addition, while in all the examples we've seen the possessor is marked, sometimes the possessee is marked. It basically alerts the listener to the fact that it's possessed by something, and that something is what follows. Here's an example from the Sondiv language from the CW's *Star-Crossed* (note: this example has been simplified for expository purposes):

ᘀᘀ *zod* [zod] "son"

ᖯ *bor* [bor] "father"

𝕺𝖝𝖜𝖟 𖼆𖼆𝖸𝖾 *zoda yabor* [zoːˈda jaˈbor] "the father's son"

𝖸𝖾𝖟 𖼆𖼆𝖜 *bora yazod* [boːˈra jaˈzod] "the son's father"

Ignore the *ya-* prefix above. Instead, focus on the *-a* suffix, which marks a noun as *being* possessed. It's, in effect, the opposite of a genitive. This is another strategy for marking possession with case or something that's caselike in a language.

Other Non-Local Cases

There are a variety of other cases that some languages have that are covered by prepositions in English, or other adpositions in various noncase languages. Below is a listing of some common non-local cases:

Instrumental: The **instrumental case** is used with a noun that's used to accomplish the action of the sentence. Below is an example from Shiväisith:

ϟ𝖸𝖝𝖠 𝖏𝖁𝖏𝖁𝖳𝖁𝖂 𝖂𝖃𝖃𝖼𝖠𝖑—

Geilää liivinith jöhär. (*jöh* "knife," nominative)
[ˈgei.læː ˈliː.vi.niθ ˈjø.hærɾ]

"The warrior attacked <u>with a knife</u>."

Comitative: The **comitative case** is used with a noun with whom another noun is associated. The instrumental and comitative cases are sometimes conflated, but they can appear as separate cases. Below is an example from Shiväisith:

ϟ𝖸𝖝𝖠 𝖏𝖁𝖏𝖁𝖳𝖁𝖂 𝖈𝖸𝖃𝖁𝖂𝖂𝖷𝖂—

Geilää liivinith domintaath. (*domintaa* "scout," nominative)
[ˈgei.læː ˈliː.vi.niθ ˈdo.min.taːθ]

"The warrior attacked <u>with a scout</u> (or accompanied by a scout)."

Benefactive: The **benefactive case** is used with a noun on behalf of whom the action of the sentence is accomplished. This role is sometimes taken care of by other cases (e.g. the dative), but it can appear as a separate case. Below is an example from Shiväisith:

ᛋᚤᛢᛦᚫ ᛢᚡᛘᚡᛏᚤᚥ ᛘᚢᛢᛚᚥᚤᛘᚫ–

Geiläa liivinith vörthevä. (*vörth* "king," nominative)
['gei.læː 'liː.vi.niθ 'vɔɾ.θe.væ]

"The warrior attacked <u>for the king</u> (or on behalf of the king)."

Vocative: The **vocative case** is used with direct address, as when calling someone out by name. Below is an example in Castithan from Syfy's *Defiance*:

ᛥᛈᚸᚦᚬᚢᚦᚱᚨᚴᛚᚢᛖ

Tando! Usholu! (*Tanda* "father," nominative)
['tan.do 'u.ʃo.lu]

"<u>Father</u>! Stop!"

There are many, many more than this, but these are some of the most common that you'll run into.

Local Cases

Local cases are so called because they refer to a location of some kind. These are all covered by prepositions in English, or adpositions in other noncase languages. Many languages, though, change the form of the noun to indicate that the action of the verb is happening on or about or somehow in some spatial relation to that noun.

In Dothraki, for example, you can modify a noun to indicate whether an action happens moving toward that noun, or moving away from it. Here's an example of each:

Anha dothra <u>krazaajaan</u>.	*Anha dothra <u>krazaajoon</u>.*
['an.ha 'do.θra kra.za.a.dʒaː'an]	['an.ha 'do.θra kra.za.a.dʒo.'on]
"I rode <u>to the mountain</u>."	"I rode <u>away from the mountain</u>."

This will give you the idea. Now imagine any other spatial relation: on, onto, out of, over, under, avoiding, through, across, between—*anything.* There is a language somewhere that has a case that does exactly that.

Of course, some of these are more common than others, so here I'll give you examples of some of the most common ones. Some key terminology to keep in mind (because the names for these are all Latin) is that -*essive* basically means "stationary" and -*lative* means "mobile." These words combine with Latin prepositions to form case names. Here we go:

Locative: The **locative case** is the most basic local case. It's used when the action of the verb takes place in some area having to do with a noun. Many languages have much more specific local cases, but a number will have a locative. The interpretation is usually based on the action and the noun. So, for example, the locative used with a verb like "stand" and a noun like "boulder" will be interpreted as "on the boulder." If it's used with a noun like "room," though, it will probably be interpreted as "in the room." Below is an example from Indojisnen from Syfy's *Defiance*:

Koraksut <u>arkonyu</u> chewtlen. (*arkon* "boat," absolutive)
['kɔ.ɾak.sut 'aɾ.kɔ.ɲu 'tʃɛw.tlɛn]

"The doctor stands <u>in the boat.</u>"

Adessive: The **adessive case** is used when the action of the sentence takes place near or at or around a noun. This case often gets used for other things, but this is its basic sense. Below is an example from Shiväisith:

ᛋᛣᛰᛘᚫ ᚦᛉᛣᛩᚢᚢ ᚹᚻᛈᛈᚷᛩᛈᛣᛏ—

Geilää höyfith <u>tukkasku.</u> (*tukka* "sheep," nominative)
['gei.læː 'høy.fiθ 'tuk.kɑs.ku]

"The warrior stands <u>near the sheep.</u>"

Allative: The **allative case** is used when the action of the sentence moves to or toward a noun. This case often gets used for other things, but this is its basic sense. Below is an example from Dothraki:

Mahrazhi dothrash <u>*vaesaan*</u>. (*vaes* "city," nominative)
['ma.hɾa.ʒi do.'θɾaʃ va.e.sa.'an]

"The men rode <u>to the city</u>."

Ablative: The **ablative case** is used when the action of the sentence moves away from a noun. This case often gets used for other things, but this is its basic sense. Below is an example from Dothraki:

Mahrazhi dothrash <u>*vaesoon*</u>. (*vaes* "city," nominative)
['ma.hɾa.ʒi do.'θɾaʃ va.e.so.'on]

"The men rode <u>away from the city</u>."

Inessive: The **inessive case** is used when the action of the sentence takes place inside of a noun. This case often gets used for other things, but this is its basic sense. Below is an example from Shiväisith:

ᛋᚤᛘᚨ �209ᚡᚹ ᚠᚤ◇◇✕◇ᛘ+—

Geilää imith <u>*djossaslu*</u>. (*djosse* "crater," nominative)
['gei.læː 'i.miθ 'ɉos.sas.lu]

"The warrior sits <u>inside the crater</u>."

Illative: The **illative case** is used when the action of the sentence moves into a noun. This case often gets used for other things, but this is its basic sense. Below is an example from Shiväisith:

ᛋᚤᛘᚨ ᚠᚨᚹᚨᚹ ᚠᚤ◇◇✕◇ᛘ✕—

Geilää pythyth <u>*djossasla*</u>. (*djosse* "crater," nominative)
['gei.læː 'py.θyθ 'ɉos.sas.lɑ]

"The warrior runs <u>into the crater</u>."

Elative: The **elative case** is used when the action of the sentence moves out of or out from a noun. This case often gets used for other things, but this is its basic sense. Below is an example from Shiväisith:

𝍖𝍖𝍖 𝍖𝍖𝍖 𝍖𝍖𝍖𝍖𝍖—

Geilää pythyth djossasle. (*djosse* "crater," nominative)
['gei.læː 'py.θyθ 'ɟos.sɑs.le]

"The warrior runs out of the crater."

This barely scratches the surface. To give you an example, the Tsez language, spoken in the Caucasus mountains, has sixty-four cases, fifty-six of which are local (not a joke). If you can imagine it, there's probably a case for it in Tsez or some other Caucasian language. There may or may not be a fancy name for it, but so long as its function can be adequately described, it doesn't matter what it's called.

NOMINAL INFLECTION EXPONENCE

The various nominal inflections—case, number, gender, definiteness, possession, etc.—will be realized on or around the noun in various ways. In this section I'll go over some of the most common strategies.

When it comes to marking a particular role, a language will use affixes, adpositions, some form of head-marking (this will be discussed later), or no marking. The closer the marking is to the noun, the tighter the connection will be between that meaning and the grammar of the language. Here's what I mean by that. Take a look at these Finnish word forms and their English translations:

talo	house	NOMINATIVE CASE
talon	of a house	GENITIVE CASE
talossa	inside a house	INESSIVE CASE
talolla	at a house	ADESSIVE CASE
talotta	without a house	ABESSIVE CASE

If you're learning the Finnish language, you have to learn how to decline a noun so that it can take on these various forms. They mean the same thing as the English translations, but no one learns about the "abessive case" in English. All you do is learn what the word *without* means, and then you use it with whatever it needs to be used with. The meaning is compositional, and the words are separate. So while the construction is a part of English grammar, it's not as integral as the abessive case is to Finnish grammar.

In many languages, one of the key differences is whether the construction is realized with an affix or with an **adposition**. An adposition is a separate word that has grammatical function, and it will generally come in one of two varieties. A **preposition** comes before a noun or noun phrase; a **postposition** comes after it. You can actually see both in High Valyrian while seeing where the language differs from English in how instrumental a given grammatical feature is to the grammar:

lenton	house	NOMINATIVE CASE
lento	of a house	GENITIVE CASE
lentot	at a house	LOCATIVE CASE
lentoso	with a house	INSTRUMENTAL CASE
hen lentot	from a house	ABLATIVE CASE
lento bē	on top of a house	SUPERESSIVE CASE

The last two examples, like English, require adpositions. In another language (like Tsez), you'd simply modify the form of the noun to create that meaning.

That said, some languages will *only* use adpositions for cases. Japanese is one such language, which uses postpositions exclusively. For a language with a split, though, the cases that are a part of the nominal inflection will be core, with the other constructions being peripheral.

How a conlang will encode all of these various things is up to the creator, though. Some languages separate each bit. In Turkish, for example, there's a separate suffix for case, for number, and for possession:

kitap "book"	"MY"	ABLATIVE	"MY" + ABLATIVE
SINGULAR	*kitabım*	*kitaptan*	*kitabımdan*
PLURAL	*kitaplarım*	*kitaplardan*	*kitaplarımdan*

Each of the suffixes is completely separable: the plural *-lar*; the ablative *-tan* or *-dan*; and the possessive *-ım*. There are rules about what order they can appear in (all languages have such rules, even if certain elements can appear in various orders), but each element can be included or excluded as one wishes.

Other languages conflate one or more of these. In Latin, case, number, and gender are absolutely inseparable, but possession is encoded with a separate word (as in English). Here's that same table in Latin:

liber "book"	"MY"	ABLATIVE	"MY" + ABLATIVE
SINGULAR	*meus liber*	*librō*	*meō librō*
PLURAL	*meī librī*	*librīs*	*meīs librīs*

Looking above, it's impossible to separate the "plural" part out of *librī* or *librīs*, or the "ablative" part out of *librō* or *librīs*. It is possible to extract the word "my," though, which is *meus* (declined in four ways above).

Notice that when different meanings get conflated into a single exponence, the words are shorter, as with Latin, and when they're left loose, the words are longer, as with Turkish. When you're learning a natural language, you're stuck with whatever you get. A language creator gets to decide what works best for the project at hand and go with that.

The last piece is the use of an **article**. An article is kind of like an adposition, except that a noun can never appear without an article, unless the grammar allows it. Articles can encode any number of features. In English, we have the articles *the* and *a* or *an*. They tell us whether a noun is **definite** (has a specific referent and/or has been referred to in conversation already) or **indefinite** (has no specific referent and/or is new to the conversation). The indefinite article *a* also tells us that the noun is singular. Only certain types of nouns can appear without an article of some kind, like mass nouns, ideas/emotions, or plural nouns. Languages that have articles will differ in their usage rules for articles. A key difference between English and Spanish is the use of articles with ideas. Consider these two sentences:

> *Life is beautiful.*   ~   *La vida es bella.*

Word for word, the Spanish sentence translates as "The life is beautiful." There's no way you could say that in English unless you were referring to some specific life. In Spanish, there's no way you could do the opposite (*Vida es bella* sounds . . . just hideous. It's repugnant). As they say in French, *C'est la vie*: That's life (or, literally, "That's the life," because, of course, French does it too).

We've already seen how Spanish articles encode gender and number. German articles are even beefier, encoding gender, number, *and* case. Take a look at these three, for example:

der Mann	the man	NOMINATIVE CASE, MASCULINE
den Mann	the man	ACCUSATIVE CASE, MASCULINE
dem Mann	to the man	DATIVE CASE, MASCULINE

It's kind of a nightmare learning German, because you have to distinguish between the "the" and "a" articles, and then each one has four case forms, three genders, and singular and plural versions. On top of that, the nouns themselves have singular and plural forms. And then the adjectives have to agree—and we haven't even gotten to the verbs! Mathematically, it seems like the language should be impossible to learn. And yet, millions get along just fine with it. Go fig.

Ultimately, one has to figure out how every possible grammatical construction is reified in a given conlang. At the very least, the meanings will be achieved by combining strings of words (e.g. *I sat on a carpet that lies slightly to the northwest of the dead center of the room.* That could be encoded by a case, but doing so would seem . . . churlish). The tools in this section will allow you to decide, essentially, how much junk you want to include on your nouns before one has to resort to stringing words together. Take it from me: noun junk can be fun. Once you create a case language, you won't go back—or at least not without a fight.

(And, yes, *without a fight* would be the abessive case.)

VERBAL INFLECTION

I've already mentioned that creating verbs is the most difficult part of creating a language. They're also the most difficult part of language, period. Verb systems are the most difficult part of a language to learn, to use fluently, to understand, and they're also the most volatile; the most prone to change. No matter how simple or clearcut a verb system is, a human user will find a way to muck it up. Nouns are pretty good at standing for what they're supposed to, but verbs? What exactly does it mean to "deliberate"? Can toddlers do it, or does it have to be a bunch of suits? And tense?! Without resorting to auxiliaries, English has two tenses: past and nonpast. How do we manage to say things like this?

> *If you would have had to have asked me first, I would have been in a position to have said "no."*

Having to translate a sentence like that for a show is my nightmare—and you'd be surprised how often sentences *very* similar to that end up in a script. Dialogue always looks simple until you have to translate it.

Unlike with nouns, verbs have so many potential inflectional categories that it's impossible to catalogue them all. In this section, I'm going to go over three main areas of verbal inflection: agreement; tense, modality, and aspect (often referred to as TMA); and valency. At the end of that, hopefully you'll understand why verbs are the onions of the language world. (Note: onions are bad.)

AGREEMENT

Verbs will often display some form of **agreement** with either their subjects or objects in one form or another. Verbs can agree with a noun in person, number, or sometimes gender. Verbs could agree with other properties of a noun (e.g. shirt color), but these are the only categories that are reified in natural languages. Agreement marking can't—

No, I'm sorry, I can't let this go. Why would anyone *ever* eat an onion or include it in food? *Onions taste bad.* Furthermore, they're the culinary equivalent of multiplying by zero: add onion to *any* food, and it now tastes like nothing but onion. In conclusion, onions are bad. Stop using them.

Agreement most often shows up as a prefix or a suffix to a verb. This is likely due to the history of agreement affixes, which most often derive from pronouns that appear next to the verb. In English, we just have -*s* for the third person singular present tense for most verbs (many auxiliaries are invariant in form, like *can, may, will,* etc.). The -*s* is just there. If you're reading a standard text, it feel wrong not to use -*s* on a verb with a third person singular subject in the present tense. How wrong? Well, how wrong did it feel to read that sentence? How much was your brain screaming, *"ARRGH! IT SHOULD BE 'FEELS'!"* as you read that? That's how wrong.

When it comes to agreement, there are two different types of behavior languages display with respect to the nouns referred to. In English, you always have to state the subject of the sentence. In other languages, though, the agreement morphology on the verb is sufficient to allow users to drop the subject entirely. This phenomenon is called **pro-drop**, since the pronouns get dropped. The more person and number marking appears on the verb, the more likely it is to be a pro-drop language (though this isn't always the case, as demonstrated by Japanese).

Verbs will generally encode the categories person (first, second, or third), number, and/or gender of a subject, object, or indirect object. Languages differ depending on how many of these categories their verbs encode, and how they do it. Chinese verbs, for example, encode none of them. Arabic verbs, on the other hand, encode them all. Languages will also differ by how vigorously they encode each category. Take a look at the difference between these languages' person marking strategies in the singular, for example:

Person	English	German	French	Spanish	Swedish
First	*sit*	*setze*	*siège*	*siento*	*sitter*
Second	*sit*	*setzt*	*sièges*	*sientas*	*sitter*
Third	*sits*	*setzt*	*siège*	*sienta*	*sitter*

Disregarding how these words are pronounced, look at that non-sense! Every possible arrangement of three potentially discrete items is present above—and all five of these languages are related! But looking at the above, if you had to guess which one allowed verbs to be used without subject pronouns, you'd probably guess Spanish—and you'd be right.

Though rarer, gender can be encoded on the verb, as mentioned. In Arabic, verbs with a second and third person subject distinguish between masculine and feminine:

كَتَبْتَ /katabta/ "you (masc.) wrote"   كَتَبْتِ /katabti/ "you (fem.) wrote"

كَتَبَ /kataba/ "he wrote"   كَتَبَتْ /katabat/ "she wrote"

And Russian distinguishes between masculine, feminine, and neuter in the past tense, but only when the subject is singular:

Я спал.	/ja spal/	"I (masc.) was sleeping."
Я спала.	/ja spala/	"I (fem.) was sleeping."
Я спало.	/ja spalo/	"I (neut. [perhaps some kind of toaster]) was sleeping."

Languages that have a dual verb form will definitely have dual marking on nouns, but the inverse isn't necessarily true.

In addition to subjects, though, many languages will mark objects on the verb. Some will even make at least passing reference to indirect objects (Georgian and Swahili come to mind). This is referred to as **head-marking**. Often languages will display object *marking* as opposed to object *agreement*. With agreement, the morphology must appear whether there's an overt object or not. By contrast, languages with object marking use it only when there is no overt object in the clause, as shown below in the Væyne Zaanics language used in Nina Post's *The Zaanics Deceit*:

ﾌﾞﾝﾄﾞ Ùﾞ Drega mufuupil.   "We will discuss the book."

ﾌﾞﾝﾄﾞ Mufuupilaw.   "We will discuss it."

Above, the only time the -*aw* suffix is used is when there is no overt object mentioned in the clause. When creating a language to be used in television or film, maximal subject agreement—and object marking, if possible—is best, as it allows for subjects to be dropped, and for lines, should they run long, to be shortened without sacrificing the basic meaning of the sentence.

TENSE, MODALITY, ASPECT

And now we get to my least favorite part of language. Not just creating languages, or conlangs: language *period*. A given language's number marking strategy may be simpler than another's, and a given language may have more agreement patterns for the verbs, but *no* language ever created has a simple tense, modality, aspect system. Even a conlang created with the intent of having a simple system ends up complicating things, often unwittingly. Placing an action in time and with respect to other actions is *the* most difficult part of language. It's also one of the most important parts, which makes everything just the worst.

So. Let's jump right in!

Tense is the grammatical encoding of the time in or at which an action occurs. Unlike with crazy number marking strategies, if there's a crazy tense you can think of, some natural language probably already has it. A special tense just for things that have been done since waking up? It's called a **hodiernal** and lots of languages have it. A tense just for telling stories? It's called the **narrative**, and lots of languages have it. A special tense for things that will take place in the distant future as opposed to the recent future?

There's a tense for each of those called, uncreatively, **distant future** and **recent future**. Makes English seem vanilla by comparison, doesn't it?

Of course, here's the catch. Every single language has the capability of expressing every single tense combination. The question is whether the verb *encodes* it or not. Taking our distant future, in English we can say *We'll all be able to teleport to the moon in the distant future*, and that conveys the concept rather nicely. In some languages, though, rather than having to say *in the distant future* or *some day*, you'd simply use a different verb form (if English had it, maybe instead of saying *we will* you'd say *we woller*). The trick in creating a language is figuring out how the system will work. So in English, we have the past tense (generally -*ed*), and we have the nonpast, and that's it. To express every other tense, we use a complex system of auxiliaries (*will, have, be*, etc.) or satellite temporal adverbs (*yesterday, soon*, etc.). When creating a system, the question I always ask is, "What do I want the verb to say on its own?" Everything else has to work itself out around it in order to express the gamut of temporal activity.

Tense interacts regularly with **aspect**, which defines how an action is presented. In English, for example, saying *I was running* is different from saying *I ran*, even though both actions occur in the past tense. In English we use an auxiliary to express this difference, but some languages take the distinction as important enough to encode on the verb itself. In Spanish, for example, the translation of those two phrases would be, in order, *corría* and *corrí*.

As with tenses, there are about as many aspects as you can think of. Below is a listing of some grammatical aspects—many of which require multiple English words to express, in contrast to the conlang exemplars (all subjects are third person singular):

Aspect	English	Conlang
Anterior	*has eaten*	*iprattas* (High Valyrian)
Perfective	*searched*	⟨𝔈⊕⊕⟩ *aklas* (Sondiv)
Cessative	*has finished/stopped working*	ꢶ *fugyupsa* (Castithan)
Inchoative	*goes/becomes feral*	*ivezhoe* (Dothraki)
Inceptive	*starts/begins to live at/in*	ꢶ *etrehe* (Irathient)
Habitual	*used to weep*	*limatis* (High Valyrian)
Continuative	*is still growing*	⊗⊗⊗⊗⊗⊗ *tiohitlen* (Indojisnen)
Stative	*is broken*	ꢶ *anizagba* (Irathient)

Each aspect focuses on an act from a different perspective in order to convey a slightly different shade of meaning. Usually a language encodes a few of these on the verb and uses multiword expressions to convey the rest, as shown in the English column.

The last prong of the mighty TMA trident is **modality**, which deals with the point of view of the speaker. Basically, if it has to do with the action of the verb, but isn't specifically about the time or manner of the action or the character of the participants, it's modality. Most examples from English make use of modal auxiliaries (hence the name), but notice how in each of the examples below, the number and person of the subject are the same, as are the tense and aspect:

We should go.
We must go.
We're supposed to go.
We may go.
Let's go!

The thing that's changing from example to example above is the mode or mood, and these are things that can be encoded on the verb. Again, all languages have a way of expressing all of them; some just have a special way of doing so. Some languages have few grammatical moods (English has just a couple), but some go overboard, like Tundra Nenets, a Samoyedic language of Russia, which has sixteen distinct grammatical moods marked on the verb. When creating a language, the two moods that come up the most often are the **indicative**, which is just the basic form of a verb when making an ordinary statement, and the **imperative** or command form used for issuing commands. Some others are shown below (all subjects, aside from the imperative, are third person singular):

Aspect	English	Conlang
Indicative	*he eats*	⬡⬡⬡⬡⬡ *oyslen* (Indojisnen)
Imperative	*Eat!*	𐐀 *əlú* (Irathient)
Conditional	*he would eat*	𐐃𐐂 *fana* (Castithan)
Subjunctive	*(that) he eat*	*iprados* (High Valyrian)
Optative	*may he eat*	*adakhi* (Dothraki)

How moods will be used in a language tends to be idiosyncratic. Strike that. How *anything* about a verb is used in a language tends to be idiosyncratic. For example, the subjunctive in High Valyrian is used in all negative statements, in addition to its usual usage (e.g. the word *eat* in sentences like *I put half of the cake in the freezer, lest he eat it all*). And in Castithan, what amounts to the conditional form for dynamic predicates is a simple past tense for stative predicates (a simple -*a* suffix below):

𐐀𐐃𐐂𐐁 𐐃𐐂 𐐃𐐁𐐂 𐐀𐐃𐐂𐐁 𐐃 𐐂𐐁𐐃𐐀

Feza do garya. *Fezo nggo uthya.*

['fe.za.do 'ga.rja] ['fe.zoŋ.go 'u.θja]

/temple OBJ demolish-CND/ /temple OBJ laugh-at-PST/

"He would demolish the temple." "He laughed at the temple."

Now, it's probably (read: definitely) my English speaker bias, but having a bunch of fancy grammatical moods is just more trouble than it's worth. Sure, it may save me one or two syllables in one line once a season, but it's a pain in the butterball to have to create a bunch of different grammatical moods and then remember how to use them. It still creeps me out to have a subjunctive in High Valyrian. *Bleh.* The subjunctive is the onion of grammatical moods. Most of them are just old future tenses vainly clinging to relevance *Sunset Boulevard*–style, anyway. Be gone with them, I say!

VALENCY

Valency refers to the number of nominal arguments a verb has and what approximate role those arguments play. Valency is just the best. It may not seem like it, but that's partly because valency is *super* boring in English. I'll show you how it can be fun. First, though, let's get our bearings.

A verb needs to get paired with some noun in order to express any meaning. This noun is called an **argument**. Some verbs require *exactly* one argument (the **subject**). These are called **monovalent** or **intransitive** verbs. A nice example in English is *sleep*. A simple sentence would be *The coyote slept.*

Verbs that require exactly two arguments are called **divalent** or **transitive**. With a transitive verb, one argument (the **agent**) interacts with the other (the **patient**) by means of the verb. In English, *disrespect* is a good example of a transitive verb, as in *The coyote disrespected the onion.*

Before moving on, notice what happens when you use either of these verbs with the inappropriate number of arguments:

The coyote slept the onion.

The coyote disrespected.

Neither of these seem like a grammatical English sentence (well, unless you play RPGs and you're familiar with spell-casting jargon). The reason is that these verbs have strict requirements about the arguments they can occur with. Many English verbs, like *eat*, have no such requirements:

- *The coyote ate.*

- *The coyote ate the onion.*

A couple other types of verbs are **avalent** or **impersonal** verbs and **trivalent** or **ditransitive** verbs. An example of each is shown below:

- *It rained.*

- *The coyote gave the prisoner an onion.*

Ditransitive verbs are few in number, and their primary example, language after language, is a word meaning "give." Many ditransitive verbs can require arguments that need to be in a particular case or sense. In English, for example, *put* requires a third locative argument of any kind. One can't say simply *I put the book* or even *I put the book the table.* The verb *put* requires an expression like *on the table, under the table, there*—anything that has to do with a location.

Impersonal verbs, on the other hand, take no arguments whatsoever. Think about the English sentence *It rained. What* rained? The clouds? The sky? The . . . weather? You can't even replace *it* with *water* in that sentence and have it mean the same thing. Rather, the verb simply describes an event, and since English requires a subject in all its sentences, we throw an *it* in there just because. (Note: Not all languages require their sentences to have subjects!)

That's valency, in a nutshell. Now that we know what it is, what can we do with it?

The fun of valency comes when we decide to take one verb and change the number of arguments it has. We do so all the time when speaking a language. These valency changing operations come in two varieties: valency reducing operations and valency increasing operations. The most common valency reducing operation is **passivization**, which is when a transitive verb is turned into an intransitive verb by deleting the agent. Passives are incredibly useful when stringing clauses together. Functionally, passives are nothing more than intransitive verbs. Often some little piece of morphology on the verb will indicate that the verb is in the passive form, though. Compare these active and passive forms of the Castithan verb *fanu* "to eat":

ᏫᎰᏘᎻᏫᎻᏯᎢ ᏫᏂ ᎮᏕᏆᎻᏣᎯ ᎥᎤ ᎻᎢᏫᏫᏂᎣ·   ᎮᏕᏆᎻᏣ ᏫᏂ ᎻᎢᏫᏂᎻᏘᎤᎢᎣ·

Vajutsa re egulina do fanupsa.   *Eguline re fanudhopsa.*

['va.dʒu.tsa.ɾe 'e.gu.li.na.do 'fa.nu.psa]   ['e.gu.li.ne.ɾe 'fa.nu.ðo.psa]

/soldier SBJ steak OBJ eat-PST/   /steak SBJ eat-PSV-PST/

"The soldier ate the steak."   "The steak was eaten."

Above, the suffix -*dho* indicates the verb is in the passive, and this triggers the change in nominal suffixes (from *egulina do* to *eguline re*), promoting *egulino* "steak" to subject position.

A common valency increasing operation is **causativization**. A causative verb is one that includes an agent who causes someone to perform or undergo the action of the verb. When an intransitive verb is causativized, its total number of arguments is increased from one to two; when a transitive verb is causativized, the increase is from two to three. In English, we usually use *make* as an auxiliary to form causative verbs (e.g. from *He slept* to *I made him sleep*). Other languages mark it directly on the verb. Here's an example from Castithan:

ᏘᎻᏫ ᏫᏂ ᏫᎨᎥᏫᎣ·   ᏔᎢᏣᏘᎩᏣᎯ ᏫᏂ ᏘᎻᏫ ᎥᎤ ᏫᎨᎥᎵᎣᏫᎣ·

Liva re rigupsa.   *Inayéne re liva do rigustopsa.*

['li.va.ɾe 'ri.gu.psa]   [i.na.'je.ne.ɾe 'li.va.do 'ri.gus.to.psa]

/child SBJ cry-PST/   /grandma SBJ child-OBJ cry-CAU-PST/

"The child cried."   "The grandma made the child cry."

Above, the suffix -*sto* indicates the verb is a causative, and this triggers the change in nominal morphology (from *liva re* to *liva do*), and adds a causer to the argument structure.

The granddaddy of all valency changing operations, though, is the **applicative**. An applicative takes a nondirect or peripheral argument and promotes it to direct object position, deleting or demoting the old direct object, if there was one. A kind of hacky English example is the prefix *out-*. For example, you can say *I shot*; an intransitive clause. You can also say *I shot better than him*. It's still an intransitive clause, but it has some extra info. This, however, is a transitive clause: *I outshot him*. You can't get away with *I outshot*. That seems odd, at the very least. By adding *out-* to a verb you make it transitive, and take a peripheral argument and make it into a direct object, producing a new, more compact, and more convenient verb along the way.

Many languages have institutionalized this practice, producing applicative affixes that target specific arguments (so one that promotes only benefactive arguments, one that only promotes instruments, etc.). It's really cool! But beyond that, why do it? Let me show you an example from one of my languages, Kamakawi.

In Kamakawi, relative clauses (sentences that tell you more about a noun, e.g. the phrase *I catapulted into space,* in the longer phrase *the onion I catapulted into space*) may only feature subjects or direct objects. In English, they can play any grammatical role (*the onion I gave a beating to, the onion whose taste I despise, the onion with whom I would not pose for a photo*, etc.), but some languages are more restrictive. What does one do if one has to build a relative clause featuring a different kind of object? This is where the applicative comes in. To see it, let's start with a simple sentence like:

°ꉯꀸ꒭ꍌꀀ꒬꒱ꉆꀸꀹꀸꍌ°

Ka lalau ei ie hate aeiu kava.
/PST throw 1SG OBJ-DEF onion into fire/

"I threw the onion into the fire."

Should be pretty easy to pick out the word for "onion" there. Anyway, by adding an applicative ꒮ *-ku* suffix to the verb ꀸꍌ *lalau*, you get ꀸꍌ꒮ *lalauku*, which means "to throw somewhere." The direct object is where the whatever it is is thrown, as shown below:

ㄹㅣ 而ㄐ ㄱ T 宗茎。

Ka lalauku ei ie kava.
/PST THROW-APL 1SG OBJ-DEF fire/

"I threw into the fire."

Now that the word for "fire," 茎 *kava*, has been promoted to direct object position, it can be promoted to the subject of a sentence with a passive verb. By adding the passive suffix ⟨ -'u to the verb, we can now produce the following sentence:

ㄹㅣ 而ㄐ ⟨茎。

Ka lalauku'u kava.
/PST throw-APL-PSV fire/

"The fire was thrown into."

If you want to say what was thrown into the fire, you can add T宗⑀ *ie hate* "the onion" to the end (as in the first sentence), and if you want to say who did it, you can add ᐳ〒 *ti'i* "by me" to the end of that.

But now here comes the exciting part. Let's say my friend Jon comes in as I'm talking to Scott about how I dispose of onions. Jon overhears me say something about a fire, and he says, "What fire are you talking about?" I'd then respond in Kamakawi (because why would I speak a language he understood?):

宗茎ㄒ ㄹㅈ宗ㅣ 而ㄐ⟨ㄑ宗⑀ᐳ〒。

E kava poke lalauku'u ie hate ti'i.
/DEF fire REL-PST throw-APL-PSV OBJ-DEF onion INS-1SG/

"The fire I threw an onion into."

Or, more accurately, "The fire that had an onion thrown into it by me." And that, dear reader, is why there's absolutely nothing wrong with using the passive voice in formal writing—and also why every language should have an applicative. Valency changing strategies exist simply to smooth transitions between disparate clauses. It's easier to have the same subject for successive clauses, as it allows the narrative to flow more smoothly. I say that as a linguist, language creator, writer, English major, English professor, *and* occasional anonymous Wikipedia editor. There's absolutely nothing wrong with any valency changing operation in any language.

WORD ORDER

Word order refers to the order of elements in a phrase and a sentence. For example, English has Subject-Verb-Object—or SVO—word order, in that that's the linear precedence of those three elements in a sentence that has all of them, as shown below:

S   V   O

David   despises   onions.

Languages make use of many different word orders, though. Natural languages have been found that utilize all six logical orderings of subject, verb, and object as their default word order, and conlangers have done the same in their work:

Order	Natlang	Conlang	Order	Natlang	Conlang
SVO	English	'Yemls	**VOS**	Malagasy	Minza
SOV	Japanese	mërèchi	**OVS**	Hixkaryana	Pasgemanh
VSO	Hawaiian	Nevashi	**OSV**	Xavante	Teonaht

The three orderings in the left-hand column are quite common; the three on the right much less so. The ordering of the verb and its object often (but not always) aligns with the orderings of several other elements. Typologists classify languages by the various orderings of the following elements, and conlangers have followed suit:

- Noun-Adjective Order: An adjective (A) can precede or follow the noun it modifies (N). English places adjectives before nouns, as in *black cat*, while a language like Spanish places adjectives after nouns, as in *gato negro*, literally "cat black." There are a number of languages that utilize both orderings.

- Noun-Genitive Order: A possessor (G) can precede or follow the thing it possesses (N). In English, "the onion's stench" is G-N ordering, and "the stench of the onion" is N-G ordering. Many languages only feature one order.

- Adposition-Noun Order: An adposition (P) can precede or follow the noun phrase it governs (N). When the adposition comes before the noun, it's called a **preposition**, and when it comes after, it's called a **postposition**. English is a language with prepositions, while languages like Japanese and Turkish feature postpositions. Some languages feature both, such as Moro, a language of Sudan and South Sudan, and High Valyrian.

- Noun–Relative Clause Order: A relative clause (R) can precede or follow the noun (N) it modifies. In English, the relative clause follows the noun, as in "The man whom I saw," whereas in a language like Japanese, Castithan, or Turkish, it would precede the noun it modifies—literally something like "The I saw man."

Linguists and conlangers combine all these orderings to determine the typological profile of a language. Depending on how the orderings align, we can say that languages are either **head-initial** or **head-final**. Below is the ideal ordering of elements for each type:

Head-Initial: V-O, N-A, N-G, P-N, N-R

Head-Final: O-V, A-N, G-N, N-P, R-N

Not all languages line up in *precisely* this fashion. Instead, many will *primarily* use one set of orderings over the other, and this allows one to determine whether a language is largely head-initial or largely head-final. We'll see more about how some of these orderings arise in the section on language evolution.

DERIVATION

Derivation refers to the ability to change via morphology one word into another. All languages have some type of derivation, even if it's **zero derivation** (no visible change to a word). Compare the word *mail* in *They'll mail it to me* and *You've got mail*. In the first sentence, *mail* is a verb; in the second, a semantically related noun. They're different words, despite looking and sounding alike.

Languages differ in how they make use of derivation. Two quick examples should illustrate. Below is a comparison between related concepts first in English and Spanish and then in English and Hawaiian:

English	Spanish	English	Hawaiian
teach	enseñar	sit	noho
teacher	maestro	chair	noho

That, in a nutshell, is derivation. Some languages will derive one concept from another in a more or less predictable fashion (*teach* vs. *teacher*); some will treat concepts as completely distinct (*enseñar* vs. *maestro* and *sit* vs. *chair*); and some will reuse the same word for different concepts (*noho* vs. *noho*).

An easy and effective way to make a language unique is to play with its derivational morphology, even if the meanings that take hold often have more to do with a language's evolution than with its synchronic morphology. For example, the word *inspiration* has an odd meaning for its evolution. It began its existence as the Latin verb *spirare*, which means "to breathe." By adding *in-* to the front, a new verb was derived that meant "to breathe in/into." This was turned into the noun *inspirationem*, which came to us by way of French. It should mean "breathing in," a generic noun, but it instead makes reference to an unseen deity literally breathing into a human being in order to give them ideas about stuff. That's *inspiration*.

Arguably, our meaning for *inspiration* is more useful than a noun that means "breathing in," but even so, derivations that produce unrelated words like this one are quite common. In Castithan, an old word for "tear," ꠰꠲꠳ꠤ *thoryo*, had a collective suffix ꠻꠲꠳ꠤ *-bun* attached to it which produced ꠰꠲꠳ꠤ꠻꠲꠳ꠤ *thoribuno*, which is the modern word for "sorrow." Using derivation in this way forces one to step back into the past (presumably spontaneous derivation is regular), but that's a good thing. Creating a language at any point is an attempt to take a slice out of an eras-long progression. It's better to accept that fact than to pretend the form one is creating is, was, and always will be.

Derivational strategies differ in whether they turn a word of one grammatical category into another or not. For example, *-ly* takes an adjective and turns it into an adverb (e.g. *sharp > sharply*). *Re-*, though, takes a verb and produces a different verb with a slightly different meaning (e.g. *work > rework*). Certain strategies will apply only to certain types of words while others will apply to many. These restrictions depend on the peculiar histories of the affixes or processes. For example, *-ity* tends to work only with Latinate words because it came from Latin. You can turn *fertile* into *fertility* but you can't turn *red* into *reddity*. There's no phonological reason this should be the case. We just know it doesn't work, because no one does it. The only reason no one does it, though, is because the words that employ *-ity* all came to us from Latin (sometimes through French), and so why would we have ever used the strategy with any other word?

To close this section I'll introduce you to an all-encompassing derivational system I created for one of the *Defiance* languages. As you look at it, though, it's a good time to start thinking about the connection between language and history. Ultimately this is what the best conlangers wrestle with. Language is nothing more than the battered baton of an endless relay race. You can take a snapshot of that baton halfway through and recreate what you see, but doing so obscures the many hands that were involved in passing it to that point. How does one replicate the entire race without simply copying the baton? That's the question I'll tackle in the next section. For now, let's look at some nominal morphology! Better than onions, I can tell you that.

Case Study

IRATHIENT NOUNS

Back in the fall of 2011, I had lunch with Tom Lieber and Rockne O'Bannon, executive producers for the Syfy series *Defiance*, which, at the time, was still in the planning stages. They'd shared with me an early draft of the pilot, and told me that they were looking for languages for two of the main alien races: the Castithans and Irathients. The only requirement was that they sound as different as possible on-screen. My first idea was that in order for them to be as different as possible, they should be opposites: one would be head-final, the other head-initial; one would be dependent-marking, the other head-marking; one would sound fast, the other slow.

Slow. Now that's a trick. As soon as I said it, I began to wonder how it could be achieved, given that an actor only has so much time to speak a line on-screen. Most of the time when we hear a foreign language, we get the impression that it's being spoken too quickly (as if slowing it down would help any!). Could a language exist that gave the opposite impression?

As it happens, I'd had indirect experience with just such a language. Many years prior, I watched the movie *Atanarjuat: The Fast*

Runner, filmed entirely in Inuktitut—the language that opened this chapter. The movie was amazing, but above all I remember my impression upon first hearing the Inuktitut language. The language was spoken slowly and steadily. Even if you'd never heard it before, you could catch every single syllable. It was still incomprehensible, of course (it's a different language), but you wouldn't ever have to say, "Hey, slow down; I didn't catch that."

Now, the Inuktitut language, as demonstrated above, does what it does by creating enormous, sentence-long words. That wasn't an option for Irathient. In order to fit the same amount of meaning into the amount of time it takes to speak an English line, the translation had to have equally short words, or fewer longer words.

My solution was to take the meaning required for a given utterance and spread it across the entire clause. That way if a sentence was running a little long, a word or two could be deleted with most of the meaning being preserved. An example sentence will help to illustrate how this works:

·ᘝᑫᒍᐦᑕᑖᑎ᷉ᐦᐱᒍ ᑫᐸᑫᒍᒍᑯᐦ·

Zahon ekesə hudi zvoshakte.
/AUX notice thief warrior/

"The warrior noticed the thief."

Above, the order is auxiliary-verb-object-subject. The order is strict, so if both the auxiliary *zahon* and verb *ekesə* were deleted, one at least could understand that the warrior (*zvoshakte*) was doing something to the thief (*hudi*). Both nouns could be deleted, because the subject (*zvoshakte*) and object (*hudi*) are marked on the auxiliary (this is head-marking). If the verb *ekesə* were deleted, we'd know that the warrior (*zvoshakte*) did something to the thief (*hudi*) in the past, and if the auxiliary *zahon* were deleted, all we'd be missing was the tense. In fact, if you just used the first word by itself, it'd mean someone did something to someone in the past, so if one already knew who was being discussed and what the context was, that'd be plenty of information.

The key to make this work, though, was to add as much information to the noun as possible while minimizing its size. Take any noun of English—like one of Nina Post's favorite words, *child*. There's nothing about *child* that tells you anything important about it. That is, if you had never heard the English word *child* before, it could stand for pretty much anything. Furthermore, in order to pluralize it, you need to make it longer by adding *-ren* to the end, meaning that plural nouns will almost always take more time to pronounce than singular nouns (not much longer, but longer nonetheless).

With Irathient, I decided to do three things to the nouns to try to minimize the space. First, stems would be short (most are mono-syllabic). Next, each noun would mark its number with a final vowel, meaning that singular and plural nouns would be the same length. Finally, each noun would have a class prefix. The class prefix would divide the lexicon into several different semantic classes so that just by looking at the first letter or two of the noun you'd know approximately what type of noun it was.

The noun class (or gender) system is reminiscent of Bantu, since the class markers are prefixes, but unlike Bantu, which changes prefixes depending on whether the noun is singular or plural (e.g. *kitabu* "book" vs. *vitabu* "books"), Irathient noun class prefixes are invariant. Nominal number is encoded by a suffixed vowel, which was directly inspired by an auxlang from the 1970s called Afrihili. Most of the time, I don't directly copy anything from another language, but the vowel triangle system Afrihili used is so cool I simply had to use it in a language. Unlike Afrihili, Irathient couldn't manage seven vowels (I didn't want to have to try to get actors to consistently distinguish between the pairs [ɛ] and [e] and [ɔ] and [o]), so I created a vowel quadrangle:

ꟼ *i* [i]   ꓳ *ə* [ə]   ꙅ *u* [u]

ꙅ *e* [ɛ]   ꟼ *a* [a]

The way it works is this: If a noun ends in a particular vowel, its plural will feature the *opposite* vowel in the quadrangle. Thus, if a singular word ends in [ɛ], its plural will end in [u], and vice versa. If a word happens to end in a consonant, it takes the neutral vowel [ə] for its plural.

In forming the noun classes of Irathient, I decided to assign a unique consonant-vowel combination to each prefix and make the singular suffix the opposite vowel from the prefix vowel. Thus, even if a given word wasn't known, if the vowels rhymed, you'd know it was a plural noun; if not, singular.

As for the classes themselves, I decided to have fun with them, since Irathients are aliens from a distant galaxy. On Earth, certain languages have made the distinction between poisonous and non-poisonous plants, so I decided to expand that model to various other areas of experience in the first ten noun classes (parentheses indicate the segment is optional):

(I)	Irathient Beings	PREFIX: *z(u)*-	SINGULAR SUFFIX: -*e*
(II)	Dangerous Irathient Beings	PREFIX: *h(a)*-	SINGULAR SUFFIX: -*i*
(III)	Animals	PREFIX: *t(i)*-	SINGULAR SUFFIX: -*a*
(IV)	Dangerous Animals	PREFIX: *k(a)*-	SINGULAR SUFFIX: -*i*
(V)	Plants	PREFIX: *d(i)*-	SINGULAR SUFFIX: -*a*
(VI)	Dangerous Plants	PREFIX: *g(e)*-	SINGULAR SUFFIX: -*u*
(VII)	Objects	PREFIX: *u(t)*-	SINGULAR SUFFIX: -*e*
(VIII)	Dangerous Objects	PREFIX: *e(k)*-	SINGULAR SUFFIX: -*u*
(IX)	Substances	PREFIX: *r(i)*-	SINGULAR SUFFIX: -*a*
(X)	Dangerous Substances	PREFIX: *s(a)*-	SINGULAR SUFFIX: -*i*

Outside of these first ten, there were others that had more specific or abstract designations, a couple of which were inspired directly by an older language of mine called Zhyler:

(XI)	Places/Passive Objects	PREFIX: *nu(n)*-	SINGULAR SUFFIX: -*e*
(XII)	Abstracts	PREFIX: *th(e)*-	SINGULAR SUFFIX: -*u*
(XIII)	Groups/Collectives	PREFIX: *i(n)*-	SINGULAR SUFFIX: -*a*
(XIV)	Actions	PREFIX: *sh(e)*-	SINGULAR SUFFIX: -*u*

The remaining four classes were designated for diminutives and augmentatives and then further split by animacy. The augmentative class takes its prefix only if the root to which it's added is monosyllabic:

(XV)	Animate Diminutives	PREFIX: *t(i)-*	SINGULAR SUFFIX: *-a*
(XVI)	Inanimate Diminutives	PREFIX: *t(i)-*	SINGULAR SUFFIX: *-e*
(XVII)	Animate Augmentatives	PREFIX: *gya(n)-*	SINGULAR SUFFIX: *-a*
(XVIII)	Inanimate Augmentatives	PREFIX: *gya(n)-*	SINGULAR SUFFIX: *-e*

Though this is where the classes began, they ended up in different places after centuries of use. For example, although Class II started out housing words like ⵏⵂⴹⵇ *hudi* "thief," ⴹⵇ *habasi* "idol," and ⴹⵇ *heimbi* "loser," when Irathients made first contact in their solar system, the class shifted to cover all aliens. Thus, ⵏⴹⵇ *zbaba* is "father" if the father is Irathient, and ⴹⵇ *hababa* is "father" if the father is alien (e.g. human).

The other semantic categories drifted in similar fashions, admitting many members that ended up being quite far from the original intent. For example, a nice pair illustrating the origins of Classes VII and VIII are the words ⵏⵂⴹⵇ *unnire* "rain" and ⵏⵂⴹⵇ *enniru* "rainstorm." As Class VIII covers dangerous objects, many weapons fall under Class VIII, like ⵏⵂⴹⵇ *eziru* "spear." Since weapons are manmade, Class VIII also came to encode words for artificial versions of natural objects, leading to pairs like ⵏⵂⴹⵇ *utame* "face" and ⵏⵂⴹⵇ *ekamu* "mask." Building off the idea of weaponry or tools, surprising pairs also began to pop up, such as ⵏⵂⴹⵇ *ulluze* "reason" versus ⵏⵂⴹⵇ *elluzu* "excuse" and ⵏⵂⴹⵇ *uttu* "advice" versus ⵏⵂⴹⵇ *ettu* "criticism."

Classes XV through XVIII collectively became the "everything else" classes, for two reasons. First, diminutives can be anything; it's all perception. Second, since Classes XVII and XVIII are the only classes that have an optional class prefix, most borrowed words ended up there. Now when a new word comes into the language— say, ⵏⵂⴹⵇ *ledo*, the Castithan word for "emblem"—it gets stuffed into

Class XVIII, regardless of whether it's an augmentative or not, just as ⟨ꞎꞟꞔ⟩ *leide* "badge" is not.

Part of the fun in having a system like this is working with borrowings that *do* fit into a class because of the phonology of the word. For example, the Castithan word ⟨ꞎꞟꞔ⟩ *dimo* "cover" was borrowed into Irathient as ⟨ꞎꞟꞔ⟩ *dim* "clothes," more commonly used in the plural, ⟨ꞎꞟꞔ⟩ *dimə*. Due to the initial *d*, it was treated as a Class V noun with a root of ⟨ꞔ⟩ *im*. This led to the production of words like ⟨ꞔ⟩ *thim* "clothing" (Class XII) and ⟨ꞔ⟩ *tim* "wardrobe" (Class XVI), regardless of the fact that the *d* isn't separable from the root in Castithan.

The best part about the system for me is that when sitting down to coin a new word in one class, I'm automatically asked by the system itself to imagine how else the concept of the root may be reified in the other seventeen noun classes. This leads to the creation of words I never would have thought of independently, like ⟨ꞔ⟩ *nunone*, a word for the usual or safe way of doing things, or ⟨ꞔ⟩ *utenye*, a mound of dirt that's been formed as a result of an animal burrowing into the ground. I didn't intend to create these words: they suggested themselves as I was coining other words. It makes coining new words fun, and that's part of what's made Irathient my favorite language of all the ones I've created thus far.

CHAPTER III

Evolution

INTRODUCTION

As is common knowledge, there are fewer content restrictions for cable television programs such as HBO's *Game of Thrones* and Syfy's *Defiance*. However, a standard of review does apply to content for broadcast television networks. For the CW's *Star-Crossed*, the first show I'd worked on that appeared on network television, one of the early words I created for an Atrian tribe, [gwa.ˈhã], got turned back because it was too similar to the Chamorro pronunciation of Guam, *Guåhån* [ˈgwa.han] (and props to CBS Legal: they were absolutely correct!). I'd never had to be concerned about things like that for the other shows I'd worked on, beyond a bit of self-policing—which, by the way, I'm usually pretty good at, despite my lack of familiarity with Chamorro beyond a relational grammar analysis of its voice system by linguist Sandra Chung.

In addition, though, most of the time when I create a word or translate a line, that's the end of it. It may get cut, or may need retranslating if the English changes, but the language part of it is always my domain. Once in a blue moon, a change would be required, as with the *Daenero* to *Daenerys* change discussed in the previous section, or when Kevin Murphy, showrunner of *Defiance*, asked me for a new Irathient word for "paradise," since my word had the potential to be said in a singsongy way (and he was right about that), but for the most part what I say goes. This is one of the things I like most about working as a language creator.

Not so on *Star-Crossed*, though. Whether it was because of legal concerns, or because the writers didn't "like" a particular word, it seemed like I was getting requests every single week for different iterations on some word or name or another. The problem is that a language's vocabulary is not a mere word list. It's rare that I go in and create a single word for a single concept. Instead, a single word will give birth to a family of related words and concepts. Here, for example, is a full entry for one root in Sondiv that stemmed from a single request:

> *ketur* [ke.'tur] (adj.) sleepy; *ktor* [ktor] (ii) bed; *bektudon* [bek.
> tu.'dõ] (vi) bedroom; *ektira* [ek.ti.'ra] (viii) dream (for "to dream"
> use a movement word with *ektira* as a destination); *ini m'ektira*
> [i.'ni mek.ti.'ra] (expr.) to dream; *iktur* [ik.'tur] (xiii) to sleep; *eketr*
> [e.'ketr] (xi) a drug that can be used to induce sleep and affect
> dreams (see *ktovor*; the part of the plant used as a drug); *soktur*
> [sok.'tur] (xv) sleep, a period of sleep (any length), nap; *ktovor*
> [kto.'vor] (xxiv) a plant that induces sleep and can be used to
> affect the user's dreams

The original request was for a drug that could be used to affect people's dreams. Everything else I created using Sondiv's derivational system. This is how I populated the language's vocabulary, and also generated words that ended up being used later on in the show. Generating the vocabulary in advance like this saves me time, and the interrelationships of vocabulary items are a big part of what produces a naturalistic result, as words in every language are similarly interconnected. Changing a word, whatever the reason, has devastating consequences on the paradigm, and usually requires ripping out everything I'd already done, so I'm not a big fan of changing things after the fact.

For episode 109 of *Star-Crossed*, I needed to generate a bunch of Sondiv vocabulary, including a word for a kind of black box from an alien spaceship. Rather than record just the audio or video of a flight in the event of a crash, though, this object would allow anyone who interacted with it to experience the crash from the point of view of the pilot. I decided to base the word on the already established root used for memory. The word ended up being 𐎓𐎚𐎐 *emern* [e.'mern], which, admittedly, doesn't sound very good, but it's a pretty cool word, as it basically means "a tool associated with memory," or a "memory machine." That, in effect, is what the thing is, after all.

News came back that the writers didn't like the word—it was too similar to Emery, the name of the show's main female character (true enough), and didn't roll off the tongue (also true). I spun a bunch of alternatives, but didn't hear anything back until poor Brian Studler, one of the show's writers, emailed me saying that while he'd tried to argue for one of my alternatives, he was over-ruled, and tried to go with a compromise: the word *mirzan* [mir.'zã].

Mirzan didn't fit any of the established nominal patterns of Sondiv. The linear ordering of vowels and consonants in Sondiv is quite specific, and so doing something small—like having the word end with *-an* instead of *-on*—made the whole word *completely* impossible.

Or so I thought.

Because before I even pulled out my Sondiv dictionary I'd thought up a solution.

Even though there couldn't be a word like *mirz*, and such a word could never end in *-an*, a word like *rzan* was perfectly possible. And even though it's used to form reflexive verbs, there is a *mi-* prefix in Sondiv, meaning that, if the verb was turned into a noun via regular derivational patterns, there *could* actually be a noun *mirzan*. Now it was just a matter of figuring out what the heck it would mean.

The first step was seeing what similar words or roots existed. Sondiv, somewhat similar to Arabic, has a series of two- and three-consonant sequences that encode general semantic ideas, and then these consonants are arranged into series to produce specific nouns and verbs. A word like *mirzan* would need to come from a root with the consonants R-Z-N or R-Z-M, since the final *n* is just indicative of nasalization on the vowel at this stage, which can be triggered by a final [n] or [m]. The reason for this is that the consonants R, Z, and N appear in that order in the word *miRZaN*. As it happens, there already existed a root R-Z, which was used for, among other things, the verb 𑀬𑀫 *idus* [i.'dus], which means "to touch." This was a start.

Jumping off from here, I looked into the ancient derivational patterns I'd created just in case I needed them. The older language—

the proto-language that gave birth to Sondiv—had a series of root extensions that altered the original meaning of the root in a series of ways. By adding a root letter *M* to the end, it'd produce a meaning that was metaphorically entailed by or related to the original concept. I used this to produce the verb *irzon* [irˈzõ], which means "to experience." By adding the reflexive prefix *mi-*, it produced the verb *imirzon* [i.mirˈzõ], which means "to experience firsthand." By retaining the *mi-* prefix and changing the root pattern, the result is 𝕏⧉𝕍⧉ *mirzan*—our word—which is an animate word that refers to someone who has experienced something firsthand.

Getting from that to a flight recorder is a step, but not a difficult one. Often when a tool is developed that fulfills one or more of the functions of a human, it can be referred to by the name of the human agent. One of my favorite on-the-fly examples is from the show *The Venture Bros.*, when Dr. Venture refers to his bedrest pillow (a back pillow with armrests) as "the husband." More generally, agentive words often can refer to humans or instruments, depending on what they do, for example, *conductor* (of electricity or a symphony), *driver* (of a car or a golf ball), *speaker* (at an event or at the end of a wire attached to a stereo), etc. Even in linguistics we routinely use the terms *mother* and *daughter* to refer to languages that have a similar genetic relationship. Anthropomorphization is a favorite human pastime, so if an alien species is sufficiently humanoid, why wouldn't it be a favorite pastime of theirs, too? And so, *mirzan* came to exist quite happily as the alien black box.

Ultimately, the question I wish to raise is how do words come to mean what they mean? In the fictional history of the Atrians, the alien species in *Star-Crossed*, presumably they created this cool bit of technology and had to call it something. Humans find themselves in similar situations frequently. What we don't do is create a brand-new root out of nothing. Instead, we use what we have to come up with an appropriate name for whatever new invention we've created. This is partly due to convenience, and partly due to marketing. After all, the best way to introduce an invention is to explain what it can do that will help make folks' *current* lives better in some way. It has to be relatable. Thus we start with known experience and extrapolate to unknown experience, until it becomes a part of our shared history. This same principle applies to language evolution.

In this section I'll discuss the three major forms of language evolution: phonological evolution, lexical evolution, and grammatical evolution. Understanding the principles of linguistic evolution is the most important prerequisite for understanding the tenets of naturalistic language creation. A fleshed-out history is what separates languages that are good enough from those that are excellent. Unfortunately, linguistic evolution is also the most difficult aspect of language creation, so, you know . . . no pressure. It'll be fun! Like a stage play of *Ulysses* where all the characters are played by kittens. (*Stately, plump Buck Kittykins* . . .)

PHONOLOGICAL EVOLUTION

Each of the three main areas of linguistic evolution has been studied by linguists, but some for a longer period of time than others. **Phonological evolution**, the way sounds change over time, has the longest academic track record of the three, and it's the best understood. Consequently, it's the best place to start.

English speakers have an unfair advantage when it comes to explaining sound changes since our gloriously appalling spelling system preserves, in many cases, an older state of the language. For example, take this word:

knight

We know how that's pronounced: [najt]. Its pronunciation is identical to *night*. Neither word really looks like it should be pronounced that way based on the spelling—a better spelling for both would be *nite*—but speaking English means swallowing horse pills like this one and memorizing the darn words.

But have you ever wondered just *why* the word is spelled that way? What's the point of it? It's not as if our writing system is anything like Chinese's, or like hieroglyphs, where pictures or abstract glyphs stand for concepts: Our writing system is *supposed* to clue us in to the pronunciation of the word. And it kind of does. But how did it even get to that point? Did someone sit down and decide to make a bunch of -*ite* words end in -*ight*—and then get drunk and decide to mess with people by creating the spelling *weight*?

Not so! Writing systems, as we'll learn, are organic things, just like languages. As words come into a language, they gain spellings. And unless a language's orthography is tightly regulated, as it is in Spanish, old pronunciations will be reflected in a word's spelling. Looking at *knight*, the word used to be pronounced [knixt]. Yes, that *k* was originally pronounced just like a *k*, and that *gh* used to be pronounced, too—kind of like the *ch* in German *Bach*. To whoever came up with the spelling, then, they were spelling the word *exactly* as it was pronounced: *k* for [k]; *n* for [n]; *i* for [i]; *gh* for [x]; and *t* for [t].

Then a bunch of stuff happened. At some point in time, we stopped pronouncing a [k] sound in front of an [n] sound at the beginning of a word (hence *knot, knee, knock*, etc.). It might seem odd to a modern-day English speaker to ever have that combination of sounds begin a word, but it happens. Initial [kn] clusters are preserved in German (cf. *Knoblauch* ['knoːblawx] "garlic") and in Russian (cf. книга ['kni.gə] "book"). We even do it sometimes if we pronounce a word like *connect* really quickly. Despite the loss of the sound, though, we kept the *k* in the word's spelling—maybe to distinguish the word from *night*, or maybe just out of habit. For whatever reason, we're stuck with it today.

An entirely separate sequence of sound changes affected the *igh* part of the word. First, we lost the sound [x] represented by *gh* before a consonant. It just disappeared. It left something in its wake, though. As if compensating for the loss of the old [x] sound, the previous vowel was lengthened. Thus, the short [i] vowel became a long [iː] vowel. This is important, because what happened next would change the face of English forever.

Ever wonder why an English speaker has to unlearn everything they know about vowels before learning another language? It's because of something called the Great Vowel Shift. The Great Vowel Shift was an innovative period of great turmoil for English. We've learned previously that when a linguist calls a vowel long or short, they're referring to literally how much time it takes to speak—not to its quality. English used to have short and long vowels like this. As a result of the Great Vowel Shift, the long vowels all became short *and* changed quality. Short vowels retained their short duration but became lax. Basically, every single vowel radically changed its pronunciation.

Spelling	Old Sound	New Sound	Example
a	*a	[æ]	*hat*
a . . . e	*aː	[e]	*hate*
e	*e	[ɛ]	*bet*
ee, e . . . e	*eː	[i]	*beet*
i	*i	[ɪ]	*hit*
i . . . e	*iː	[aj]	*bite*
o	*o	[ɔ]	*hot*
oo, o . . . e	*oː	[u]	*hoot*
u	*u	[ʌ]	*hut*
u	*uː	[aw]	*house (orig. hus)*

As you can see, it was a mess—and not super consistent (consider *lose* and *rose*). For our purposes, though, we saw that what was [ix] became [iː]. And, thanks to the Great Vowel Shift, what was [iː] became [aj]. A sensible spelling system would have altered the spelling of the word, but instead we're stuck with *knight*: the ghost of a former stage of the English language.

So, yeah, languages change pronunciation over time. All languages. There are three main reasons that languages do so, and they are:

1. **Ease of Articulation:** As a language is spoken more quickly or casually, certain distinctions maintained in careful speech can be lost. Consider how often the first *t* is left unpronounced in words like *argumentative, preventative,* and *Sacramento.*

2. **Acoustic Interference:** If a distinction isn't always easily heard or is routinely obscured by its phonetic environment, it can be lost. This is what happened to the *l* in words like *talk, walk, folk,* and *yolk.* It's also why many (including me) don't

have a rounded [w] sound before rounded vowels in words like *quart* or *quarter.*

3. **Innovation:** This is another way of saying that sometimes it just happens. Sometimes a group of speakers just ends up sounding different, and the change appears to be unmotivated— or the simple motivation is that speakers want two similar sounding words to sound different. The Great Vowel Shift is one of those changes, as are many of the subsequent vowel changes in English (consider the New Zealand pronunciation of *rest,* which sounds almost identical to the American pronunciation of *wrist*).

One of these motivations lies behind every sound change that has occurred in natural languages the world over. They also help lay the groundwork for what a language creator does in creating a naturalistic language. I'd call it the cheater's way of introducing complexity into a system if employing naturalistic sound changes were actually cheating. But, no, it's legit; it just *feels* like cheating. (Best of both worlds!)

There are innumerable sound changes that have occurred in the history of language, and an entire universe populated by sound changes that are plausible yet have never occurred. I'll show you some of my favorites from each of the three categories introduced above.

Ease of Articulation

Sound changes that take place in order to maximize the ease of articulation are the simplest to understand. We've seen a little bit of this with tone sandhi, described in the first chapter of this book. The trick is defining what "ease" is. Let's start with a basic example (thesaurus's getting a workout! Wonder if I can work "facile" in?). Consider this nonce phonetic form:

[ˈɑ.tɑ]

It's already pretty simple to pronounce, but what would make it simpler? Well, we have two identical [ɑ] sounds and a naughty [t] separating them. One way to simplify the pronunciation would be to make the [t] more like the sounds around it. Now how to do that? For starters, the vowel [ɑ] is voiced, but [t] is voiceless. That means to pronounce this word, your vocal folds will have to start vibrating to pronounce the [ɑ], go still for the [t], and then start vibrating again for the [ɑ]. Wouldn't it be nicer to our poor old vocal folds if they could just vibrate right on through the whole word? Let's give it a try!

['ɑ.dɑ]

Now we're cooking with gasoline! This is what in linguistics is known as **assimilation**, where one sound becomes similar to a sound before or after it. But you know what? Even though it's voiced, that [d] is still a stop. Airflow through the mouth is completely closed off in the middle of the word. That's a bummer. Why not speed things up a bit by reducing the duration of that closure as much as humanly possible? In other words, why not turn that [d] into a flap, [ɾ]? It'll still be alveolar, so it won't have lost its identity; it'll just come out a little smoother. So . . .

['ɑ.ɾɑ]

Voilà!

But you know what? It's a pain to have to pronounce a full [ɑ] vowel like the *a* in *father* at the end of the word. We put so much effort into pronouncing the first part of the word that we're all out of breath by the time we get to the end! Wouldn't it be easier if we just reduced the effort we put into pronouncing that vowel? Just a little bit! We'd still know it was a vowel—and not a high one, like [i] or [u]. Just something like . . .

['ɑ.ɾə]

Yeah, *that's* it! That's the money melon!

And notice what we've done. That is exactly how we pronounce the end of the word *ciabatta* in English—far different from its Italian pronunciation [tʃɑ.'bat.ta]. This is a pronunciation that was a couple centuries in the making, but we did it for words like *knotted* ['nɑ.ɾəd], *rotted* ['ɹɑ.ɾəd], *cottage* ['kʰɑ.ɾədʒ], *oughta* ['ɑ.ɾə], etc., and we now apply it to relevant words borrowed into our language.

Ease of articulation can produce some interesting alternations in language. Compare some of these High Valyrian words to their reflexes in one of the daughter languages of High Valyrian, Astapori Valyrian:

High Valyrian	Astapori Valyrian	Meaning
obar ['o.bar]	*uvor* ['u.vor]	"curve"
rāpa ['raː.pa]	*raba* ['ra.ba]	"soft"
letagon [le.'ta.gon]	*ledagho* [le.'da.ɣo]	"to frustrate"
jikagon [ɟi.'ka.gon]	*jigagho* [ʒi.'ga.ɣo]	"to put"
brāedion ['braːɛ.dion]	*braedhe* ['braj.ðe]	"copper"

In the table above, look only at the sounds [p, t, k, b, d, g] in the High Valyrian column, and see what happened to them in the Astapori Valyrian column. To sum up, High Valyrian [p, t, k] became [b, d, g], respectively, in Astapori Valyrian in between vowels. A separate change also turned High Valyrian [b, d, g] into Astapori Valyrian [v, ð, ɣ] in the same environment. Each set moved one step closer to being more like the vowel sounds around them to make pronunciation easier. Notice that it occurred only in between two vowel sounds, though. That makes for some interesting alternations, as the one shown below:

High Valyrian	Astapori Valyrian	Meaning
obar ['o.bar]	*uvor* ['u.vor]	"curve"
obri ['o.bri]	*ubri* ['u.bri]	"curves"

Notice in the plural, the [b] is retained in Astapori Valyrian. This is because the original High Valyrian [b] occurs in between a vowel on the left, [o], and a consonant on the right, [r]. That blocks the sound change from occurring, and so an irregular plural is produced.

Also notice that the two sound changes—the one that turned [p, t, k] into [b, d, g], which is called **intervocalic voicing**, and the one other that turned [b, d, g] into [v, ð, ɣ], which is called **intervo-calic spirantization**—had to occur in a precise order. Specifi-cally, intervocalic spirantization *had* to occur before intervocalic voicing. If the inverse had happened to, for example, *rāpa*, "soft," it would first have become *raba* in Astapori Valyrian, and then would immediately have become *rava*. As that didn't happen, we have evi-dence of rule ordering—that is, when chronologically one change occurred with respect to the other.

Some other sound changes driven by ease of articulation are touched on below:

• **Vowel Harmony** causes affixed vowels to change their quality to be closer in quality to the vowels closest to them. In Shiväisith from *Thor: The Dark World*, for example, a suffix will have either a back vowel or a front vowel, depending on whether the previ-ous vowel is a back vowel or a front vowel. Below is an example illustrating the distinction between the *-a* [ɑ] variant of the dative suffix, and the *-ä* [æ] variant:

ᛉᚹ8 *djesh* [ɟeʃ] "door"   ᛉᚹ8Δ *djeshä* [ˈɟe.ʃæ] "to the door"
ᛉΔ8 *päsh* [pæʃ] "stone"   ᛉΔ8Δ *päshä* [ˈpæ.ʃæ] "to the stone"
ᛨᛝ *yydh* [yːð] "wave"   ᛨᛝΔ *yydhä* [ˈyː.ðæ] "to the wave"
ᛐᛣᛐ *koun* [koun] "shore"   ᛐᛣᛐᛝ *kouna* [ˈkou.nɑ] "to the shore"
ᛚᛩ8 *rash* [rɑʃ] "sky"   ᛚᛩ8ᛩ *rasha* [ˈrɑ.ʃɑ] "to the sky"
ᛘᛯᛐ *luun* [luːn] "nose"   ᛘᛯᛐᛩ *luuna* [ˈluː.nɑ] "to the nose"

The original suffixed form was simply *-a* [ɑ]. Internal pressure to ease pronunciation, though, caused the vowel to move forward for words that had all front vowels. Thus, an older form would have been **djesha* [ˈɟe.ʃɑ], and then, over time, it became modern *djeshä* [ˈɟe.ʃæ], producing the modern vowel harmony system.

• **Word-Final Devoicing** sees voiced stops or fricatives becom-ing voiceless at the end of a word. When speaking, we start out with the highest volume of air coming out of our lungs, and wind up with less as it passes out of our mouths. If there's less air at the end of a phrase, then it's harder to maintain voicing. Consequently, a number of languages simply allow voiced consonants at the end of a word to lose their voicing. Indojisnen, from Syfy's *Defiance*, is one such language. Compare the nominative and vocative forms of the pairs of words below, focusing on the final consonant of the stem:

[vik] "light"   ['vi.ɡa] "O, light!"

['kɔ.ɾak.sut] "doctor"   ['kɔ.ɾak.su.da] "O, doctor!"

To illustrate that this isn't simply intervocalic voicing, though, compare the following forms, where the word-final voiceless consonants remain voiceless:

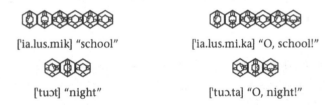

['ia.lus.mik] "school"   ['ia.lus.mi.ka] "O, school!"

['tuɔt] "night"   ['tuɔ.ta] "O, night!"

- **Neutralization** can affect segments in less prominent environments, as in unstressed syllables. In English, most vowels come out as schwa [ə] in unstressed syllables, as shown in the pairs below:

syllable ['sɪ.lə.bəɫ]	~	*syllabic* [sə.'la.bək]
divinity [də.'vɪ.nə.ɾi]	~	*divination* [ˌdɪ.və.'ne.ʃən]
positive ['pʰa.zə.ɾəv]	~	*positivity* [ˌpʰa.zə.'tʰɪ.və.ɾi]
politics ['pʰa.lə.ˌtʰɪks]	~	*political* [pʰə.'lɪ.ɾə.kəɫ]

In the history of Castithan, the high vowels [i] and [u] were lowered to [e] and [o], respectively, at the end of a word, so that the tongue could rest in a more relaxed position at the end of an utterance:

Orthographic Form	Old Pronunciation	Modern Pronunciation	Meaning
௨ს௮	['fiː.li]	['fi.le]	"first"
ஃℎℾ℧	['na.pu]	['na.bo]	"edible"

You may also notice that old Castithan was subject to intervocalic voicing, as evidenced by the modern word ['na.bo] "edible."

These are three examples among many. And one need not rely exclusively on what has happened in the history of a natural language. I often set up some word forms based on my phonotactics and then try to pronounce them as quickly and fluently as possible. What I do with my mouth naturally to accomplish that will often be a clue as to how the system would evolve over the course of centuries.

Acoustic Interference

If I had to guess, I'd say that the majority of sound changes are driven by acoustic interference—that is, one speaker says *x*, and the other speaker thinks they hear *y*, and, pretty soon, the new way to say *x* is *y*. This won't happen if the new form is heard by only one person: it has to be heard by thousands over and over again in order to take root.

An easy example comes from a set of English last names like mine that should be fairly transparent. My last name is *Peterson*, which breaks down as *Peter's son*. Simple. And so we have *Jackson* which is *Jack's son*; *Ericson* which is *Eric's son*; *Dixon* which is *Dick's son*; and *Thompson* which, logically, is *Thomp's son*.

But hang on. There's no such name *Thomp* (though there should be. Or no, wait. I'm thinking of *Thwomp*). In fact, the name comes from *Thom*, the original spelling of *Tom*, a shortening of *Thomas*. It should be *Thom's son*. So where on earth did that *p* come from?

Thinking back to articulatory phonetics, moving from an [m] sound (lips closed, air passing through the nose, vibrating vocal folds) to an [s] sound (lips open, air passing through the mouth, vocal folds still) is not simple. It can be done, sure, but in casual speech, what ends up happening is we stop our vocal folds vibrating *before* opening our lips but *after* raising our velum. The result? Our vocal folds are still, our lips are closed, and the air is released through the mouth. That's the textbook definition of [p]. Thus, an **epenthetic** or spontaneous [p] is produced in between the [m] and [s] sounds.

This satisfies the first part of the definition. The speaker *believes* they're saying something like *Thomson*, but the hearer hears the speaker saying *Thompson*. Since the epenthetic [p] is a common phenomenon in this environment, *Thompson* will happen quite a bit. Thus, after centuries of English speakers saying *Thompson* with a [p] over and over again, eventually people began spelling it that way, and pronouncing the [p] *on purpose*, rather than by accident.

That's the standard life cycle of a sound change based on acoustic interference. Here are a few other common sound changes based on acoustic interference:

- **Gemination** or consonant doubling can be caused by mishearing a consonant cluster. This happened in the history of Italian. Compare the Latin words on the left with the Italian words on the right (just look at the consonant clusters in the middle of the word):

octo ['ok.to]	>	*otto* ['ot.to]	"eight"
somnus ['som.nus]	>	*sonno* ['son.no]	"sleep"
relaxāre [re.lak.'saː.re]	>	*rilassare* [ri.las.'sa.re]	"relax"

  Complex clusters like [kt], [mn], and [ks] were ironed out, producing doubles of the second member. Based on the fact that it can be difficult to determine the quality of the first member of a consonant cluster in environments like these, it's understandable that, at least in Italian, the first member got replaced by a copy. This produces a consonantal event of the same duration, resulting in a similar acoustic effect. This type of change is quite common.

- **Nasalization** has a muddying effect on a previous vowel. This effect is incidental and can be avoided in careful speech. Its presence, though, is enough to indicate to a hearer that the vowel coloring is the important distinction, rather than the final nasal. One potential result is that coda nasals can be lost, producing nasalization on a previous vowel, often affecting its quality. This happened in Sondiv, the alien language from the CW's *Star-Crossed*, as shown below:

Orthographic Form	Old Pronunciation	Modern Pronunciation	Meaning
ꝏꝯꝅꭓ	[bia.'tim]	[bja.'tẽ]	"liar"
ꝯꝅꭓ	[bua.'lum]	[bwa.'dõ]	"gate"
ꝏꝅꝅꝳ	[nua.'lan]	[nwa.'lã]	"flood"

Notice that the high vowels [i] and [u] were lowered to [e] and [o], respectively, in Sondiv. In Irathient, from Syfy's *Defiance*, a following nasal consonant remained, and while it didn't affect the quality of high vowels, it did affect the quality of low vowels, raising them up from [a] and [ɛ] to [o] and [e], respectively.

Orthographic Form	Old Pronunciation	Modern Pronunciation	Meaning
ꝲꝳꝯꝯꝯꝅ	[u.'tɛm.nɛ]	[u.'tɛm.nɛ]	"foot"
ꝳꝯꝲꝵꝅ	['trɛŋ.gɛ]	['trɛŋ.gɛ]	"distraction"
ꝏꝯꝯꝵꝅ	['ɟam.mə]	['ɟom.mə]	"again"
ꝏꝯꝯꝯꝲꝵꝅ	[ɟa.'nan.tɛ]	[ɟa.'non.tɛ]	"sunrise/ sunset"

- **Compensatory Lengthening** is when a vowel is lengthened to compensate for the loss of a following consonant. Basically, a vowel followed by a consonant takes *x* amount of time to pronounce. Remove the consonant, and that unit now takes less time to pronounce—a noticeable difference. If the vowel, though, is lengthened so that it alone takes up *x* amount of time, the loss of the consonant might be less noticeable—and, in fact, one may be confused for the other. And that's how this sound change works. We saw a real world example of compensatory lengthening with the elongation of the vowel in the English word *knight*. Compensatory lengthening also occurred for certain words in High Valyrian. This, for example, is what happened to the irregular verb *emagon*, "to have," in the perfect:

Old Pronunciation	Modern Pronunciation	Meaning
endan ['en.dan]	*ēdan* ['eː.dan]	"I had"
endā ['en.daː]	*ēdā* ['eː.daː]	"you had"
endas ['en.das]	*ēdas* ['eː.das]	"s/he had"

Above, the first *n* in the stem was lost, and the previous *e* vowel was lengthened to compensate for the loss of the *n*.

There are more, of course, and these types of sound changes are fun to play with, because the question one needs to ask is, "How might a given word/phrase be misheard?" Misapprehension is one of the driving forces of language change.

Innovation

A language that changes very little is called conservative; one that changes a lot is called innovative. For example, Icelandic has allegedly changed very little in about a thousand years. On the other end of the spectrum, Portuguese split away from Spanish to the point of mutual unintelligibility in about the same time frame. Why does one language change while another remains stable? Happenstance, really. But it's important to note that the Spanish and Portuguese *wanted* to sound different from each other—to distinguish themselves. Their social and political differences were magnified in language.

Another fine example is teenagers. Slang comes and goes every decade. Why? Because teenagers of every generation want to distinguish themselves from the previous generation in how they dress, in what they buy, in how they act, and in how they speak. Some of it sticks around (*cool*'s been around for more than seventy-five years), while some of it gets left in the dust (no one can—or should— say *gnarly* unironically). The same is true of speech patterns. Younger generations, if allowed to flourish, are endless sources of innovation. If they hang on to their innovations into adulthood, their innovative patterns solidify into regular patterns.

The key is, though, that *none* of these changes may have any motivation whatsoever. It's not speakers trying to speak more quickly, or speaking more casually, or mishearing one another: They're just doing it. Just. Because.

Of course that doesn't mean the sound changes are totally random. They all have their own sense to them. Here are a couple examples of innovative sound changes:

- **Dissimilation** is when one sound spontaneously changes next to another similar sound. The idea behind dissimilation is to make the sound that changes *more* distinct, so that it doesn't get lost in pronunciation the way the initial consonants in Italian consonant clusters from above did. In Dothraki, a stop will become a fricative when it occurs before another stop. This is easiest to see in compound words:

dothrak		qoy		dothrakhqoyi
[do.ˈθɾak]	+	[qɔj]	=	[ˈdo.θɾax.qo.ji]
"rider"		"blood"		"bloodrider"

lajo		qoy		lazhqoyi
[ˈla.dʒo]	+	[qɔj]	=	[ˈlaʒ.qo.ji]
"fight"		"blood"		"feud"

vorto		qoy		vorthqoyi
[ˈvoɾ.to]	+	[qɔj]	=	[ˈvoɾθ.qo.ji]
"tooth"		"blood"		"fang"

Since the final consonants in these words are not in an acoustically salient position, Dothraki speakers make them more distinct by turning, for example, /t/ into [θ]. One of my favorite dissimilations that I tend to overuse sees the glides /j/ and /w/ becoming the fricatives [ʒ] and [v] before [i] and [u], respectively, as happens in Sondiv from *Star-Crossed*:

	*ayat*	/ajat/	[a.ˈjat]	"loved"
	*iyit*	/ijit/	[i.ˈʒit]	"loves"
	*awar*	/awar/	[a.ˈwar]	"died"
	*uwur*	/uwur/	[u.ˈvur]	"dies (generally)"

The idea with the above is that a glide like [j] is almost identical to a vowel like [i], so in order to alert listeners to its presence, it becomes even more of a consonant by becoming the fricative [ʒ] sound.

- **Breaking** is one example of an unmotivated change to a vowel, where a single vowel becomes a diphthong or triphthong. This is a *great* way to produce differing accents from a single linguistic source. In the history of Castithan, short high vowels broke in stressed syllables, such that old /i/ and /u/ became modern [je] and [wo]. This change, though, did not affect long high vowels in stressed position—which later shortened—as shown below:

Orthographic Form	Old Pronunciation	Modern Pronunciation	Meaning
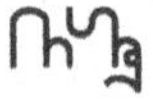	[ˈpi.ɾau]	[ˈpje.ɾo]	"girl"
	[ˈku.fai]	[ˈkwo.ve]	"deadly"
	[ˈɾiː.^{n}du]	[ˈɾin.do]	"wall"
	[ˈpuː.mi]	[ˈpu.me]	"dignified"

A similar change happened in the history of Spanish, as is seen in certain verbs in different conjugations, for example, *tienes* "you have" versus *tenemos* "we have."

- **Epenthesis** is the spontaneous insertion of a sound to prevent two sounds from occurring next to each other. Epenthesis happens in just about every language in one form or another. In the history of Castithan, an epenthetic [l] was introduced whenever a long vowel or diphthong would have occurred next to another vowel, as shown with the following verb forms:

Orthographic Form	Old Schematic Form	Modern Pronunciation	Meaning
⋂ᐟᒫᒣ	/paɾ-aː/	['pa.ɾa]	"investigates"
ᒍᘓⵀhᒕᔐ	/ɾaggi-aː/	['ɾa.gi.la]	"answers"
⋂ᒔᕼᒕᔐ	/θiːka-aː/	['θi.ga.la]	"glides"
ᒐᘳ⥅ᒕᔐ	/vuːzˤu-aː/	['vu.zu.la]	"dies"

In Irathient, an epenthetic schwa [ə] is inserted to break up difficult consonant clusters:

Orthographic Form	Old Schematic Form	Modern Pronunciation	Meaning
ᘔᒣᒪᒺ	/tlans/	['tla.nəs]	"short visit"
ᖴᖯᒼ	/uŋers/	['u.ŋɛ.rəs]	"stalactite"
ᘔᒲᒪᒺ	/tidams/	['ti.da.məs]	"ladder"

Notice that even a simple sound change like the epenthesis rule for Castithan can produce complexity that wouldn't be there otherwise. For example, now in Castithan the present tense form has two suffixes—/-a/ and /-la/—and they're added depending on whether the verb stem ends with a consonant or a vowel—this despite the alternation arising from a more or less regular system in the prehistory of the language. As a language creator, I'm constantly researching the histories of the languages we speak on Earth in order to add to my repertoire of potential sound changes. It's one of the easiest ways to take a simple system and turn it into a complex, realistic one.

LEXICAL EVOLUTION

The easiest of the three types of language evolution to understand is **lexical evolution**: the way words change meaning over time. Anyone who's been alive at least sixteen years should be intimately familiar with this process. For those younger, I'll catch you up to speed.

Last millennium, I started college as a freshman at UC Berkeley, which is in the middle of California—about four hundred miles north of where I grew up, as the dragon flies. In my first year I lived in the La Loma dorm at the northeast corner of the campus along with eleven other guys. Three of them came from a place known as Half Moon Bay, a short drive from Berkeley. Shortly after getting our new internet hooked up, the Half Moon Bay three were testing their download speeds, and one of them exclaimed in excitement, "*Sick!*"

This pronouncement—of joy, apparently—took me completely off guard. *Sick?!* Why would anyone describe superior download speeds as sickly? How does that make sense? It's not even a lifeform; it can't *get* sick. How could anyone say that about a . . . process or phenomenon? And why?

This was my very first encounter with the positive use of the word *sick*. I've had many more since then, of course, but that first one was quite jarring. It shouldn't have been, though, because this type of semantic change is quite common. It's a process whereby a word that expresses some extreme negative trait or quality is turned into a positive exclamation (a technical term for it is **autoantonymy**). Back when I was a kid, the one we would say was *bad* (thank you, Michael Jackson). I've also heard *stupid* and *ill* used positively, and if you come from an English-speaking area, you can probably come up with a dozen others. Some last (typically the adverbs expressing scale or extremity, like *terribly, awfully, horribly,* etc.); some don't. But new ones always have—and always will—keep popping up.

As a conlanger, it's very tempting to look at the vast lexical possibilities that exist and encode them all as if each meaning deserved a basic term—something like:

mantak (n.) the hair on the right side of a human's head (from a viewer's perspective), if the hair is parted exactly down the middle

lumit (n.) the sudden joy at realizing that one is not a squid, followed by a lingering feeling of melancholy over the plight of squids in general

bolku (n.) the piece you would need to finish a puzzle if you were putting together a puzzle

nipak (n.) the piece you need to finish a puzzle that you are actively putting together

karev (n.) an anecdote misremembered while you're visiting your paternal aunt for lunch on a weekend when you have work or school the next day

There are limitless numbers of things that can be encoded in language, but most languages don't do it with single words that arise ex nihilo. In English, for example, what's the word for when you're picking up your very first slice of pizza and your favorite topping tumbles off and falls to the floor *right* as you're taking a bite? Is it *blorpy*? No. It's nothing. There is no word for this. It doesn't mean we can't talk about it. And if we had to create a word for it, we wouldn't go to our letterboard and come up with a brand-new form: we'd come up with a euphemism—like a DiCaprio, since that topping was *so* close to enjoying the lasting safety of your stomach acids if it'd just hung on to the pizza life raft for a few more milliseconds . . .

There are a number of principled ways that words change meaning over time. In this section, I'll go over some of the most common or most important ones.

- **Specialization** is when a generic term comes to be used for something specific. An example from English is the word *salsa*, which we borrowed from Spanish. In Spanish, *salsa* just means "sauce" (both *salsa* and *sauce* even come from the same Latin root). In English, though, *salsa* refers only to a specific type of spicy sauce that comes from Mexico. In Castithan, the word **ꓭꓛꓘ** *tilo* used to refer to any type of veil, but now refers exclusively to the face covering worn by brides during their wedding. This is basically how the change works: anything that has a generic reference becomes associated with a particular item or event, and so the word comes to refer exclusively to that item or event.

- **Generalization** is the opposite of specialization and is quite common. It's when a specific term comes to be used for something generic. Most modern examples refer to products. *Kleenex*, for example, used to refer exclusively to a brand of facial tissue, and now refers to facial tissue in general. *Google* is now a verb, regardless of what search engine one uses. And *pants*? It's a shortening of *pantaloons*, which were named after a character in Italian comedies from the sixteenth century named *Pantaloun*. They were so named because *Pantaloun* used to wear a very specific type of (for lack of a better word) pants. So saying someone was wearing *pantaloons* at that time was like saying someone has a Janelle Monáe hairstyle nowadays. It eventually just became a word. In Castithan, the old word for water, ꓠꓥꓘꓳ *tholo*, now refers to any type of fluid or liquid.

- **Metaphor** is referring to something as something else, in its most generic sense. Using a metaphor implies some kind of similarity between the two. For example, in English, the word *face* is used to refer to any flat surface. As a result of the fact that we consider where a person's face is to be the front of the person, we also consider the face of an inanimate object to be the front or interactional side of that object. Metaphor deserves its own book, but luckily it's got one: *Metaphors We Live By* by George Lakoff and Mark Johnson, which I *strongly* recommend all humans read. For a conlang, metaphorical concepts often come in bunches. Thus, in Dothraki, if the word for "head," *nhare*, is the leafy part of a tree, *lenta*, "neck," is used to mean "tree trunk"; *fotha*, "throat," is used to refer to the interior of a tree; and *gadim*, "lungs," begat *gadima*, the word for a tree's subterranean root system. The result is a series of interconnected terms that describe an entire system of related concepts. Metaphor *must* be taken into consideration or metaphors from a conlanger's own language will be unconsciously borrowed into the conlang.

- **Metonymy** is referring to one thing by means of something related to that thing. A simple example is referring to the entertainment industry as *Hollywood* or to the U.S. government as *Washington*. While such names are largely situational, metonymy can operate over the course of a language's history. For example, the Castithan word 🅡🅤 *chango* used to mean "fist." It now is used to refer to a thug or a bouncer. Another very common example found not just in conlangs, but in all manner of natural languages—including English—is the use of the word for "tongue" to refer to "language." The difference between metonymy and metaphor is that the two objects compared in a standard metaphor have nothing to do with each other (like a neck and a tree trunk). With metonymy, one object is used in the production of or involved with the other (as a tongue is with a spoken language).

- **Synecdoche** is a specific type of metonymy where an object that's a small part of a larger object or system is used to refer to the whole thing. An oft-cited English example is the use of the word *hand* to refer to a worker (who, presumably, will be using their hands while doing the work in question). Another historical example from Castithan is the word 🅨🅝 *wozo*, which was a word that used to refer to the top or crown of the head. It's now a second person pronoun ("you"), where the idea was to use a body part to make reference to the entire person.

- **Ellipsis** refers to the creation of a new word from the shortening of a phrase or longer word. In English, both *cell* and *mobile* have attained new meanings referring to mobile phones, even though they already had other meanings. The same thing happened decades earlier with *phone*, which was a shortening of the word *telephone*. In Irathient, from *Defiance*, the same thing happened with the phrase ⌣ꞶꞶꞶ·ꞶꞶꞶ *thanaku parko*, literally "fall of an Ark," which is used for when the huge Ark ships in orbit fall to Earth. Now arkfall events, as they're called, are just referred to by ⌣ꞶꞶꞶ *thanaku*, which is simply the word for "fall."

While these and other processes operate on lexical material throughout the history of a language, there are four outcomes that are often the result of the various changes words undergo. They are:

- **Augmentation:** A word with a neutral or lesser meaning intensifies. An easy example would be use of the word *whack* to mean "kill." In Castithan, the word ꞶꞶꞶꞶ *furíje*, which meant "beautiful," now means "perfect."

- **Diminution:** A word with an extreme meaning weakens. For example, the English word *peruse* used to mean "to pore over intensely," whereas now it means "to casually glance through." In Castithan, the word ꞶꞶꞶꞶ *dailu*, which meant "to burn," now means "to cook."

- **Amelioration:** A word with a neutral or negative meaning becomes positive. The example that opened this section, *sick*, is an example of amelioration. In Castithan, the word ꞶꞶꞶ *cheni*, which meant "quiet," now means "nice" or "proper."

- **Pejoration:** A word with a neutral or positive meaning becomes negative. In English, *gross* used to mean "large"—and its German cognate, *groß*, still does. In Castithan, the word ꞶꞶꞶꞶ *zembalu*, which meant "to harvest," now means "to kill."

Before moving on, there is one specific area of lexical change in natural language I'd like to address. All languages—or if not all, most of them—have experienced what I'll call **feminine pejora-tion**. This is a specific and frustrating type of change whereby if there are two otherwise equivalent words—one referring to a male, and the other to a female—the female-referring word has a much greater chance of undergoing pejoration than the male-referring word. In English, the word *cow*, which at one time referred primarily to female cattle, can be used in a derogatory fashion to refer to a woman. The same can't be said of gender-neutral or male words for bovines (*bull, steer, cattle*, etc.), and some even have positive connotations (*strong as an ox*). The word *wench* used to be a rather neutral word for a girl, but attained negative connotations rather early on. Numerous words with negative connotations referring to females—*slut, whore, temptress, seductress*—have no obvious or equally negative male counterparts. And while the occasional word will pop up for use exclusively with males in roughly the same way (*bastard*, which originally only meant illegitimate child, appears to be an insult that can only be used with men), the overwhelming majority of such words refer exclusively to women. All the examples here are English, but the pattern is borne out in just about every natural language.

The pattern of misogyny illustrated here is a product not of language, but of those who use it. At any point in time users can put a stop to certain practices, and the results can be successful (cf. the ascendance of singular "they"). As a language creator, it's often a difficult thing to balance realism and ethics. The Dothraki, for example, appear to be a fairly patriarchal bunch, all things considered. The language they employ is often misogynistic—and the same is true of the slavers in Slaver's Bay and the Castithans from *Defiance*. Their histories would likely not be vastly different from our own with regard to patriarchy.

Even so, I've always kept in mind that creating a language means creating the vocabularies of *all* speakers. A language's lexicon contains words used by the privileged and the disenfranchised; the elderly and the very young; warriors and artisans; men and women. The speech and behaviors of one character don't define a language, and there's always room for representation of all aspects of a culture in a single lexicon.

Getting back to lexical change in general, of paramount importance to me is the role semantic change plays in the construction of
a lexicon. Though one thinks of a conlanger as someone who creates words, creating a *brand* new word is always my last resort. If a
new word is needed, I always ask myself this question first: What
have I already got? Recycle, reduce, reuse. This is what we do with
our own languages, so it stands to reason that if one's conlang is
supposed to *look* like one of our languages, one should do the same.

GRAMMATICAL EVOLUTION

Grammatical evolution is the most difficult, least described,
and most exciting aspect of linguistic evolution. Grammatical evolution is how grammar itself emerges—basically, everything you
saw in the last chapter: plurals, verb conjugation systems, noun
marking systems, etc. When it comes to historical linguistics and
language modeling, this is the final frontier. We know a lot, but
there's still a lot of fog out there in the depths of our linguistic
history—and that means there's a lot of territory for a conlanger to
explore.

The idea behind grammatical evolution is that every single piece
of grammar ultimately has a lexical source. That means a plural suffix, a past tense marker, an adverb marker, an evidential marker—all
of that will ultimately come from one or more concrete words that
have been eroded over the centuries. This is a bit of a counterintui-
tive notion, but it's actually fairly simple to demonstrate.

Let's start with a familiar example: -*ly*. We know that you add -*ly*
to an adjective in English to form an adverb: *jaunty* > *jauntily*; *fanci-
ful* > *fancifully*; *robust* > *robustly*. Of course we also see this word
added to nouns to make adjectives, which is a bit odd if you know
the first rule: *friend* > *friendly*; *knight* > *knightly*; *king* > *kingly*. You
can't say "I greeted him friendly"; despite its looks, the darn thing
really isn't an adverb. Why is that?

As it turns out, it has to do with the history of the suffix. It came
from an actual word. You might be able to guess it by looking at it,

but if not, maybe this will help. The *-ly* suffix in English is cognate with the *-lich* suffix in German. Starting to look familiar? It actually comes from a stem meaning something like "like" (and before that, meaning something like "body," but the suffix derives from the "like" stage of its existence). Thus, someone who is knight-like is *knightly*, and if you perform an action quick-like, you do it *quickly*. We can even witness changes like this one happening in modern times. For example, *alcohol* is a thing I don't drink, but someone who drinks a lot of it is called an *alcoholic*. Some clever ad executive some time in the twentieth century thought, "Well, if an *alcoholic* is someone who drinks alcohol to excess, then a *sugar*holic is someone who eats sugar to excess!" And so we were gifted with sugarholic—soon to be followed by shopaholic, workaholic, rageaholic, blogaholic, cheese-aholic—pretty much whatever-you-want-aholic. A similar story can be told with the *-ous* suffix which came to us from a Latin word that originally meant "smelling of wine."

It's also worth noting that as much as these things may start out as lame jokes, they eventually become grammar. No one looks askance at you now for saying *vicious, cautious, gracious, strenuous*, or any of the many other words ending in *-ous*: it's just a part of the language. The *-oholic/-aholic* suffix is on the way there, too—as is *-gate*, if things keep going the way they're going (i.e. controversy + *-gate* = the social interest in and/or furor over the named controversy).

Imagine if you didn't speak English, and you were being introduced to the suffixes of English and what they mean. Your instructor tells you, "And you add this suffix to any word and it forms a noun that means a media frenzy about the controversy associated with the word you added the suffix to." That sounds *sooooooooooo* fake. Why would a language have a suffix for that?! If a conlanger did that, they'd be strung up by their ears!

And yet it exists. The reason *always* lies in the history of the language—in this case, in the scandal regarding a team working on behalf of Richard Nixon stealing documents from the opposing party in the 1972 presidential election (the scandal was named after the hotel where the documents were stolen: the Watergate). If you know the story, it actually becomes a little less mysterious. It makes sense.

And stories like this one lie behind *all* grammar.

There are several books on these processes, which, collectively, are called **grammaticalization**, and I strongly recommend them, as they're *fascinating* (they also stack well). In this section, I'll go over some of the general principles, and some of the common pathways of grammaticalization that I've utilized in the languages I've created.

Semantic Bleaching

The first step on the path of grammaticalization is **semantic bleaching**: when a common word loses some of its specific meaning, leaving behind a more general meaning. A nice way to break this down is to *really* tease out the meaning of a given lexeme that has evolved away from its original source. Take *can*, for example—the one that means "be able to." It comes to us from a root that meant "to know" (in fact, it comes from the *exact* same root that gives us the word *know*). When used with another verb way back when, it meant "to know how to"—somewhat equivalent to if someone told me I couldn't make stuffed mushrooms, and I replied, "Don't tell me I can't make stuffed mushrooms! I *know* making stuffed mushrooms!" Because I do. And they're *great*.

When used in this context (that is, with *can* as the main verb and some other verb being used as the thing one knows how to do), here are the meanings associated with or entailed by *can*:

1. The subject has the mental capacity for performing the action in question.

2. The subject has the physical capacity for performing the action in question.

3. The subject knows what the action in question is.

4. The subject understands the process involved in performing the action in question.

So that's what *can* meant way back when. What happened gradually over time is that meanings 3 and 4 began to be deemphasized, leaving behind simply 1 and 2: the subject has the physical and mental capacity to perform an action. That's pretty close to our modern meaning of *can*, but it's still a little too specific. What about a sentence like *That knife can cut a watermelon in half*? Certainly a knife has no mental capacity whatsoever. Furthermore, a knife can't cut anything on its own: it needs an agent to operate it. What happened is that meanings 1 and 2 blended together and the mental and physical requirements were lost. Now we can say things like *That plan can work if everything falls into place*. A plan isn't even a thing! Now *can* can refer simply to the plausibility of the assertion made by the clause.

And yet, all this started with a word that functioned almost exactly like our modern word *know*—and still does, in German, where *kennen* means "to know a person" (e.g. *Ich kenne deine Katze*, "I know your cat"). Little by little the meaning was eroded until the word had no function but its grammatical function (so you can no longer say *I can a lot about music* and expect that to mean anything). This is the beginning of the process: a potential future grammatical particle is targeted in a specific construction (e.g. the "know how" construction for *can*), and in that construction, it starts to lose its specific meaning, leaving grammatical meanings behind— eventually losing its ability to be used outside such constructions.

Phonological Erosion

As a word is becoming grammaticalized, it undergoes a process of **phonological erosion**. In so doing, its phonemes are "reduced" in a language-specific way, the form is shortened, and, ultimately, it becomes an affix. A great example is the English future tense—the *real* English future tense, not *will* or *shall*. One has always been able to say something like *I'm going to LA to see Eleni Mandell*. *Go* is a simple motion verb and we use it to imply generic motion of any kind. Looking at that sentence, though, the following meanings are implied:

1. The subject is traveling from somewhere that isn't LA toward LA.

2. The subject is currently in the process of traveling there.

3. If the travel is successfully completed, the subject will see Eleni Mandell at some indefinite point in time in the future.

Presumably one could also leave out the destination, if one so wished, since a destination is implied when travel is happening. Looking at the last section, you can guess what happened: with the destination left out, the requirement for actual motion was lost, and all that was left was the assertion that something was going to happen at some indefinite time in the future. But that's not the story. The story is what happened to its phonological form. It started out as *be going to*: three separate words, the first conjugated depending on the subject of the verb and the desired tense. The first reduction that occurred was with *to*. The vowel changed from its usual [u] to [ə], which is a reduced vowel in English. Then the words got smushed together, and the final velar nasal [ŋ] in *going* ['go.ɪŋ] became an alveolar nasal [n], assimilating in place to the following [t]. Next the [t] got deleted entirely (cf. *Sacramento*), and you got something like *goin'a*. Finally the complex vowel sequence [oi] was reduced to [ə], and we got *gonna*. Then the [g] actually got reduced, so we were saying something like *unna*, that is, *I'm'unna see Eleni Mandell*. And as a final step in recent history, *the whole thing was reduced to a single schwa!* Thus, though it might be nonstandard, you can now say *I'm'a see Eleni Mandell*.

Now, this is a fairly extreme case of phonological erosion (a full phrase like *going to* reduced to a single lax vowel), but such things aren't at all uncommon. This is how affixes are produced. And even though the origins may be obscured due to the lack of records, every affix has a story in a natural language. As a conlanger, I have the opportunity to write those stories myself.

Unidirectionality

Unidirectionality is a hypothesis that holds that words go from fully lexical to grammatical, and not vice versa. The history of *can* shown above is a nice example. It can never go back to meaning something like "know," and even if it drops out of the grammar one day, it won't lexicalize into another lexical form.

That said, this is a hypothesis, and there are some counterexamples. One of my favorites is *ish*. The suffix *-ish* attaches to adjectives and means "kind of"—hence, *reddish, bluish, oldish, youngish,* etc. Modern speakers have taken that suffix, loosed it from its moorings, and now use *ish* as a stand-alone adjective (or even adverb) meaning "kind of." It's made the jump, and others can too, but these instances are few and far between, so the unidirectionality hypothesis serves as a good guideline for grammaticalization.

Keeping these principles in mind, here is a nonexhaustive list of some of my favorite grammaticalization tricks—and "tricks" is really the best word for it. The more I learn about grammaticalization, the less mysterious language becomes. It really is like seeing a magician explain a magic trick. If you don't want to see language spoilers, you may want to skip this section, because a'spoiling we will go!

- **Adpositions:** Adpositions derive most often from nouns and verbs. Whether they come before the noun they modify (as a preposition) or after (as a postposition) depends on how the language works. For example, if verbs come before their objects, and adpositions derive from verbs, then they'll likely be coming before the nouns they modify and be prepositions. This happens in Irathient, where objects always follow verbs. Below is an example showing the verb *shebaktu*, which came to be used as a preposition:

Abaktə nushaise skir.	zushure shebaktu skir
/pass meadow boy/	/tall pass boy/
"The boy passes the meadow."	"taller than the boy"

In Castithan, a lot of the postpositions developed from nouns. Originally, the relationship between the two nouns was understood to be a genitival relationship, where the modified noun was the owner of the grammaticalized noun. Since possessors precede possessees in Castithan, it's no wonder that grammaticalized nouns became postpositions. Below you can see the old word *nat-, which came separately to mean both "roof" and the postposition "on top of" (notice how the postposition has been reduced phonologically):

ﾌﾞﾊﾊﾆｿﾞﾙ ﾔﾞﾄﾟ   ﾌﾞﾊﾊﾆｿﾞ ｾ

lorishwano nado   *lorishwana nda*

/house top/   /house top/

"the roof of the house"   "on top of the house"

Some of the most common lexical items that grammaticalize into adpositions are listed below:

Adpositional Meaning	Lexical Source
under, underneath, below, beneath	foot, animal belly, buttocks
on, on top of, over, above	head, animal back, top, cover
in, inside	belly, cover, contain, hold, swallow
away	outside, outdoors
with (instrumental)	use, hold, accompany, take, touch
with (comitative)	accompany, together, take
at, near, around, by	stay, live, sit, stand, touch, lie
from	leave, go, fall, turn
than (comparative)	exceed, pass, surpass, from
front, in front of	face, body, chest
behind, in back of	back, buttocks, turn

In addition, many adpositions are composed of several different adpositions (e.g. *in back of*). This is especially likely with adpositions derived from nominal sources, as illustrated by the example from Castithan below:

ˀ乃ˇ ਨੋੜਿ੨ੵ ਗੁੜਿ ੨ੵ

lorishwano dime no
/house back from/

"behind the house"

- **Number Marking:** First, specific nonplural/nonsingular number marking almost always comes from numerals. That is, a singulative number will come from the numeral "one" plus the noun, a dual number will come from the numeral "two" plus the noun, a trial will come from the numeral "three" plus the noun, etc. That source is so common I almost want to say it's without exception, but I can't, because there's always exceptions to everything (this is language, after all). In my language Kamakawi, the combination is quite transparent:

ka alama [ka a.'la.mə]   *alamaka* [a.'la.mə.kə]
   /two sand-crab/   /sand-crab-two/
  "two sand crabs"   "sand crabs (two of them)"

Plural marking comes from a variety of sources, including words for "all," "people," "children," reduplication (doubling all or part of the word), or even the numeral "three." You can see the connection between the word for "all," *eghi*, in old Dothraki and the plural suffix, *-i*, though the relationship by this stage is entirely opaque:

feshilh eghi [fe.'ʃiɬ 'fe.ɣi]   *feshithi* ['fe.ʃi.θi]
      /tree all/   /tree-all/
     "all trees"   "trees"

In modern Dothraki, the word *eghi* became *ei*, and is now used in front of the noun it modifies, so you can actually say *ei feshithi*, which means "all the trees." Etymologically, that breaks down to "all tree all." Etymological redundancies like this one occur all the time in natural languages.

- **Perfective/Past Marking:** Past tense marking usually comes from perfective marking, which indicates that an action has been completed, regardless of tense. Perfective marking arises in a number of ways. Some lexemes that give rise to perfective marking are verbs meaning "finish," "stop," "cease," "end," or similar lexemes, or words like "have" or "get." In Castithan, an old verb **pasu* meaning "finish" became the suffix *-ps* indicating the perfective aspect, and then separately became a verb *pazu* meaning "to conquer." So, if one wanted to say, "The army conquered the city" . . .

ᚸᚱᚼᚾᚢᚦᚼ ᚢᚻ ᚲᚨᚱᚻᚢᚻᚷᚱᚱ ᚲᚢ ᚾᚲᚢᚾᚷ°

Tegibuna re fajiráwala do pazupsa.
/army SBJ city OBJ finish-finish/

"The army conquered the city."

Of course, at this stage, Castithan speakers don't recognize a connection between the *-ps* suffix and the verb *pazu*. In forming these constructions, it's important to note that new suffixes will fossilize from old constructions. So, for example, in older Castithan, the *-u* form of a verb was a nonfinite form that one would use in conjunction with another verb. The expression "finishes *x*-ing," then, where *x* stands for any verb, would be *x-u pasa*. The latter got shortened to a single form in *x-upasa*, and eventually to *x-upsa*. That *u*, though, stems from the old multiword expression, which is why the past tense looks like a suffix has been added to an infinitival form.

- **Future Tense Marking:** Future tense marking comes from *everywhere*. A future tense is probably the easiest thing to evolve in a conlang because so many natural language future tenses are so transparent. Take the *go* future in English. We know *exactly* where *gonna* came from because it's obvious. The *will* future is a little less obvious, but we still have phrases like *free will* and *do what you will*, so it's somewhat figure-out-able. Future tenses arise from lexemes for "go," "come," "arrive," "love," "have to," "want," "be," and adverbs like "tomorrow," "then," or "later." An example of the latter is illustrated below in my language Kamakawi:

A nemei ei male.
/PART leave I later/
"I'm leaving later."

A male nemei ei.
/PART later leave I/
"I'm going to leave." *or* "I will leave."

In the example on the left, *male* is in the position of an ordinary adverb. On the right it's been moved in front of the verb where tense particles go, making it a part of the verb inflection system. In Irathient, one takes the standard present tense (an auxiliary plus a present participle, roughly equivalent to a phrase like "be sleeping") and changes the main verb to an infinitive (roughly like "be to sleep"). This produces the future tense:

Emegnə eneliga.
/AUX sleeping/
"I'm sleeping."

Emegnə sheligu.
/AUX to-sleep/
"I will sleep."

We have a similar construction in English, where one might say something like, "We are to arrive next Monday" (sounds a little stuffy, but it's grammatical). This type of expression has conventionalized to become a standard future tense in Irathient, as it has in a number of other languages (e.g. Russian).

- **Case:** Case marking usually derives from adpositions, for which see above. The difference between a case and an adposition is slight, and varies language by language. Usually if the marking comes in the form of an affix, it's safe to call it a case. If it's not an affix, then a case phrase (a noun plus an adposition) can be so called if it's obligatory, or required by certain verbs, and occurs closer to the verb than actual adpositional phrases, but even then, with languages that have *huge* numbers of cases, it's sometimes tough to say. What we can say, though, is where a lot of these cases come from. Here are lexical sources for some of the key grammatical cases:

Case	Lexical Source
nominative, absolutive	— (default, unmarked noun)
ergative, agentive	from, with, at, near, hand
accusative, objective, patientive	to, at, on, against, take
dative	to, for, give
genitive	from, for, to, home, property, thing, at

Other cases have more obvious historical antecedents:

Case	Lexical Source
ablative	come from, leave, from
allative	arrive, go to, see, to
instrumental	with, take, use, from
comitative	comrade, follow, take
partitive	from, child, of

One way that languages with large case inventories get all the nongrammatical cases is by building them off grammatical cases. In Shiväisith from Marvel's *Thor: The Dark World*, I built twelve of the fifteen cases off the genitive, accusative, or dative. Here are examples of some that were built off the dative (marked by a suffixed -*a*):

	ᏙᎷᏒᎯᏓ			♢ᎮᏍ♢			ᏙᎷᏒᎯᏓ♢	
GENITIVE	jova ['jo.vɑ]	+		sos [sos]	=		jovas ['jo.vɑs]	
	"to the wife"			"possession"			"of the wife"	

	ᏦᏙᎥᎯ			ᏔᏫᛕ			ᏦᏙᎥᎯᏫ	
COMITATIVE	kira ['ki.ɾɑ]	+		athu ['a.θu]	=		kirath ['ki.ɾɑθ]	
	"to me"			"comrade"			"with me"	

	ᏉᎷᎥᎯ			ᏝᎦᏔ			ᏉᎷᎥᎯᎥ	
INSTRUMENTAL	tora ['to.ɾɑ]	+		ryh [ryh]	=		torar ['to.ɾɑɾ]	
	"to the sword"			"master"			"with the sword"	

How grammatical marking is typically reified in a language will determine how it will appear with respect to a noun, of course. The nice thing is that once a language has established the *idea* of case, future cases are easier to construct, and end up looking less and less mysterious.

- **Pronouns:** First and second person singular pronouns tend to be pretty old and may be semantic primitives in many languages. Plurals of these also tend to be pretty old, but those that aren't are often formed from the singular plus some plural formation strategy (e.g. "we" could come from something like "I-person" or "I-people"). Third person pronouns routinely come from demonstratives ("this," "that," etc.). This is the source of all third person pronouns in the Romance languages (French, Spanish, Italian, Romanian, etc.). The presence of grammatical gender in Latin is what gave the Romance languages separate male and female third person pronouns. Indojisnen, from Syfy's *Defiance*, lacks grammatical gender, and so its third person pronoun, drawn from the demonstrative series, is genderless:

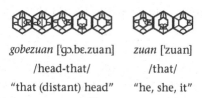

gobezuan ['gɔ.bɛ.zuan]	zuan ['zuan]
/head-that/	/that/
"that (distant) head"	"he, she, it"

Beyond the basic level, though, second person pronouns—especially formal, official, or polite second person pronouns—derive regularly either from second person plural pronouns, third person plural pronouns, or words referring to "proper" individuals like "master" or "lord" (cf. "your grace" or "your highness" or "your honor" as a form of address), or from family terms for respected (usually older) individuals, like "aunt," "uncle," "grandfather," or "grandmother." Beyond that, such pronouns can come from pretty much any word referring to an individual (specific or otherwise) or to a quality. Castithan has a number of these, like ᘯᘰᘲ *yelako* (from "lowered one" or "sinner"), ᘯᘰᘲ *voritso* (from "biter," a slang pronoun used only among men), and ᘯᘰᘲ *pozwo* (a form of "they" used only with groups of sentient beings that comes from a verb for "gather" plus an honorific suffix).

* **Articles:** Indefinite articles pretty much always come from the numeral "one." Definite articles can come from demonstratives (the same sources from Latin give Romance both its articles and pronouns) or pronouns. In the Slaver's Bay variety of Valyrian, the definite articles all came from accusative forms of pronouns or the numeral "one," depending on the article:

High Valyrian	Low Valyrian
mēre ['meː.re] "one"	*me* ['me] "a"
ziry ['zi.ry] "him/her (accusative)"	*ji* ['ʒi] "the (singular, gender 1)"
ūī ['uː.iː] "it (accusative)"	*vi* ['vi] "the (singular, gender 2)"
pōnte ['poːn.te] "them (accusative)"	*po* ['po] "the (plural)"

To get the sense of how this originally worked, think of colloquial English sentences like, "I don't like them onions." Now imagine English didn't have the word *the*. This might not be a bad way to get one!

There have been books written on grammaticalization and historical change that go into greater detail and greater variety than I've got space for here. The lack of records we have regarding the very earliest days of language affords a conlanger a lot of leeway, though. There are processes we have evidence of, and then there are processes that seem plausible, but for which we have no direct evidence. A conlang itself is an argument for its own plausibility. One need not be constrained by what a natural language has done in the past: a conlang blazes its own trail. How successfully it has done so is up to its author and its audience to determine.

HIGH VALYRIAN VERBS

In 2012 I was asked by Dave Benioff and Dan Weiss to create High Valyrian for season three of *Game of Thrones*. At that time, High Valyrian consisted of a ton of proper names and six words: *valonqar, valar, morghulis, dohaeris, dracarys,* and *maegi.* That might not seem like a lot to go on, but George R. R. Martin gifted me with these two phrases, written and translated precisely as follows:

> *Valar morghulis.* "All men must die."
>
> *Valar dohaeris.* "All men must serve."

These two phrases inspired the number system of High Valyrian along with its entire verbal framework.

As I stated before in discussing Dothraki, one of my goals in developing the *Song of Ice and Fire* languages was to preserve the spellings used in the books, save for the sake of regularity (e.g. *dracarys* became *drakarys* in spellings used on scripts for the sake of consistency). I also had extra motivation for keeping these phrases just as they are. In addition to their being rather famous in the books, I met a guy named Sean Endymion at a popular culture conference in Albuquerque who had VALAR tattooed on his right arm and MORGHULIS tattooed on his left arm. I didn't want to invalidate his tattoo!

Despite only being asked in 2012 to create the language, I'd started toying with Valyrian as early as the fall of 2009—after I'd finished my work on the *Game of Thrones* pilot, but before *Game of Thrones* received its first-season pickup. I already knew fans of the books would be most excited about seeing High Valyrian of all the possible *Song of Ice and Fire* languages, and I knew if the show was successful, I'd eventually get the opportunity to create it. The verbal system was going to be the crux of the project, so I wanted to start working on it as soon as I could.

By giving us two phrases, George R. R. Martin gave us some important information. However the details worked out, I knew that *valar* would correspond to "all men," *morghulis* would correspond to "must die," and *dohaeris* would correspond to "must serve." It's possible to come up with other interpretations, but they require some trickery, and this interpretation seemed to me to be the most obvious. Tying "men" to *valar*, "die" to *morghulis,* and "serve" to *dohaeris* was simple; figuring out what to do with "all" and "must" would require more thought.

Since we're here to talk about the verbs, I'll deal with *valar* quickly. As the phrase is "all men" and not just "men," I had to figure out a way to encode the "all" part on the noun. Rather than having suffixed adjectives (something I definitely did not want to do), I decided to do it with traditional number encoding. If High Valyrian had not only a singular and plural number but also a collective, that collective number could be interpreted as "all" given the right context. I decided, then, that *valar* would be the collective of a singular *vala*. I added a paucal number, as well, to give some balance to the system, which ended up looking like this:

	Number	Verb Agreement	Logic
Singular	one	singular	one actor
Plural	many	plural	multiple actors not treated as a cohesive unit
Collective	all	singular	multiple actors treated as a unit
Paucal	a few	plural	small number of actors not treated as a cohesive unit

The argument *valar*, then, would be treated as third person singular. All men are being treated as a cohesive, indivisible unit.

With that settled, I turned my attention to the verbs. George R. R. Martin gifted me with identical endings on the two verbs for two identical senses. Both *morghulis* and *dohaeris* end in -*is*, which means that that's the part that's going to contain "must" and whatever other tense/aspect information is in there. But what would that be?

To start, let me back up and talk about High Valyrian a little bit. The High Valyrian language is meant to be the language of the old Valyrian Freehold and its vast empire on Essos in ancient days. The Valyrians conquered many lands—including the old Ghiscari empire—thousands of years before the action of the *Song of Ice and Fire* series, and their influence stretched all the way to the Isle of Dragonstone across the Narrow Sea. At some point in time a cataclysmic event destroyed the Valyrian Freehold, and the empire was wiped out. Many languages descended from the old High Valyrian language. These came to be known as the Bastard Valyrian tongues. The history of Valyria was modeled somewhat after the history of the Roman Empire, and High Valyrian was intended to have the status of Latin, with its daughter languages intended to have the status of the Romance languages descended from Latin. I wanted to honor this intention with High Valyrian without simply copying Latin, so I decided to take some cues from it without actually using it as a model.

First, it seemed relatively uncontroversial to have the verbs agree with their subjects in person and number, giving each verb at least six different forms. Next, since Latin verbs had independent passive forms, I decided to add passive forms for each verb, bringing each paradigm to twelve unique forms. I also decided to have a formal subjunctive set, bringing each paradigm to twenty-four unique forms. After that all that was left was to determine how many tense/aspect combinations there would be.

The fact that the key phrases were translated as *"must* die" and *"must* serve" added a bit of a wrinkle to the formula. The word *must* in English is used in a few ways. Notice that there's a difference between these three uses of the word *must*:

1. To get to the Emerald City, one must follow the Yellow Brick Road.

2. If the ball is put in play, the batter must run to first base.

3. Humans must breathe air.

The uses are all very similar, but the first phrase indicates volition on the part of the subject. That is, if one wishes to get to the Emerald City, one is obligated to follow the Yellow Brick Road. One could ignore this information; it's being provided to indicate what's needed to achieve the stated goal. In the second sentence, on the other hand, the rules of baseball state that a batter *must* run to first base if the ball is put in play. The batter has no choice in this if the batter wishes to follow the rules of baseball. Finally, humans *must* breathe air. There are absolutely no ifs, ands, or buts about it: humans must breathe air.

So even though all of these uses of *must* imply some sort of obligation, the immediacy of that obligation differs. In the phrases "all men must die" and "all men must serve," it seems that the intended implication is closer to sense (3) than either sense (2) or (1). The phrases are meant as definitions—as prerequisites for being in the group "all men." It's a kind of obligation where volition simply isn't a part of the equation.

Obligation is something all languages encode, but few encode it as, say, an affix on the verb, or as a form of the verb, especially at such an early stage. I didn't want to get sucked into creating an "obligative" form of the verb for High Valyrian. After all, if there's an obligative form, is there a permissive? A potential? A conditional? A dubitative? An optative? This didn't feel right—especially since this is such a marginal case of strong obligation. Plus, as a conlanger, the question should always be "What have I got?" rather than "What new thing can I create?"

Looking back at Latin, one of the key features of its conjugation system is a dual stem system. Latin has two basic sets of personal endings, and then two basic stems associated with two different sets of tenses. With a verb like *portāre*, "to carry," the imperfect stem is *port-*, and the perfect stem is *portāv-*. Each of these combines with two sets of person marking and a unique suffix (*-āb* for the imperfect stem and *-er* for the perfect stem) to form six unique tenses. Throw in a little irregularity to make sure similar-sounding forms aren't too similar, and that's the Latin tense system.

I *loved* this idea, so I decided to do my own version of it. I decided each verb would have an imperfect and perfect stem, as well, with the perfect having some added irregularities. The next step was creating this perfect stem. Going into the prehistory of High Valyrian, I decided the perfect stem would be formed from the imperfect (the basic or unmarked) stem by adding a basic form of *tat* to the end. *Tat* became the verb *tatagon*, which means "to finish." Its perfect form, *tet*, would ultimately become attached to verb forms as *-et*, often being reduced further based on regular sound changes. For our two verbs, for example, the history looked something like this:

Stage 1	Stage 2	Stage 3	Stage 4
dohaer-tet-	*dohaer-tət-*	*dohaertt-*	*dohaert-*
morghuli-tet	*morghultət-*	*morghultt-*	*morghult-*

More often than not, *-et* would be reduced to a simple *-t* suffix.

Once the stems were set, the next step became forming the tenses. I decided to form three different sets of personal endings: regular endings, past endings, and tenseless or gnomic endings. These endings were added to verbs in different waves, based on the history of the language.

In the first stage, there were two sets—regular and gnomic—which, schematically, looked like this:

	REGULAR		GNOMIC	
	Singular	Plural	Singular	Plural
First Person	dohaeran	dohaeri	dohaeria	dohaeriti
Second Person	dohaerā	dohaerāt	dohaeria	dohaeriat
Third Person	dohaerza	dohaerzi	dohaeris	dohaerisi

The personal endings themselves were derived from proto-forms that eventually became the pronouns of High Valyrian—*nyke* "I (first person)," *ao* "you (second person)," *ziry* "s/he (third person)," etc. The set of past tense personal endings that were originally applied directly to the stem were replaced by the new perfect stem forms, as shown below:

	OLD PERFECT		NEW PERFECT	
	Singular	Plural	Singular	Plural
First Person	dohaeren	dohaerin	dohaerta	dohaerti
Second Person	dohaerē	dohaerēt	dohaertā	dohaertāt
Third Person	dohaeres	dohaeris	dohaertas	dohaertis

These innovative forms entirely replaced the old perfect (and part of the motivation for that replacement may have been that the forms were too similar acoustically to other tenses). At the time, this might have been like replacing a regular past tense like "I walked" with something like "I done walked." Eventually it became the new standard, producing four forms: a regular stem with regular and gnomic endings, and a perfect stem with regular and gnomic endings.

A separate innovation occurring at around the same time caused a new tense to form, filling in a gap in the past tense. An auxiliary verb *ilagon*, "to lie," came to be used in the past tense with main verbs to indicate that an action was ongoing in the past tense. Eventually these verb forms fused to produce a new past tense progressive—or past imperfect—tense. Even though the old perfect was abandoned with main verbs, it stuck around for these suffixed verbs (*ilagon* and *tatagon*) which were understood to be irregular and treated as auxiliaries. Thus, the old perfect endings surfaced as part of a new past imperfect construction. They were also used with the perfect ending to produce a past perfect or pluperfect construction, resulting in two new tenses. The irregular auxiliaries, in effect, licensed the presence of the old perfect endings which had been lost for other verbs. These forms are shown below:

	Past Imperfect		Pluperfect	
	Singular	**Plural**	**Singular**	**Plural**
First Person	*dohaerilen*	*dohaerilin*	*dohaerten*	*dohaertin*
Second Person	*dohaerilē*	*dohaerilēt*	*dohaertē*	*dohaertēt*
Third Person	*dohaeriles*	*dohaerilis*	*dohaertes*	*dohaertis*

The lone remaining combination was the auxiliary *ilagon* used with the regular endings (the auxiliary construction wasn't used with the gnomic endings). If the past imperfect construction meant "I lay serving," the regular construction would mean something like "I lie serving," which is roughly equivalent to the present tense. This forced a new interpretation of the construction, which was something like, "I lie to serve," which was interpreted as a future tense. That produced the final tense of High Valyrian:

	Future	
	Singular	**Plural**
First Person	*dohaerilan*	*dohaerili*
Second Person	*dohaerilā*	*dohaerilāt*
Third Person	*dohaerilza*	*dohaerilzi*

In order to better distinguish it from the imperfect, the form of the first person singular eventually became *dohaerinna*, and passive verb forms arose from an original auxiliary *kisagon*, which meant "to eat," but otherwise those are the modern tenses of High Valyrian. The lone missing combination (something like *dohaertil-* or *dohaerilt-*) never occurred because the perfect and imperfect auxiliaries were never used in conjunction in the oldest form of the language. This is why there is no distinct future perfect form in High Valyrian.

The final question in figuring out the tense associated with *valar morghulis* and *valar dohaeris* is the modern interpretation of the gnomic or tenseless forms. The verb forms themselves are third person singular gnomic (or aorist, as they're called in the modern language). These tenseless forms are used to denote habitual actions or general truths. A simple way to illustrate the difference is with the two sentences below:

Jaohossa rhovis. "The dogs are barking." (PRESENT)

Jaohossa rhovisi. "Dogs bark." (AORIST)

If this is the generic interpretation of these two tenses, what distinction would, say, using the collective of "dog" (*jaohor*) versus the plural of "dog" (*jaohossa*) make? The only possible distinction that could be made would be having emphasis placed on the fact that one was talking about *all* the dogs. Thus, the use of the collective *combined* with the use of the aorist is what produces the sense "all men" in "all men must die."

Regarding "must," the interpretation here is based on the pairing of the phrases "all men must die" and "all men must serve." Dying is one of the few things that all humans do (go us?), but serving is not. Consequently, *valar dohaeris* is interpreted as "all men *must* serve," since it couldn't be a generic statement about the lives of men. Pairing it with the additional phrase *valar morghulis*, accompanied by the fact that the two phrases are inextricably intertwined, is what gives us the interpretation "all men must die."

Some detail has been left out for the sake of brevity (ha!), but this is how I created the verb system of High Valyrian. Regarding the spelling, I thought I'd add one final note. Since I work for the canon within the show, I had to wait (somewhat breathlessly) for the last episode of season two of *Game of Thrones* to air in order to see how the actor who played Jaqen H'ghar, Tom Wlaschiha, would pronounce *valar morghulis*. There are a number of ways it could have been pronounced, and several would have proved disastrous for what I was planning for High Valyrian. As it turns out, he pronounced it the way I thought an average English speaker would: *VA-lar mor-GHU-lis* ['vɑ.lɑɹ mɔɹ.'gu.lɪs]. When I heard that, I breathed a huge sigh of relief. The fact that the *gh* was pronounced as a regular [g]—along with the English pronunciation of the *r*'s—could be easily explained by the fact that Jaqen H'ghar is not a native High Valyrian speaker.

Unfortunately, it did mean I had to do something with the stress system. As I'd planned it, High Valyrian would have a weight-sensitive stress system that would default to the penultimate syllable. Outside of resorting to some clever trickery, there was no way I could argue that the syllable *mor* was light. That meant that in order to get the stress on *ghu*, I had to make the vowel in that syllable long—which means that what is spelled *valar morghulis* should technically be *valar morghūlis*.

Of course, that isn't that big a deal. After all, even in a language that uses macrons to mark long vowels, like Hawaiian, long vowels are often left unmarked. The program I use for the show, Final Draft, doesn't even accept characters with macrons, so long vowels are never marked in the script. Plus, if Sean Endymion *really* wanted his tattoo to be 100 percent accurate, he could always add a macron (there's room!). Even so, I say it's all right. Nobody cares about macrons! They're just crazy little vowel hats that the poor vowels don't even want to wear. Set them free, I say!

As fun as creating this system was, it was even more fun to see the system destroyed as it evolved into Low Valyrian. Verb systems are highly complex and highly unstable. It's like a game of Jenga that nobody wants to play. Nevertheless, the hallmark of any con-lang will be its system of verbal conjugation, so it pays to put in the time and effort.

CHAPTER IV

Phrases

INTRODUCTION

Even now, ten years after I started working on *Game of Thrones*, a full five years after this book was first published, the two words I dread reading the most when I open up an email—even more than "Dear Peter" (MY NAME IS DAVID! DAVID PETERSON! FIRST NAME DAVID, D-A-V-I-D! HOW BY THE TAIL OF SUN WUKONG, GREAT SAGE EQUALING HEAVEN, DO YOU SCREW UP ONE OF THE SIMPLEST MOST COMMON NAMES WE'VE GOT HERE ON THIS EARTH OF MANKIND?!)—are "*quick* translation." Why, you might wonder, would I care about a quick translation? Shouldn't I fear a long, complicated translation? Of course I *do*, dear reader, I do. The issue, though, is that "quick" is in the eye of the beholder—or, in this case, the estimation of the emailer.

Take this request from a different *Star-Crossed* Brian—script coordinator Brian Fernandes (again, just the messenger)—who asked for a "quick translation" for casting (more on that later). What was the line? Take a read:

Is that the woman that crashed the ship?

Quick. *Quick.* Forget the lexical items for the time being (this was for episode 109; I had words for "woman," "crash," and "ship" by then) and focus on the structure. In one sense, it is quick—after all, it's only one sentence, not fifty. But bearing in mind that a declarative sentence is the simplest type of clause, look at all that's going on in this sentence:

1. Rather than a declaration we have a question:

   The woman crashed the ship. > *Did the woman crash the ship?*

2. We also have a question in place of a simple copular construction:

   That is the woman. > *Is that the woman?*

3. The two are combined, so that we have a relative clause built off *woman*:

   Did the woman crash the ship? + *Is that the woman?* > *Is that the woman that crashed the ship?*

Producing a translation like this is nothing to a native speaker, but as I believe I've mentioned already—or wait, did I . . . ? Let's see . . . *Return of the Jedi* . . . Onions . . . Reference that didn't age well . . . Onions again . . . Son of a gun, I didn't! Okay, revising—I am by no means fluent in any of the languages I've created, and I certainly wasn't fluent in Sondiv before we'd even finished filming the first season. Consequently, whenever I get a request like this, I briefly go through the five stages of grief, and then I sit down, open up the grammar, and mutter, "Okay, how the heck did I decide to do relative clauses in this language?"

And we're just talking about casting! We're sitting here, and I'm supposed to be the creator of the Dothraki language, and we're talking about casting. Not a live shoot, not a live shoot, we're talking about casting. In other words, they needed this thing translated quickly because they were casting actresses for the roll and wanted them to practice with the real line. The indignity! This was the greatest injustice in the history of the world!

So, naturally, I translated the line as quickly as I could and sent it back; I don't call the shots. (Because, seriously, I'm a language creator. I'm generally valued slightly less than the on-set caterer—which . . . fair,

I get it, they do amazing work: we had *lobster tails* one day on *Bright!* Seriously, *lobster tails!*) But this helps to illustrate one of the greatest disconnects between those who create or translate languages and those who don't. In my experience, many who work on a show or film view complexity as a function of length: the more lines, the more difficult the job. While it certainly will take longer to do more translations than fewer, what takes the most time is the level of grammatical complexity present in the requested translations.

But what, exactly, *is* grammatical complexity? What makes translating "She's the sister I got the book for" so much more difficult than translating "I quickly tossed all three yellow onions into the raging fire in the deepest circle of Dante's Hell"? I've got nowhere to be. Let's find out!

CLAUSE INTERACTION

The basic tends to be simpler and easier to tackle than the complex. In language, the basic involves the simplest form of each element (singular nouns are usually simpler than plurals; indicatives are usually simpler than passives; subjects are usually simpler than objects, etc.), while the complex involves the edge cases. We've seen this in morphology in chapter II. When it comes to full-on sentences, simple is a single clause where each element is where you expect it to be. Complex is when there are multiple clauses crammed into one, and/or when elements are out of their expected places—or doing more than one expects them to.

The best way I've found to illustrate this complexity is with a single line from the Janelle Monáe song "Electric Lady." Aside from being our lone, shining hope for a brighter future, Janelle Monáe created this line that leaves me absolutely dumbfounded when it comes to the economic complexity of the English language. That line is as follows:

You've got the look the gods agree they want to see.

Look at that! Eleven words, twelve syllables, and yet there are at least four separate things going on in that sentence. To begin to parse it, let's reintroduce a couple of missing words:

> You've got the look that the gods agree that they want to see.

I honestly don't even know if that makes it any simpler. An English speaker will understand the original line effortlessly, but can they explain it? If you either speak another language or have even ever studied another one for five minutes, can you *imagine* trying to translate this line into that language? Forget trying to make it fit the syllable count and meter!

To try to tease out this line, let's iterate, starting from the top and moving down into the depths of its complexity:

> You've got the look.
> You've got the look the gods see.
> You've got the look the gods want to see.
> You've got the look the gods agree they want to see.

What a journey! And all this to further emphasize that Cindi Mayweather is all that. Shock me one good time!

What makes this line complex is the presence of one relative clause and two different subordinate clauses. What are those? Let's dig in and find out!

QUESTIONS

Gotcha! Ha, ha, ha . . . Yeah, I started writing up a section on relative clauses when I realized that, of course, many languages use *interrogative* pronouns as *relative* pronouns, and if I haven't yet *introduced* interrogative pronouns, then . . .

Anyway, QUESTIONS! We introduced the main types of questions in chapter I, but here we'll go into greater depth—starting with yes/no questions. Let me take a moment to introduce the Méníshè language,

created for the Freefrom show *Motherland: Fort Salem* by myself along
with the amazing, spectacular, sensational, and indefatigable professor
Jessie "Sassafras" Sams, PhD:

Kháà 'èlá t'analì azwà bà.
[xaː51 ʔe11.la55 t'a33.na33.li11 a33.zwa11 ba11]
"The witches are singing about the moon."

That's a basic declarative sentence. Now here's the yes/no question version of it:

Kháà 'èlá t'analì azwà bà jìnà?
[xaː51 ʔe11.la55 t'a33.na33.li11 a33.zwa11 ba11 dʒi11.na11]
"Are the witches singing about the moon?"

Above, Méníshè uses the question particle *jìnà* in sentence-final position to form a yes/no question from a declarative sentence. That's actually the most common way to form a yes/no question, looking at the world's languages, but there are three other fairly common strategies in addition to that one. Here's a summary of those four strategies:

- **Question Particle:** Many languages use a completely invariant question particle that appears in the same place every time to differentiate a yes/no question from a statement. We saw this with Méníshè above, where the question particle *jìnà* occurs at the end of a yes/no question. In Arabic, the question particle هل [hal] appears at the beginning:

نامت. ['naː.mat] "She slept."

هل نامت؟ [hal 'naː.mat] "Did she sleep?"

Question particles generally occur sentence-initially, sentence-finally, directly before or after the verb, or in second position.

These particles often derive from words or longer phrases whose purpose is to seek confirmation or otherwise ascertain the truth of the proposition. For example, the emerging sentence-initial particle *est-ce que* [ɛs.kə] in French derives from a phrase meaning roughly "Is it that . . . ?"

- **Interrogative Verbal Morphology:** This can take the form of a special verbal conjugation, or a verbal auxiliary used for asking questions. In Indojisnen, the suffix ⊕ [-va] becomes a part of the verbal complex in yes/no questions (notice the lenition of the [k] below):

  ⬡⬡⬡⬡⬡ [ˈfa.na.tlik] "They are sleeping."

  ⬡⬡⬡⬡⬡ [ˈfa.na.tlih.va] "Are they sleeping?"

  Interrogative auxiliaries are often co-opted from other auxiliaries (cf. "do" in English). Otherwise, interrogative verbal morphology often derives from the same sources as particles.

- **Word Order Change:** Sometimes a particular type of inversion is associated with a yes/no question. In older forms of English, this used to be the standard way to form yes/no questions—so rather than "You slept well" you'd say "Slept you well?"—but I guess we got tired of it, so now we only invert the copula or auxiliaries ("be," "have," "can," "should," etc.) if they're there, otherwise we throw "do" in and invert it. German still does it, though, so if you have *Ich sehe einen respektlosen Leichenbestatter*, "I see a disrespectful mortician," you'd rephrase it *Sehe ich einen respektlosen Leichenbestatter?* "Do I see a disrespectful mortician?"— literally "See I a disrespectful mortician?" Though somewhat common in Europe, this strategy is fairly uncommon crosslinguistically. For all such languages, the subject goes from being in front of the verb to immediately following the verb.

- **Intonation Change:** The second most common strategy for forming yes/no questions involves a simple change in intonation with no structural change. Spanish speakers will be well familiar with this, and the same strategy is used by Trigedasleng, the language of the CW's *The 100*:

Kepon-de na kik thru.

['kɛ.pɔn.dɛ nə 'kik 'θɹu]

"The hostages will survive."

Kepon-de na kik thru?

['kɛ.pɔn.dɛ nə 'kik 'θɹu]

"Will the hostages survive?"

Though not indicated in the IPA, there is a general intonational rise in Trigedasleng yes/no questions when compared to their corresponding non-interrogative forms. While it's common for an intonational rise to accompany a yes/no question, it's not universal. In fact, in Dothraki (a language which uses a question particle), there is a sharp *falling* intonation associated with yes/no questions.

As a final note, a word for "yes" often derives from words like "true," "this," "that," "already," or even the third person singular positive form of the copula (a kind of short way of saying "it is so").

WH-questions, also called nonpolar or content questions, are questions featuring any of a number of **interrogative pronouns** or **question words** that ask for some specific kind of information. For example, in English, "what" asks for a thing, "who" asks for a person, "where" for a place, etc. In addition to having basic question words, English also has a few compound terms like "what kind," "how much/many," but the moment you try to put these things into a table, there is a certain type of conlanger who will get the irresistible urge to do something like this:

Thing	*ufa* "what"	Reason	*ufe* "why"
Person	*ufo* "who"	Manner	*ufæ* "how"
Place	*ufu* "where"	Height	*ufə* "how tall (?)"
Time	*ufi* "when"	Color	*ufi* "what color (?!)"

You don't need to do this. If anything, I'd encourage you, at least at first, to go in the opposite direction. Some languages get by with a small number of question words and instead use compound terms (like "how much" or "what kind") or even the same term to cover other categories. For example, there doesn't *have* to be a difference between "what" and "who." It's nice, I guess, but not necessary.

A basic interrogative pronoun is something that is likely to be quite old in a language, but that's not necessarily the case for any individual question word—in fact, many are likely to be compounds, with older ones having eroded to the point of being single words. This is why, for example, English has a bunch of words that begin with "wh": it started as one word that declined in a number of ways and combined with other derivational strategies to produce a number of stand-alone words that stood in for different types of phrases and ended up sticking around.

In terms of placement, question words are likely to be found in one of two places: Right at the beginning of the sentence, or right where they would be if they were in a non-interrogative phrase (i.e. **in situ**). Crosslinguistically, the latter is more common. Here's an example of a fronted question word in the Ravkan language from Netflix's *Shadow and Bone*, based on the novel by Leigh Bardugo, whom you may know from the inside cover of this book:

ᒋᘐᕼᴑ ᴕᓀᒋᴑᔕ ᴣᴑᴙᴗᴖᴐ.

['ve.la 'dʒa.fan 'baʃ.ni]

"The girl is eating spinach."

ᗷᴗᴐᴄ ᒋᘐᕼᴑ ᴕᓀᒋᴑᔕ꞉

['ʒov 've.la 'dʒa.fan]

"What is the girl eating?"

Notice in the first sentence, ᴣᴑᴙᴗᴖᴐ "spinach" is at the end of the sentence, which is where objects go in Ravkan. In the corresponding question, ᗷᴗᴐᴄ "what" comes at the beginning, even though it's the object of the verb. In Irathient, by contrast, the question word

ཨཤཔ [na.zə] "what" sits in the exact same spot as the object ཨོཤ [ri.za] "a snack" in the non-interrogative clause:

ཨཤཔཨཤཔཔ
['za.ra 'ɛ.lu 'ri.za 'za.grɛ]

"The rider is eating a snack."

ཨཤཔཔཨཤཔ
['zɛ.na 'ɛ.lu 'na.ze'za.grɛ]

"What is the rider eating?"

Despite the fact that creating what you need to do questions in your language can seem daunting, it's really a short series of relatively painless decisions. Possibly the most difficult thing is coming up with a good set of question words, but even that isn't too bad, since a lot of question words in the world's languages wear their etymologies on their sleeve. If you're searching for inspiration, check out some online etymological dictionaries! You'll get some ideas before long.

NEGATION

Speaking of "not as difficult as it looks," negation really isn't that bad, even though I personally dread it. And, before going on, let me be clear about what I dread (because a lot of the topics in this chapter keep me up at night). When I create a negation strategy in a language, I want it to be unique and authentic. It's a difficult thing in conlanging to transcend the limitations of one's native language, or the other languages one has studied. Where it's most difficult are the invisible aspects of language that operate beneath the surface: subordination, negation, topicalization, etc. In developing something for a language, one is often asking, "Is this simply the way this works in human language, or is it just my native language?" It's easier to answer that question with concrete topics like nominal morphology or sound inventories; much more difficult with syntax and pragmatics.

Negation in language is a way to assert that the action in question did *not* occur—or, in the case of nonverbal phrases, that the element or quality does not exist. In developing a negation strategy, one has to decide on a predicate negation strategy, decide where the negative elements will appear, and then evolve them. Let's go through these steps one at a time.

Standard sentential or predicate negation negates the main proposition of the clause. Here's an example from Trigedasleng:

> *Yu gonplei ste odon.*
> [ju 'gɔn.ple stɛ 'ɔ.rɔn]
>
> "Your fight is over."

> *Yu gonplei **nou** ste odon.*
> [ju 'gɔn.ple 'no stɛ 'ɔ.rɔn]
>
> "Your fight is **not** over."

Above the negative particle *nou* negates the entire clause. There are other types of negation, but we'll set those aside for the moment. Simple negation like this tends to appear in particle form or as a part of the verbal complex—and, in both cases, either before or after the verb. This Trigedasleng example illustrates the most common situation: a negative particle, as opposed to an auxiliary or verb form, which occurs directly before the verb. Nevertheless, other strategies are hardly uncommon. Here are some examples:

Nonadjacent Preverbal Negation (Kamakawi)

> ⊙ꗧꗑ *Male kelea ei.*
> ['ma.le ke.'le.a 'e.i]
>
> "I will be sad."

∘ 用 冈禾 **Oku** *male kelea ei.*

['o.ku 'ma.le ke.'le.a 'e.i]

"I will **not** be sad."

Prefixal Negation (Méníshè)

Pèlá.

[pe11.la55]

"We are singing."

Péwèlá.

[pe55.we11.la55]

"We are **not** singing."

Adjacent Postverbal Negation (High Valyrian)

Zaldrīzes sōves.

[zal.'driː.zes 'soː.ves]

"The dragon is flying."

Zaldrīzes sōvios **daor.**

[zal.'driː.zes 'soː.vios daor]

"The dragon is **not** flying."

Nonadjacent Postverbal Negation (Kinuk'aaz, from Syfy's *Defiance*)

𝔶 ʊ𝔧𝒴 𝔧ᵖ𝔏ᵖᵲ𝔧𝔦 𝒴ᵖ𝔧ᵲ

['vak k'u.'zu.naz 'svon]

"A man drank water."

𝔶 ʊ𝔧𝒴 𝔧ᵖ𝔏ᵖᵲ𝔧𝔦 𝒴ᵖ𝔧ᵲ 𝔧/𝔧

['vak k'u.'zu.naz 'svon 'ar]

"A man **did not** drink water."

Suffixal Negation (Indojisnen)

['jɔs.lɛn]

"It is shining."

['jɔr.tu.tlen]

"It is **not** shining."

Full Negative Auxiliary (Engála, from *LangTime Studio*)

Chesi imé.

['tʃe.si i.ˈme]

"The rabbit twitched her ears."

O imé chesi.

['o i.ˈme 'tʃe.si]

"The rabbit **didn't** twitch her ears."

This isn't every possible negation strategy, but almost every language on Earth uses one of these strategies. Sometimes you'll find more than one used at the same time, or other oddities. English, for example, requires postverbal negation—sometimes as a particle (i.e. *not*) and sometimes as a suffix (i.e. *-n't*)—but it's picky about which verbs allow negation. I mean, one *could* say "I slept not" and be understood, but it's antiquated. Instead, we have what we call *do*-support. If the verb isn't a copula or auxiliary, the auxiliary *do* is inserted so that either *not* or *-n't* can sit after it.

Do-support is an interesting instantiation of the can-do attitude humans have when it comes to their languages. We decide, "Our language *must* do this!" The language says, "Uhh . . . actually, that's not allowed, for the following very sensible reasons . . ." Then we chuckle and throw down our Exodia card: "How about I do anyway?"

Remember that when designing your own language: There's *always* a way to make it work—even if your language hates it.

Negation particles are quite old. Something like English *no* ultimately derives from Proto-Indo-European *ne, which, as far as we know, has been a negator with no other function since time immemorial. That said, there are younger negators, and we know where they come from. Verbs like "lack" or "lose" commonly become negators, as well as verbs like "leave," "abandon," "let go," and drop. You'll also find complex negators that have older negators inside them. In Swahili, *hapana* comes from a phrase meaning "to not have," which was used in negative existential constructions (i.e. "there isn't"). English *not* comes from *naught,* which is *ne aught* (i.e. "not anything"). German *nicht* comes from an older compound that means "no person." And then French . . .

Okay, let's pause a moment. You're going to want to sit down for this one. (I know you're reading this standing in line at a bookstore where you're getting a card for your aunt. It can wait. This is important.)

I'm about to teach you about something they gave the amazingly pretentious name *Jespersen's Cycle*. They actually named this silly bit of grammaticalization like it's a multipart epic fantasy series. It's as if they called intervocalic devoicing *The Trembling Fold.* I both love it and hate it at the same time. In keeping with that theme, I have further named the parts of Jespersen's Cycle, and shall present them, in order, below:

The Dawning Void: Book the First of Jespersen's Cycle

Our story begins with a humble adjacent
preverbal negative particle . . .

*Je **ne** vais.* [ʒə nə ve] "I do **not** go."

A Solitary Echo: Book the Second of Jespersen's Cycle

A challenger emerges from the East! Negated verbs begin to co-occur with nominal objects that represent the *smallest part* of the verb in question—for example, "I don't move *a step*" (*pas*), "I don't write *a dot*" (*point*), "I don't see *a thing*" (*rien*). These objects are reanalyzed as a standard part of negation!

*Je **ne** vais **pas**.* [ʒə nə ve pa] "I do **not** go."

Hope's Twilight: Book the Third of Jespersen's Cycle

In a shocking twist, the object is reanalyzed as
the actual negative particle, and the original negative
particle is defeated! The hero is slain!

*Je vais **pas**.* [ʒə ve pa] "I do **not** go."

And thus a word that means nothing more than a small part of something comes to be a negative particle in and of itself!

In addition to predicate negation, there is another type where variation can occur—something I call phrasal negation. It's the distinction between "I don't see the pencils" and "I see no pencils." These negators modify noun phrases, adjectival phrases, adverbial phrases, etc.—everything but verbal phrases. Often the two differ—sometimes slightly (cf. English *not* vs. *no*), sometimes sharply (cf. German *nicht* vs. *kein*, the latter coming from a shortening of a larger word, *nehein*, "not any"). The key difference seems to be that a negative particle wants to modify a verb or a sentence, not anything smaller. To modify something smaller, the particle must combine with something else (e.g. "not any," "not one," "not a person," etc.). This is also how languages get negative pronouns ("no one," "nothing," etc. Rather transparent in English. By contrast, consider the French *rien*, "nothing," which originally meant "thing"!).

Languages also differ in how much of a negated item is present. In English, we're fine with *"There are no pencils here."* In Spanish, on the other hand, we don't use the plural: we use the singular. *No hay lápiz aquí*—"There are no pencils here" or "There isn't a pencil here" (the logic being if there isn't even one of them, certainly there aren't *more* than one).

As a final note, let's talk about double negatives. In English, double negatives are considered nonstandard. That is, one oughtn't say "I don't see nothing," one ought to say either "I don't see anything" or "I see nothing." The logic is that if you don't see *nothing*, then you must be seeing *everything*, I guess . . . ? Turns out most of the world thinks that's bunk. Indeed, it is *overwhelmingly common* for a language to prefer the structure *I don't see nothing*, with many languages disallowing the standard English single negation. The reason seems to have nothing to do with the "logic" of the phrase. Instead, it's simple agreement: the clause is negative, so the pronoun ought to be negative as well. Apparently Western languages were just copying Latin, and Latin was an outlier. Go fig.

RELATIVE CLAUSES

A **relative clause** is a full sentence that modifies a noun phrase. You read a bit about these in Kamakawi, but here we'll go into greater depth. Below is a noun from Chakobsa, a language originally conceived in Frank Herbert's *Dune*, and later fleshed out for the Legendary feature film adaptation:

ᴚᏕᏈ

['le.kis]

"dune"

Now here's that noun modified by an adjective:

ᴚᏕᏈ ᎋᏖᏋ

['le.kis vaː'hiː]

"the large dune"

And here's that entire noun phrase modified by a relative clause:

ᴚᏕᏈ ᎋᏖᏋ ᏗᏚᏖᏚᏞᏙᏜ

['le.kis vaː'hiː 'heʃʃja.ha.bit 'bi.li]

"the large dune **that the woman saw**"

The phrase "that the woman saw" is a relative clause. It's a full sentence pretending to be something less than a full sentence. The full sentence is "The woman saw the large dune." In a way, that full sentence has been combined with the phrase "the large dune" with a variable dropped in place of "the large dune." In this case, that variable is the suffix ᨠᨅᨒ [-bit]. This suffix co-occurs with a relativized object. Rather than saying "the large dune that the woman saw the large dune," using ᨠᨅᨒ [-bit] alerts the listener that the object of the verb (the thing that was seen) is identical to the noun phrase that is being described by the relative clause.

Almost all languages allow relative clauses, but they differ in how they deploy them. A relative clause may appear before or after the noun it modifies, or the noun may be a part of the relative clause itself (these are called **internally headed relative clauses**). A relative clause may be introduced by one or more relative particles, or may use a relative pronoun. They also may have no marking at all and simply place a **gap** where the modified noun would appear in an ordinary clause. Most languages allow a copy pronoun to be retained in a relative clause, though languages will differ in how extreme the relative clause must be before a copy pronoun is warranted.

To start someplace simple, let's look at the placement of relative clauses. Relative clauses overwhelmingly appear after the noun they modify when the object occurs after the verb in standard clause structures. When the object occurs before the verb, it's fifty-fifty. As a result, you can say there's a general preference for postnominal relative clauses, but that doesn't mean prenominal relative clauses are at all uncommon. Here are examples of both (prenominal from Castithan and postnominal from Trigedasleng):

ᑎᕈᖕ ᕈᖕ ᕿᕆᖕᕦ ᓓᕆᖕᐅᖁ

['pje.ɾa ɾe 'ba.no.zo 'de.ɾun.dʒa]

"the animal **the girl saw**"

bis gada-de don sin in
['bis 'gæ.ɾə.dɛ dɔn 'sin 'in]

"the animal **the girl saw**"

Both languages above employ a gap strategy (it's not "the animal the girl saw it"). They also have a null complementizer—that is, there's nothing equivalent to the English "that," "who," or "which." For English speakers trying to wrap their head around the prenominal strategy, think of it as an extended adjectival phrase—that is, instead of saying "the animal the girl saw," say "the girl saw (it) animal," but without the "it."

Now let's turn our attention to internally headed relative clauses. They are rare (about 3 percent of the world's languages have them), and they give you a real "horse raced past the barn fell" vibe. Here's an example from Quechua (Perú):

> **Nuna** bestyata **rantishqan** alli bestyam karqon.
> /**man** horse **bought** good horse was/
> "The horse **that the man bought** was a good horse."

Remembering that the relative clause modifies a noun phrase, how exactly do you describe the placement of that relative clause? The noun being modified is right in the middle of the phrase and occurs where it would in an ordinary sentence. It's a bit like saying "The man bought a horse (and it) was a good horse," but without the "and it." That's precisely how internally headed relative clauses work. I recommend reviewing a few languages with internally headed relative clauses if you'd like to use them in a conlang.

Languages differ in how obvious their relative clauses are. They run the gamut from . . . well, the above, to having a gap, having a special introductory *and* closing particle, having a special verb form, having marked word order, etc. A simple distinction is whether there is or isn't something in between the relative clause and the noun it modifies. Here's a comparison between Castithan and High Valyrian:

ᚾᚺᚱ ᚢᚺ ᚨᚩᚦᚾᚲ ᚢᚺ ᚱᚲᚢᚺᚷ

['pje.ra re 'ba.no.zo 'de.run.dʒa]

"the animal the girl saw"

*riña ūndas **lȳs** dȳñes*
['ri.ɲa 'uːn.das **lyːs** 'dyː.ɲes]

"the animal the girl saw"

Both examples above have the order "girl saw animal," but the High Valyrian example has a fourth word, *lȳs*, which does nothing but sit in between the relative clause and the noun it modifies. In English we have a few of these: "that," "who," and "which." Their usages overlap a bit, and that's not uncommon. This spot can be filled by a bare complementizer (a word that does nothing but say "a relative clause is next to this"), a relative pronoun that may or may not inflect for case, number, and/or gender, an adjective that also may or may not agree, or a wild card like "where." Ever heard one of these in English?

That's the girl I told you about where I used to babysit her younger brother.

That's a double relative clause there, and the *where* basically says "something relevant's coming! Look out!" It's like giving up. Sure, one could go through the mental gymnastics it takes to say "That's the girl about whom I told you whose younger brother I used to babysit," but why bother when you can just say "where" and dump the whole clause after it? German's a big fan of this strategy. Probably a lot of languages rely on it. If the relative clauses in your conlang get too complex, your speakers may make use of it, too. Beware!

These relative complementizers/pronouns have a number of sources, but one of the most common places is either demonstrative pronouns (e.g. "that") or interrogative pronouns ("who," "which," where"—even "what," informally). Almost all relative clause markers derive from one of these sources. And again, like we see in English, German, Serbo-Croatian, and many other languages, you can have more than one relative clause marker in the same language.

Now that we've seen some of these markers, let's talk about how they work with copy pronouns. In English, "the man I saw" is good, but "the man I saw him" is bad. On the other hand, "the really tall man with the huge bushy beard I'd told you that I totally remember asking my brother if he saw him the other day" seems to be okay. Notice how you read that and didn't have a problem with the word *him* that time? It's because the darn thing got too long and complex so your brain just sat there amid the flames and said, "This is fine." All languages do this, because our brains are meat and have more important things to do than say, "Hey! Wait a minute! They didn't need that pronoun!" every time someone decides to get "crafty" with their verbiage.

Leaving overly complex examples aside, though, many languages use copy pronouns even in basic clauses. In Arabic, if the role of the modified noun is anything other than a subject, a copy pronoun is used in addition to the relative pronoun:

الرجل الذي عرفته

[ar.'ra.ʒul al.'la.ði: ʕa.'raf.tu.ha]

"the man **that I knew**"

The ه [-ha] suffix on the end of the verb عرفت [ʕaraftu] is a clitic third person masculine pronoun. Not a relative pronoun, mind you: a regular one (for the curious, الذي [allaði:] is the relative pronoun). The sentence literally reads "the man that I knew him." Of course, these object pronouns in Arabic are *incredibly* lightweight, so adding them doesn't require a lot of effort or space. That plus the added redundancy, which increases the signal strength of the message (cf. grammatical gender), is probably why the copy pronouns are still used in relative clauses—and probably why they're not used when the embedded noun is the subject of the sentence (they don't add enough, since verbs already agree with their subjects, and Arabic *subject* pronouns aren't lightweight).

As noted in our discussion of applicatives, languages differ in which nouns are allowed to be modified by a relative clause. It depends crucially on the role the noun plays *in* the relative clause. As we saw in Kamakawi, something like "the onion that bit me" would be fine, but "the onion I incinerated" would not be. This is because Kamakawi only allows relative clauses to modify nouns that occupy the *subject* role in the relative clause. As it turns out, there's a continuum with these called the accessibility hierarchy:

Subject > Direct Object > Indirect Object > Oblique > Genitive > Object of Comparative

That is, if you have a language that will allow a relative clause to modify a noun that acts as, say, an indirect object in the relative clause, that language will also allow nouns that act as direct objects or subjects in relative clauses. The same isn't necessarily true of the members to the right of that (e.g. obliques). Languages draw a line somewhere on this continuum (or nowhere, as the case may be), and everything to the left of that line is okay, while everything to the right is not. In those instances, another strategy is required (say, passivization and/or applicativization), or one simply has to use two sentences (e.g. "This is an onion, and I am more handsome than it.").

This should get you started with relative clauses, though there's lots of other fun stuff to dig into. For example, ever wondered about adjectives? Adjectives tend to come from one of two sources: nouns or verbs. Nounish adjectives tend to agree with the nouns they modify in number, case, and gender, because they arise from appositive constructions (e.g. الكلب السعيد [al.'kalb as.sa.'ʕiːd] "the happy dog" or "the dog the happy one"). There are also stative verbs that give rise to adjectives. For example in Engála, you could say *Mislen imé* ['mis.len i.'me] "The rabbit is sweet." You could also have a relative clause like *imé **mislen*** "the rabbit **who is sweet**." Now guess what order the adjective and noun come in if you were to say "the sweet rabbit"! [Note to Editor: Please embed *Tim and Eric* "mind blown with fireworks" .gif when we achieve the technology to embed animated .gifs in real paper.]

PRAGMATICS NOTES

As I take a quick gander at my word count, I see I'm rapidly running out of real estate, but there are a few quick notes I'd like to make. Get ready!

Subordination: Subordination is a lot like a relative clause, except that it's a verb that takes an entire sentence as its complement. Subordinate clauses are introduced by verbs like "hope," "think," "say," "feel," "hear," want," "like," "hate," "expect," etc. Example: "I heard that onions are not the way." In English you have *that* + clause subordination, but you also have a couple of other strategies that a language may or may not use. As one example, in English, you would say "I want him to go" rather than "I want that he goes." In German, a *very* closely related language, however, this is precisely what you must say: *Ich will, dass er geht* "I want that he goes." Saying something like *Ich will ihn gehen* "I want him to go" is catastrophically impossible. The key takeaway here is that a conlanger can decide how subordination will work; it's not the same in every language.

Fronting: Almost every language allows you to drag a phrase up front to emphasize it (e.g. *I like her!* > *Her I like!*). This has nothing to do with word order or constituent order. Since spoken language is linear, what you say first *always* has the opportunity to receive special emphasis. Some languages require a change in verb morphology, a change in case, or a special particle to license this fronting; some require nothing at all but maybe special intonation.

De-emphasis: Also referred to as an anti-topic, these are phrases like *I love going there, the beach.* It's intentionally replacing some element of a sentence with a pro-form and then throwing it at the end. There's also a special kind of de-emphasis where subject pronouns are placed after a verb. I raise this because this is actually how a lot of subject-verb-agreement suffixes arise. It happened with certain verbs in Spanish, even though Spanish *already had* subject-verb agreement. Ever wonder why certain first person singular present tense verbs end in *-oy* instead of *-o*? It came from phrases like *Esto yo en la casa. Esto* was the verb, and *yo* was a de-emphatic pronoun added after the verb. It eventually reduced to *estoy.* The same is posited for a number of subject-agreement endings throughout many of the world's languages.

Commands: Imperatives are divided into positive and negative. Positive command forms are often simply the root (very basic), but they can also have agreement (usually but not always exclusively with a second person argument), or accrue unique morphology designed to make the command heard better over a long distance (adding a vowel, lengthening a vowel, adding an [s] or some other loud consonant on the end). Negative commands can be as simple as negating a positive command, but they can also be quite different. For example, Latin has a whole host of specialized forms for positive imperatives, but for negative imperatives, the verb *nōlle*, meaning "to not want," is put into the positive imperative and followed by an infinitive. Thus *scrībe* "write," but *nōlī scrībere* "do not write" (cf. *non scrībis* "you are not writing").

Tag Questions: These are basic sentences that have something like *isn't that so?*, *no?*, or *eh?* on the end. They often feature negation. Tag questions can evolve into actual yes/no question marking or simply continue as an informal alternative, but there is something important to note about negative questions in general. Some languages have a special answer that avoids the whole "you said yes, so that means no!" phenomenon. In French, for example, if one asks a basic question, *Est-ce que tu as un chat?* "Do you have a cat?," you can answer simply *oui* "yes" or *non* "no." If instead one asks a negative question like *Tu as un chat, non?* "You have a cat, no?," if you answer with either *oui* or *non*, it means you don't have a cat. If, on the other hand, you answer *si* [si], it means you *do* have a cat. The latter derives from Latin *sic* [sik] "thus," and is kind of like saying, "As you say." A conlang may or may not have a distinction like this—your choice!

There is, of course, more to say on each of these topics—and on pragmatics in general—but I've got a strict word count here, and if I go over it my editor will

Case Study

ENGÁLA NEGATION

Back in April 2019 I was hired to create a language for the witches of Freeform's *Motherland: Fort Salem*, and they granted me the unique opportunity to hire an assistant. For all other projects up to that point I'd worked alone, occasionally with help from my wife, Erin, when she wasn't busy (she, too, had a full-time job). For the most part, that's how I liked it. Since having a child (hi, Meridian! You weren't born yet when this book was first published, but thanks to Auntie Elda, you made it in!), I discovered I had to work quicker than I was accustomed. When I was working on *Game of Thrones* and *Defiance*, I'd often put in eighty-hour workweeks—not because I *had* to, mind, but because . . . well, I was conlanging! *On a TV show!* What the hell else would I want to do with my time? I loved it! As it turns out, though, toddlers don't really tolerate eighty-hour workweeks, so having an assistant seemed essential, since I had about ten days to create a full language.

Ideally, my assistant would be a conlanger with a solid grounding in linguistics who was able to learn on the fly and work quickly. I wanted someone who could easily handle the basic stuff (flesh out inflectional paradigms, figure out phonological alternations, suggest sound changes, etc.) and also be a real asset when it came to the creative end of it: semantic evolution, idioms, pragmatics—the fun stuff! After running my own search process, I hired Jessie Sams.

I'd known Jessie for some time (we once bonded over David Schulner's hit medical drama *New Amsterdam* in the midst of a traffic jam on our way to the Intercontinental Airport in Houston where I ended up missing my flight to Victoria, Texas, despite the fact that I was standing at the counter *and could see the damn plane out the window*, and yet they *still* wouldn't let me on, and the guy at the counter straight up walked away from me while I was talking to him!), but I didn't really know her as a conlanger. To say that she more than exceeded my expectations is a gross understatement. Jessie had an absolutely intuitive grasp of the way a noun class system like Irathient's can be used to flesh out a lexicon and was able to adapt quickly to creating and working with a register tone language—this despite the fact that she had never had a conlang with either. She was also able to work quickly, which was vital, as, again (I feel like I kind of glossed over this part), we had about ten days to create this language from scratch. She was nothing short of phenomenal.

As we joined the production fairly late, it wasn't long before we had a language, translated our dialogue, and had finished with the first season. This left us both wanting to work on another project, and so we decided to create something of our own. Thus the YouTube series *LangTime Studio* was born. On *LangTime Studio*, Jessie and I create a language from scratch and stream the whole process live. Our first project was a language for anthropomorphic rabbits called Engála [e.'ŋæ.la].

In episode 116, Jessie and I decided to turn our attention to negation. Up to that point, Engála had grammar for nominal marking and for verb conjugation, but we hadn't dealt with any kind of negation. As with any other naturalistic language, our first step was to figure out what kind of lexical material leads to negation. An early one we toyed with was *limhe* "leave," but we already had a lot of function words that began with l (*lu* "to," *las* "that," *li* "now," the interrogative particle *lai*) and had also used *limhe* to create our ablative preposition *linyá* "from" and our elative preposition *linyús* "out of." We didn't need another *l* function word. As we pondered other lexical sources, one of our viewers, YouTube user [i.ˈzaːk], suggested "fall" as a source—and I completely missed it until Jessie noticed it and told me about it. That seemed like an avenue worth exploring.

Syntactically, Engála is an ergative language. Thus you can have a trio of sentences like this:

*Chechenu **imé**.*
[ˈtʃe.tʃe.nu iˈme]

"**The rabbit** is sleeping."

*Chulya wika **'n imé**.*
[ˈtʃu.ʎa ˈwi.kan iˈme]

"**The rabbit** held the mouse."

*Chulya **imé** 'n wika.*
[ˈtʃu.ʎa iˈmen ˈwi.ka]

"The mouse held **the rabbit**."

The little **'n** bit is an ergative preposition that has become a suffixed clitic (it attaches to the word that precedes it if it ends in a vowel). In Engála, the argument that is most affected by the action of the verb is the one that appears closest to the verb. In the case of a word like **ogo** [ˈo.go] "fall," the most affected argument is the one that falls. The verb, however, is intransitive.

This is where things got a little difficult.

Tying falling to negation is simple enough: If one falls while attempting to walk (or hop), then one has failed to walk (or hop), meaning that it didn't happen—hence negation. Given that the one falling is causing the action to fail, though, it stands to reason that the faller must be the *cause* of the action. In the case of a transitive verb, that is often the agent, rather than the patient, which means that in Engála, negation would be nominative-accusative, whereas ordinary clauses would be ergative-absolutive.

But that can be a feature, rather than a bug! Most ergative languages are actually split-ergative in one way or another. Engála could have a split in polarity—something I hadn't seen before, but given that we were evolving it naturally, it seemed reasonable that such a thing could exist. The first step was to take the full verb and erode it a bit, turning it into an auxiliary, per YouTube user Chris Helvey's suggestion:

Perfective Aspect	Full Verb		Negative Auxiliary	
	Singular	Plural	Singular	Plural
First Person	*ogun*	*ogo*	*on*	*o*
Second Person	*oges*	*ogesís*	*wes*	*wesís*
Third Person	*ogo*	*ogosás*	*o*	*osás*

As you can see, we relied heavily on intervocalic lenition to get us our auxiliary. The next task was figuring out how it would work. We could use an invisible coordinative structure—something Jessie called an asyndetic construction, much to my delight—but that didn't seem quite right ("The rabbit fell and held the mouse" seemed like the rabbit fell first and then went on to hold the mouse). Then I remembered my old friend that I can always rely on: the de-emphatic construction. By using a nonfinite form of the verb, we could push the rest of the verb phrase to the end of the clause, giving us a literal translation of something like "The rabbit fell, holding the mouse." This is what it looked like:

O *imé chulya wika.*
['o i.'me 'tʃu.ʎa 'wi.ka]

"The rabbit **didn't** hold the mouse."

O *wika chulya imé.*
['o 'wi.ka 'tʃu.ʎa i.'me]

"The mouse **didn't** hold the rabbit."

And so we had our negation strategy: a full negative auxiliary that resulted in nominative-accusative alignment in negative clauses while retaining ergative-absolutive alignment in positive clauses. That's part of the fun in naturalistic conlanging: you never know where you'll end up!

CHAPTER V

The Written Word

INTRODUCTION

While creating the spoken languages for the Syfy show *Defiance*, I realized that the setting provided us with a unique opportunity to develop one or more novel writing systems for our aliens. In the show, eight alien species band together and seek refuge on Earth. The civilizations are at least a thousand years more advanced than Earth's, so it stands to reason that they would have discovered computing, robotics, space travel, and, it goes without saying, writing. I created sketches for the three writing systems that would feature prominently in the series—Castithan, Irathient, and Indojisnen—and showed a sample to executive producer and showrunner Kevin Murphy:

Irathient

Castithan

Indojisnen

Of course, the sample didn't look like that—that's a finished product—but fortunately Kevin was able to see the potential that existed, and so he gave me the green light. Once I'd created the fonts for each of the writing systems and handed them over to the art department, they ran with it. The writing systems show up *everywhere* in the show: on street signs; as graffiti; on playing cards— even on a series of pill bottles that will only ever be seen in the background of a few interior shots for no more than a couple seconds. The day I set foot on the set and saw all of this with my own eyes was indescribable. While my work played only a small role in it, I'll never forget the day I saw what Stephen Geaghan, Suki Parker, and the rest of the art department had done with the backlot of *Defiance*. It was the greatest professional moment of my life.

In this section, we'll take a look at what it takes to go from doodling on a page to creating a full-fledged, fully functional writing system. First I'll go over some background on the history of writing in our world, and then discuss how to create a writing system. I'll introduce some of the basics of font making, and then go over how sound, history, and writing interact in a case study on the Castithan writing system.

Before going any further, though, if you're interested in creating your own writing system and you're the type of person who describes themselves as "not artistic," worry not! Designing a good writing system has everything to do with the *system*, and nothing to do with the glyphs—and designing good fonts has more to do with copying and pasting and math than being able to draw a nice Bézier curve freehand. I firmly believe that designing writing systems is within the reach of anyone who can use a writing system— and if you can read this, you can use a writing system. So you're set!

ORTHOGRAPHY

Before we get too far in, let's discuss some terminology. The term **orthography** comes to us from Greek, where it translates to something like "correct writing" or "the correct form of writing." That translation is important to understanding the use of the term. Orthography implies a value judgment, and that value judgment is made by the users of a given language. In this book, I'm writing in the orthography for the English language. If ay disaydid to swich to som odhur form ov rayting, may editur wud pich o fit. Why? Because it's not correct—that is, it's not the form that the speakers of English agree is the correct way to write the language.

When creating a new language, the conlanger has to decide what the imaginary speakers think is correct for their own language. For example, the Dothraki have no written form of their language. This was made explicit by George R. R. Martin in the *Song of Ice and Fire* book series. Consequently, the language has no orthography. For the convenience of those of us in the real world, though, Dothraki does have a **romanization** system. A romanization is a way to transcribe a language using the Roman alphabet (what we use to write English). It exists purely to help speakers of languages whose orthographies use the Roman alphabet to read other languages that have a different orthography—or no orthography, as the case may be. While a romanization system and orthography *can* be the same thing (as they are in English), they are not generally the same thing. Below is a sample of the Arabic language written in its own orthography:

أنا مترجم في الأمم المتحدة.

Now here's that same passage written in an ad hoc romanization system I've devised to help you read what the above says:

Ana mutarjim fil'umim al-mutahida.

This is different from a narrow phonetic transcription, which would look something like this:

[ʔa.na mu.ˈtar.ʒim fil.ʔu.mim al.mu.ˈta.ħe.da]

And that, of course, is different from a translation, which would be "I am a translator for the United Nations" (a key phrase all students of Arabic learn in their first year of study).

It's important to distinguish these key terms as their functions should be quite different. For example, have you ever been reading a book with a "fictional" people in it and gotten annoyed by names like Sqrellexxx, or Mhanh'thor'acc, or Bt'uoôelỳ? If not, I envy you. This is a thing that authors will do to make names *look* foreign. And while they can't be blamed for hitting the "random" button for their fictional world, given the history of romanization systems on Earth (there is an African language called !Xóõ, after all), in the real world, where the only relevant person is the reader, such names are simply uncooperative. Unless the characters in the book use the Roman alphabet for their own languages (something that may happen, but which seems unlikely in a fantasy setting), a romanization system should be as uncreative as possible. Anything else is a layer of complexity that has no reality in the fiction. Such quirks should be saved for the *actual* orthography, if it exists.

For example, in Syfy's *Defiance* the Irathient Spirit Rider Sukar has a pet name for Irisa, one of the show's main characters. The name is *tishinka* [ti.ˈʃiŋ.ka]. In Irathient's orthography, one spells it thus:

If I were to do a direct romanization for that word, it would be *tishingkka*. Why? First, you use a different glyph for the velar nasal [ŋ] than for the alveolar nasal [n]. In English, we don't bother, when it comes before [k]. Second, Irathient doubles the glyphs for the sounds [t], [p], and [k] when they occur after nasals. The reason is lost to history (has to do with an old sound change), but such words are pronounced as if there's only one of those sounds there. *Tishingkka* is a more accurate representation of how the word is spelled in the orthography, but such a spelling would be nothing but a distraction to the actors or to anyone simply trying to learn the language. Learning the orthography of any language is a challenge, but learning a romanization system should be a mere matter of minutes, if not seconds. I favor a *purely* functional romanization, if all the romanization is doing is conveying the sound of the language. After all, learning a language is enough work as it is!

TYPES OF ORTHOGRAPHIES

Often I get questions about some of the systems I've developed that go something like, "How do you write my name in the Castithan alphabet?" Such questions make a presumption the askers are likely not aware of—namely, that Castithan's writing system is an *alphabet*. In the coming sections, I will introduce you to the different types of writing systems that exist in the world. They are many and varied, and go far beyond the alphabet.

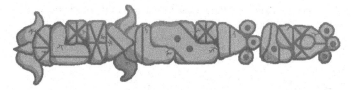

Gweydr's Stone Script (David Peterson)

Idrani's Ksatlai (Trent Pehrson)

Kēlen's Ceremonial Interlace Alphabet (Sylvia Sotomayor)

ALPHABET

Let's start with what will be most familiar. An **alphabet** is a writing system that uses a distinct glyph for a distinct sound, whether it's a vowel or a consonant. English uses an alphabet, as do all the languages of Europe. There are different alphabets, to be sure—compare the name Maria written in five different European alphabets below—but they all operate on the basis of one symbol = one sound.

Maria (Roman)

Мария (Cyrillic)

Μαρία (Greek)

Մարյա (Armenian)

მარია (Georgian)

Many alphabets on Earth have what's known as **case**. This is a confusing term, as it's identical to the term we use for noun case, but the relationship is incidental. All it refers to is a writing system having capital (majuscule) and lowercase (minuscule) letters. In our sample, the first four alphabets have an uppercase set, while Georgian does not.

In alphabets, one letter stands for one sound in an ideal case, but those letters aren't always used for the same sounds. Consider the varying pronunciations of *O* in American English:

- *tome* [tom]
- *prom* [pʰɹɑm]
- *lose* [luz]
- *Peterson* [ˈpʰi.ɹɚ.sən]
- *women* [ˈwɪ.mɨn]
- *woman* [ˈwʊ.mən]
- *ton* [tʰʌn]
- *button* [ˈbʌ.ʔn̩]

In addition, sometimes combinations of letters are used for single sounds:

- *shoe* [ʃu]
- *those* [ðoz]
- *thin* [θɪn]
- *tack* [tʰæk]
- *beautiful* [ˈbju.ɾɪ.fəɫ]

And on certain occasions, single letters are used to express series of sounds:

- *fox* [fɑks]
- *jam* [dʒæm]
- *I* [aj]

Crucially, though, alphabets take as basic the sound, rather than the syllable or some larger unit. Cases like the letter *X* in English or the letter Ψ in Greek which stands for [ps] are the exception, rather than the rule.

Historically, the alphabet is the latest writing system developed by humans. Though writing has evolved independently in several different areas, the alphabet, to the best of our knowledge, was developed once (outside of modern conscious creations, all alphabets are related to one another). For those creating a writing system for a fantasy setting, this fact should be taken into consideration. An alphabet would likely *not* be developed by an ancient society—or at least not initially. An alphabet is usually the *last* stage of development of a writing system, and often doesn't evolve at all (as has been the case with many scripts from South, East, and Southeast Asia).

ABJAD

Moving on to the next most familiar, an **abjad** or consonantal alphabet takes as its base the consonant rather than the vowel. Arabic and Hebrew both use abjadic writing systems. An abjad has one symbol for each *consonant* in a language's sound system, but not necessarily for each vowel. Vowels are treated as secondary, and, in many cases, unimportant. This might seem less than ideal to an English speaker, but consider this sentence:

Wht r y dng rght nw?

Probably no English speaker has a problem understanding that that says, "What are you doing right now?" It also probably isn't hard to see how you could take some of those same words and have them mean something totally different, as shown below:

Dng! Tht's Sgfrd nd Ry's wht tgr!

Now *dng* stands for "dang" instead of "doing," and *wht* stands for "white" instead of "what." Context helps to determine what precisely is meant, and, for the most part, there aren't really any problems.

Here's an example from Arabic. Below are the consonants *k*, *t*, and *b* written in a row (note: the script is read from right to left, and the letters connect, like English cursive):

كتب

That's the equivalent of writing *ktb* in English. What does it mean? That all depends on the context. Take a look at the examples below (remember: read from right to left, and look for the word that looks just like the one above in the examples below):

كتب رسالة.   ['ka.ta.ba ri.'sa:.la.tan]   "He wrote a letter."

رأيت كتب الرجل.   [ra.'ʔai.tu 'ku.tub ar.'ra.ʒul]   "I saw the man's books."

Notice that the word spelled كتب is pronounced ['ka.ta.ba] in the first sentence, but pronounced ['ku.tub] in the second sentence. That's because the first instance of the word means "he wrote," and the second means "books." It's hard to imagine the top sentence meaning "Books a letter," or the bottom sentence meaning "I saw he wrote the man's." The context helps determine which pronunciation is meant, and, consequently, which word is meant.

Most abjads have ways to indicate vowels if it's absolutely necessary, but they usually appear as diacritics. For example, the two different *ktb* words can be written as follows in Arabic:

كَتَبَ   ['ka.ta.ba]   "he wrote"

كُتُب   ['ku.tub]   "books"

But in day-to-day life, this is never done. Really the only place you'd see it is in elementary textbooks, or in the spellings of foreign names or words that aren't a part of common discourse.

One interesting feature of many abjads is that they will occasionally have full-fledged letters for vowels. These vocalic letters will often have consonantal uses in addition to vocalic uses, and will be used both as consonants and as vowels depending on the context they appear in. In Arabic, the two simplest ones to work with are the glyphs for [w] and [j], which double as the long vowels [uː] and [iː]. Here are examples of each:

و = [w]/[uː]   ي & ﻳ = [j]/[iː]

يويو   ['juː.juː]   "sparrow hawk"

والدي   ['waː.li.diː]   "my father"

Because abjadic scripts tend to give short shrift to the vowels, the scripts can be more economical, albeit less precise. As with alphabets, they can be the end point of an evolutionary chain, but they also appear at an earlier stage of development than alphabets. Such scripts work very well for languages with smaller vowel inventories, and work far less well for vowel-heavy languages.

ABUGIDA

The most common type of writing system found in India and many parts of Southeast Asia is the **abugida**. An abugida (also referred to as an alphasyllabary) is a script that, for the most part, adheres to the maxim that one glyph = one syllable. An abugida, though, will have a very obvious base glyph with a more or less predictable set of variations. The base glyph is usually a consonant, though it need not be, as vowels *do* have separate glyphs (for when two vowels come next to each other, for example). Below is an example of some syllables from a number of different abugidas:

	[ka]	[ki]	[ku]	[ke]
Hindi	क	कि	कु	के
Tamil	க	கி	கு	கெ
Sinhalese	ක	කි	කු	කෙ
Tibetan	ཀ	ཀི	ཀུ	ཀེ
Kannada	ಕ	ಕಿ	ಕು	ಕೆ
Malayalam	ക	കി	കു	കെ
Castithan	ꓱ	ꓱ	ꓳ	ꓱ

As you may have been able to guess, the first six of these scripts are related (the last, of course, is one of my scripts for *Defiance*). All seven scripts, though, have two things in common. The first is that the base consonantal form, whatever it happens to be, remains constant, with mandatory diacritics being added to produce CV syllables. The second is that the base form on its own stands for a syllable, not a bare consonant. This is the crucial difference between an alphabet and an abugida: the most basic form of any glyph is always a syllable, never a bare consonant.

Abugidas may vary as to which vowel is taken as its inherent vowel for a base glyph. In all the languages above, a short [a] is taken as the inherent vowel. As shown above, a vowel diacritic may combine with a base glyph in any number of ways, including coming before the base glyph. A base glyph may also combine with a vowel that comes before a consonant, or after a consonant, though the latter is much more common. Here's an example of each from the *Defiance* abugidas:

Castithan Abugida   Irathient Abugida

[da]   [de]   [əd]   [ed]

Abugidas will differ in how they deal with single consonants. For example, neither of the *Defiance* scripts has any special marking for single consonants. The Irathient script allows a reader to pronounce any glyph as either a bare consonant or a bare consonant preceded by the reduced vowel [ə]. In Castithan, all characters have an inherent or specified vowel, and phonological rules determine whether the vowels are pronounced. Hindi's Devanagari script, on the other hand, has a special symbol called a virāma which indicates that the inherent [a] vowel has been suppressed, as shown below:

क	क्	प	प्	च	च्
[ka]	[k]	[pa]	[p]	[tʃa]	[tʃ]

Overall, the key to remember with an abugida is that the base glyph is the major feature, but that the vowel diacritics are *never* optional. That plus the fact that a base glyph stands for a syllable, not a sound, are the key distinctions between an abjad and an abugida.

SYLLABARY

A full **syllabary** is like an abugida, except that there are no base glyphs. Instead, each symbol stands for a full syllable, and there may be little to no relationship between symbols that encode the same consonant or vowel. The most canonical examples are either of Japanese's kana systems: katakana or hiragana. Below is a sample of some of the glyphs in Japanese's hiragana:

か	き	く	け	こ
[ka]	[ki]	[ku]	[ke]	[ko]
ま	み	む	め	も
[ma]	[mi]	[mu]	[me]	[mo]
な	に	ぬ	ね	の
[na]	[ni]	[nu]	[ne]	[no]
ら	り	る	れ	ろ
[ɾa]	[ɾi]	[ɾu]	[ɾe]	[ɾo]

As you can see, this system is kind of a mess. It looks like a little loop is the only thing that distinguishes め [me] from ぬ [nu], and while ね [ne] and れ [re] look related, we don't see the little vertical stick elsewhere, really. A loop appears to turn ろ [ro] into る [ru], and we see a little line on か [ka], な [na], and ら [ra] that *could* be indicative of an [a] vowel, but it's not there for ま [ma]. Basically the association between the form and meaning is arbitrary and must be memorized, just like an alphabet. The only difference is that each glyph stands for a syllable, not a sound.

Outside of the two Japanese scripts, there are no pure syllabaries in use by any natural language today that wouldn't have an asterisk next to them. For example, the Vai syllabary, used to write the West African Vai language, is barely used today, and was a conscious construction of one man in the 1830s. The Yi syllabary is currently used to write at least one form of the Yi language in China, but it was developed in 1974. The Cherokee syllabary used to write Cherokee was developed by Sequoyah, who based the letterforms on the letters in an English-language Bible he owned, and so this too was a conscious construction. For whatever reason, it seems that pure syllabaries are disfavored as natural writing systems, despite the simplicity of their construction.

One possible reason that syllabaries don't appear in greater numbers is the difficulty such systems have in rendering coda consonants. For example, if we wanted to build a syllabary for English that would handle coda consonants, the resultant system would need more than one thousand glyphs—all of which would need to be memorized. As nonsensical as English's spelling system is, a syllabary—even a regular one—wouldn't be an improvement. The same is true of many languages.

If a syllabary is going to encode coda consonants, it has a few options. One option is to do what Japanese does. Japanese has, in effect, only one coda consonant—a nasal—so it has a letter to spell its coda nasal, ん. Thus, Japanese's kana systems can be said to be pure syllabaries with one additional letter. Other potential solutions include synharmonic spelling (e.g. a spelling of *sa-ba* at the end of a word will be understood to be *sab*, since the vowel in the second syllable is the same), or just not writing the codas at all. This is apparently how Linear B was used to encode Ancient Greek (i.e. not very well). Despite their impracticality, syllabaries remain fruitful possibilities for language creators, depending on the phonology of the language.

COMPLEX SYSTEMS

Any natural language writing system is bound to be more complicated than its label implies. The very fact that we as a people have allowed a movie with the title *Se7en* to exist should be cause for deep concern. The fact that it can make any kind of sense simply points up the fact that learning the twenty-six letters of the English alphabet is *not* enough to understand how to use and interact with our writing system.

But beyond innovative uses of the systems already discussed, there are systems that exist that are already fairly radical. One obvious one is the system of Chinese characters employed by the various Sinitic languages. In this system, which comprises more than 100,000 characters (not a typo), a glyph can stand for a syllable, a word, a concept, or a piece of a word. Sometimes a change in glyph is only indicative of a different meaning, rather than a different pronunciation (compare spellings in English like *here* and *hear* or *their, they're,* and *there*):

- 籲 [yˈl] *"to implore"*
- 鬱 [yˈl] *"gloomy"*

Notice both of these words are pronounced the same; they're just "spelled" differently.

Some systems, like Egyptian hieroglyphs, have different systems layered one on top of the other. Hieroglyphic features an abjad (a consonantal alphabet), along with a series of glyphs that stand for two, three, or four consonant groups. In addition, it has a series of **pictographs**, which are glyphs that depict what they stand for.

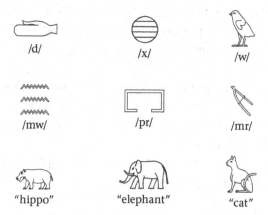

For the sake of accuracy, a usual Egyptian pictograph would have some sort of a phonetic clue as to how it was pronounced in the spelling of the word. The word for "cat," for example, was spelled like this:

/mjw/ "cat"

In order from left to right, the four glyphs that make up the word for "cat" serve the following functions:

1. ⊖ is a biliteral sign that stands for /mj/.

2. ⎮ is a sign for the sound /j/, and is there to remind you how the sound for ⊖ is pronounced.

3. 🐦 is a sign for the sound /w/ and is serving a purely phonetic function.

4. 🐈 is a cat, to remind you that this is the word for "cat."

Most full words written in hieroglyphs are written in this way. A lot of redundant information is built in to help writers and readers keep track of the comparatively large list of glyphs that constitute the system.

While the glyphs in a complex system can be pictographic, often they're not—or are not obviously so (consider modern Chinese). Glyphs can be built up in various ways, as illustrated by one of my older languages, Kamakawi.

In Kamakawi, some of the glyphs are pictographs, and their designations are fairly obvious:

keva	tetu	uvo
"shark"	"shrimp"	"swordfish"

Others are formed in a variety of ways. For example, Kamakawi has a supplementary syllabary used for certain words and in conjunction with other types of glyphs. These syllabic glyphs have been used to form complex glyphs that spell out words:

po	+	te	=	pote
—		—		"fight"

Other glyphs are formed by combinations of meanings, even if the words whose glyphs are used to create the new glyph have nothing in common with the new glyph's pronunciation:

ta	+	maka	=	alama
"sand"		"crab"		"sand crab"

Above, even though neither the words *ta* nor *maka* appear in the word *alama*, the meanings associated with their glyphs are combined to form the new glyph for a sand crab. This association exists only in the writing system, not in the language proper.

Still other glyphs are formed by changing the orientation of fully formed glyphs. Here, for example, is a complex syllabic glyph, like *pote* above:

mo	+	*ka*	=	*moka*
—		—		"metal"

And here's a word that's formed by flipping the glyph for *moka* horizontally and vertically:

late

"rust"

When a glyph is turned thus, the idea is that the opposite or a negative version of the word is meant. Thus, if you know *moka* is "metal," you can look at this glyph and know it has something to do with the opposite of metal, or something deleterious with respect to metal—that is, rust.

Many glyphs in Chinese and in other complex scripts like Kamakawi's have stories like these. Ultimately, the construction of a writing system is a *conscious* decision on the part of a group of speakers, unlike language. It's subject to the whims of evolution, like everything else, but efforts to consciously change a writing system are much more effective than efforts to change a language ever are.

As a final note on complex systems, the larger the number of glyphs in a system, the more redundancy is built in. Memorizing twenty-six letters is child's play. Memorizing ten semipredictable yet distinct forms for a set of thirty-three glyphs is challenging.

Memorizing more than ten thousand glyphs is soul-crushing. To make the task possible, systems are set in place to aid the learner in assimilating and maintaining the information as quickly and efficiently as possible.

USING A SYSTEM

Designing glyphs is only one part of the system. Before leaving writing systems in general, I just wanted to note a couple things about how systems are used. For example, in English, we put spaces in between each word. Notallwritingsystemsdothis. Those that don't tend to have glyphs that are fairly evenly spaced. Chinese, for example, doesn't put any spaces between its glyphs, but every glyph fits in a nice little glyph box that doesn't impinge on the space of any other glyphs. As a result, adding extra space is unimportant.

The direction that one writes also is not fixed. In English and most Western languages, we write from left to right. Arabic and Hebrew are written from right to left. A nice illustration of the difference can be shown with Hindi and Urdu—in effect, the same language written in two different scripts:

मैं खा रहा हूँ।

میں کھا رہا ہوں۔

Both the top and bottom line say [mɛ̃ khaː ˈrɛ.haː hũː], which means "I'm eating." The difference is that Urdu, on the bottom, is written with a variant of the Arabic script that is written from right to left, and Hindi is written with Devanagari, which is written from left to right.

Languages can also be written from top to bottom. Both Chinese and Japanese use this as a stylistic variant. Mongolian traditionally is written from top to bottom. Egyptian hieroglyphs were frequently written from left to right, right to left, *and* top to bottom (both right-facing and left-facing). Writing from the bottom to the top is possible, but extremely rare. All directions exist as a possibility, though.

Some other variables to consider when developing a writing system are where the next line will start. In English, we write from left to right, and the next line starts on the bottom; it could very well start on the top. In book binding, one can also decide where the next page will be. Japanese books are fairly similar to English books, in that writing usually goes from left to right and then goes from top to bottom. The next page in a book, though, is in the opposite location an English speaker would expect, leading to manga books appearing "backwards" to English-speaking readers.

Something else to consider is what happens to the letters at the end of a line. What if, for example, when one got to the end of the line writing from left to right, one started over and wrote from right to left on the next line? Such systems existed, and that style of writing is referred to as boustrophedon. An example is given below:

Don't look now, but
ᵷuᴉoᵷ sᴉ ǝɔuǝʇuǝs sᴉɥʇ
crazy on you, just like
¡ʇɹɐǝH

All of this is in play—plus whatever else you can imagine.

Practically speaking, though (if you don't want your parade rained on, stop reading here; if you can deal with it, turn up the Mazzy Star and let the rain parade begin), a system that works *exactly* the way English's does (distinct glyphs written from left to right, with new rows appearing below, and the characters always facing the same way) will be the easiest to fontify and work with. If you don't care about creating a font or using a word processor, there are really no constraints. Font creation programs and word processors and web browsers and graphics programs, though, *despise* writing systems that don't work *exactly* like English's. There's probably a better way to do the boustrophedon example I constructed above, but using Photoshop Elements, I just created four distinct text lines in four different layers and flipped them around till they looked the way I wanted them to. There is no boustrophedon setting in Word (though I think there is a paperclip that laughs at you if you try to search for one). Pencil and paper is far superior when it comes to working with "deviant" systems. There's nothing truly deviant about them, of course, it's just that computing systems don't support them. We're gradually getting better and better, but the fact that inserting a single word of Arabic into an English sentence *destroys* the entire paragraph's formatting and makes me want to rip out and devour my still-beating heart tells me that we've got a long way to go before our programs and apps can deal with the great variety of writing styles available to us.

DRAFTING A PROTO-SYSTEM

Just as a naturalistic language starts off with a proto-language, so does a naturalistic writing system start off with a proto-system. This is how I created the Castithan and Irathient scripts for *Defiance* and the Sondiv script for *Star-Crossed* (the Indojisnen script for *Defiance* was a postdigital creation by the Indogene people, and so needed no proto-stage), and it's the best first step to creating a naturalistic orthography.

Before you sit down to create glyphs, several questions have to be answered first—specifically, who are the speakers of the language who need a writing system? Where do they live? What plants and animals are around them? What resources are available to them? These are the same kinds of questions a language creator has to answer, but in drafting a writing system, they take on a different significance.

If you look at the history of our writing system—the Roman alphabet—you'll discover that it came from an old pictographic system. Check this out:

Proto-Sinaitic 18th Century BCE	Phoenician 13th Century BCE	Greek 8th Century BCE
/ʔalp/ "ox"	/ʔ/	A
/mem/ "water"	/m/	M
/ʕen/ "eye"	/ʕ/	O

The Proto-Sinaitic system utilized pictographs, and Canaanite speakers were happy with that system. When the Phoenicians got hold of it, they took some of those pictographs and formed an abjadic writing system from them, taking the first consonant of each pictographic word and turning it into a consonantal letter. When the Greeks inherited the Phoenician system, they saw letters for a bunch of consonants that weren't in Greek (e.g. /ʔ/ and /ʕ/), but no letters for vowels, so the Greeks took the unneeded consonant letters and turned them into vowels.

Making reference to Proto-Sinaitic as stage 1 and Phoenician as stage 2, we can now discuss where a language creator begins. Obviously, for any type of system, one can always start at stage 1. The system that began as a simple pictographic system went all the way to an abjad in Hebrew, an abugida in Hindi, and an alphabet in English. An old series of pictographs affords one a *lot* of latitude. Certainly if one wants a complex system like that of Chinese or Egyptian, a simpler pictographic system is the way to start. Aside from a few art experiments (the works of Xu Bing, for instance), we've never seen a language go from an alphabetic/abjadic orthography to a complex/ideographic/logographic orthography; we have, however, seen the opposite, so starting at stage 1 keeps your options open. Starting at stage 2, though, is not a bad way to go if you haven't got all the time in the world. That's where I began for both Castithan and Irathient. Given that we'd be picking up with these aliens about a thousand years *after* they mastered space travel, going into their proto-history wasn't feasible (working on a TV show means working with deadlines). Starting with a stage 2 system wasn't a problem, though, and it helped to add to the realism of the systems.

In order to start drafting glyphs (after one has settled on stage 1 or stage 2), the next subject one has to tackle is resources—specifically, what did the people who speak this language have to write *on* and to write *with*? The importance of these two questions *cannot* be overstated when it comes to drafting a writing system. For example, have you ever seen cuneiform? It looks like this:

I don't know what any of that means or how it's pronounced, but just look at it. Who could possibly *tolerate* a system like that?! It looks so impractical! And it is, if you're trying to draw these things with a pen or pencil on paper. But that's not how cuneiform was written. Instead of paper, writers used a wet clay tablet upon which impressions could be made, and the thing they used to make these impressions had an end that looked a lot like this:

It was a long, blunted reed called a stylus that had a triangular end. If that was your implement and you were making impressions into wet clay, you should be able to see why it'd be easier to write ▷ than something like *R*, for example.

Old forms of writing often included making impressions into wet clay tablets; carving onto solid materials like rocks, bones, shells, or wood; or painting on uneven surfaces like rock faces. Whether you're developing a stage 1 or stage 2 system, the shapes you come up with should suit the writing implement and writing surface. Drawing shapes freehand was simply not an option for users of cuneiform. Similarly, the Ogham runes used to write Old Irish contained no curved characters at all. Since the runes were cut into wood or stone, curved characters would be impractical, or at least very difficult. An example of some of the runes is shown below:

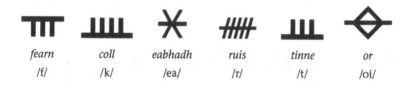

fearn	*coll*	*eabhadh*	*ruis*	*tinne*	*or*
/f/	/k/	/ea/	/r/	/t/	/oi/

Someone painting on a cave wall, though, would have no problem with curvilinear shapes. The original medium *strongly* delimits what's possible in a proto-system, whether it's stage 1 or stage 2.

Creating the glyphs goes hand in hand with the language as it exists when the glyphs are supposed to have been created. Conspiracy theories aside, there are no cave paintings of catapults or airplanes. The things ancient civilizations chose to encode with writing were things they had and which were important: livestock, plants, goods, family members, tools, etc. An advanced alien civlization would likely have discovered writing centuries before they discovered machinery, let alone space travel. A stage 1 writing system has to start there.

For stage 2, all one has to do is establish the phonemic inventory that was current at that stage. In English, for example, we spell words like *wet* and *whet* differently because they were actually pronounced as different words at the time that we started regularizing our spelling system. If a language has a phoneme [h] when writing is encoded, the stage 2 writing system will probably have a glyph for [h], whether or not the modern language has that phoneme any longer.

Finally, remember that an alphabet, an abugida, and a syllabary are a later development than an abjad or a pictographic system. Most older systems were *really* imperfect. Often words that sounded similar were spelled the same; many details considered important by modern standards were completely omitted from the system;

writing direction was a matter of style; glyph shapes weren't standard; and spellings themselves weren't standardized, either. All of
these "necessities" are later developments. This makes proto-systems
simpler to develop, but more difficult to understand.

When it comes to the glyphs themselves, remember: simpler is
better. Simple pictures or simple shapes were how *all* our systems
began their existence. The stylized elements arose as a matter of
course—something we'll examine in the next section.

EVOLVING A MODERN SYSTEM

There are exactly two things that have revolutionized writing systems in our world: (1) using one system to write a language for
which it wasn't intended; and (2) technological advancement. Both
of these steps can be utilized to take a proto-system and evolve it.

Looking back at cuneiform, that system started out as a pictographic system. Here are three key stages of its development:

The first stage on the left there was written on clay tablets with something sharp, but they were drawn, not stamped. The second stage is
when the glyphs were put onto walls. The curves and details are
gone, primarily to make it easier to carve. Then the last stage is the
wedge stage which we're familiar with, and you can see how what
they were trying to do was create the stone carving using the wedge-
shaped reeds. The lines are all there, basically, they just look funky.
Eventually this stage would evolve too, as they tried to make it easier
for reed stamping, and pretty soon people didn't even know that
what they were stamping was supposed to represent a human head.

Changing either writing implements or the writing surface
requires a revision of the *entire* system. In evolving a system, then,
you start out with a stage 1 or stage 2 system and make a decision

about what comes next: A move from stone walls to clay tablets? From tablets to paper? From a stick to a stamping implement? From a stamping implement to a brush? A chisel to a stylus? Once the decision is made, the system will start to morph and take shape.

For those designing their own systems, it's my strong recommendation to try, as practically as possible, to find the actual implements you're considering and try them out. Trying to write one system with a different implement will prove quite illuminating. For example, when you move to pen and paper, it's *really* easy to see how cursive emerges. Writing happens so quickly that picking the pen up between *every single word* is just a bother! Natural connections will emerge of necessity. Whether or not those connections become a part of the system (as they did in Arabic) or not (as they didn't in Roman type) depends a bit on how quickly the language's speakers develop typesetting and on happenstance. These are decisions the language creator must make.

For an example of how to evolve a script over the centuries, I implore you to take a look at this absolutely *outstanding* chart of the evolution of the Tamil script (and *thank you* to Wikipedia user Rrjanbiah for taking a photo of this chart and releasing it into the public domain)!

HISTORY OF TAMIL SCRIPT

A photographic chart showing the evolution of Tamil script glyphs from BC 3rd Century through AD 19th Century. The left portion covers vowels (a ā i ī u ū e ē ai o ō), and the right portion covers consonants (k ṅ c ñ ṭ ṇ t n p m y r l v ḻ ḷ ṟ ṉ), with rows for each century: BC 3rd C, AD 2nd C, AD 3rd C, AD 4th C, AD 5th C, AD 6th C, AD 7th C, AD 8th C, AD 9th C, AD 10th C, AD 11th C, AD 12th C, AD 13th C, AD 14th C, AD 15th C, AD 16th C, AD 17th C, AD 18th C, AD 19th C.

Enjoy the whole thing, but just *look* at some of the incredible changes! Look at the column headed by η. In the third century BCE, the thing was basically a capital I, and now it looks like this: ணை! In the ṭ column, a character that looks like a big capital C ends up looking like ட, and in the n column, a character that in the fourth century CE looked like a capital L now looks like this: ந! It's insanity! Or it would be, if you weren't able to look at the incremental changes that occurred to each character along the way.

You can see that there are certain points in time where a greater variety of changes occurred. For example, around the ninth and tenth centuries CE, lots of characters get noticeably funkier. One important driving force in the funkification of Tamil's script was a shift to writing on palm leaves, which were apparently *really* easy to puncture. As a result, writers would try to have fewer points—so fewer places where you'd pick your writing implement up and put it down. This helped preserve the document (fewer tears led to a longer-lasting writing surface). Consequently, straight edges and sharp connections got smoothed out a bit. Evidently they switched to more permanent paper by the thirteenth century CE, because, as you can see, the straight edges returned. But by then the damage was done, and the system started on a path to becoming what it is today.

Once you've settled on a writing utensil and medium that's supposed to last for several centuries, the key to evolving a writing system is the same as evolving a language. Each generation will learn how to write based on how the previous generation writes, not based on how the original generation wrote. What you need to do is simulate how the generations hand down knowledge from one to the next, and how each generation adds innovations. The latter is simple. If you're working with pen and paper, for example, just try to write *faster*. Work with the script. See what happens naturally when you increase the speed of transcription; what your hand does to try to form the same characters in half the amount of time you usually do. Once you've got this down, look at the quickly written version of the old characters and form a new standard version of the script from those quickly written characters. After that, repeat the process until the script looks the way it ought.

Moving a script from one language to another is a great way to stretch a script to its limits. The Roman alphabet itself is just a modification of the Greek alphabet—as is the Cyrillic alphabet. The Roman script was developed for Latin, to which it was well suited. As it was extended to languages like Spanish, French, Italian, Romanian, English, German, Swedish, Albanian, Finnish, Turkish, Hungarian, Vietnamese—you name it—the script was stretched to its very limits. And so digraphs were introduced, as well as a supplemental cast of thousands: é, ê, à, ɗ, ü, ß, ä, ø, ı, ñ, u̇, ž, etc. (Side note: Many diacritics—including vocalic modifications in abugidas and abjads—are formed from shrunk-down versions of other letters. The tilde on top of the ñ began its existence as a second letter n written directly above the main n.)

The same principle can work for a created script. One fun trick to do is to create a sound system and writing system for a different proto-language and then use that writing system with the language one is actually creating. It will of necessity need to expand—or contract—in order to fit the sound system and phonotactics of the new language, and that will help to produce a realistic spelling system and little irregularities here and there.

Ultimately, it's up to the creator to decide when the script is finished. The nice thing is that, unlike a lexicon of thousands of words, there is usually a fixed set of glyphs, so it's possible to produce iteration after iteration without spending too much time. A writing system is probably the one area of language where a conlanger can reproduce a *perfect* example of a realistic linguistic subsystem.

TYPOGRAPHY

Movable type changed humanity's relationship to writing irrevocably, so at this stage it's hard to conceive of writing without thinking about typesetting. In order to create a realistic system, one has to start at the oldest stages, but the truth is, we now spend most of our lives working with some sort of computer. As a conlanger, dealing with virtual typesetting is inevitable.

In this section, I'll give you a brief introduction to font making, but be warned: it can be *quite* difficult. I'm not really a math guy, but getting deep into font making is kind of like being Neo and seeing the Matrix as just a mess of numbers (sorry for that spoiler, if you're reading this in the year 1999). I spend more time on my calculator app than with the mouse when I'm creating a large font. If you want to create a more or less WYSIWYG font, you can probably find an online resource with a web interface that will let you create a simple font for free. If you want more, keep reading.

To start, let me define a couple of terms that are a part of our everyday vocabulary. A **writing system** is an abstract entity: a loose set of rules for how a number of glyphs are supposed to look, and how they're supposed to fit together to form words. An **orthography** is a specific set of rules about how a writing system is used to encode a language. A **font** is a single instantiation of a writing system. On a computer, we can flip through tons of fonts: Helvetica, Palatino, Times, etc. Each of those is a single, unified encoding of the Roman alphabet. They look different because they've been designed by different people for different purposes. When talking about a created language, there's usually only one font (i.e. not a lot of language creators create different fontified versions of their writing systems, since the one is tough enough). Even so, that font is not synonymous with the writing system: it's just one version of it. And just as there are thousands of fonts with which to write the Roman alphabet, so could there be thousands of fonts to write Tolkien's Tengwar script. The original version of a constructed script need not be the *only* version of a constructed script.

All the font programs I've worked with make use of the traditional U.S. letterboard (though most are now updating to Unicode, which is a good thing). The first step in creating a font, then, will be mapping the sound system of a conlang to the letterboard. Since I'm an English speaker and use a Qwerty keyboard, what I do first is develop a romanization system for the language I'm working with, and then map the romanization system to the letterboard. Technically, this is dishonest: when you type an *a* on your keyboard, it returns Unicode point 0061, which should look roughly like *a*—not ȧ, which is what you get if you type *a* in the font I created for the

Sondiv language from *Star-Crossed*. The proper method—assigning all the characters to points in the Private Use Area of Unicode and creating either a special keyboard layout or a series of contextual ligatures to activate the correct keys by using the romanization system—takes *way* too much work, though, and not all word processors will recognize the result. Instead, I always decide to do something like this, as I did for Sondiv:

Sondiv Character	Phonetic Equivalent	Keystroke
౭	/a/	*a*
Ƴ	/b/	*b*
⊕	/k/	*c*
Ψ	/d/	*d*
௮	/e/	*e*
௡	/f/	*f*
O	/g/	*g*

A mapping like this makes Sondiv look like an alphabet, even though it's an abjad. It also ignores the fact that ௡ is only ever used in foreign words, ௮ is just a rarely used ligature, and ⊕ is a duplicate, since there is no equivalent of the English letter *c* in Sondiv. The font program expects the font to be an alphabet, and so it works like an alphabet. That makes creating a nonalphabetic font very difficult.

That aside, this will produce a typeable font. Until any of my writing systems make it into Unicode, that's good enough for me.

Once the mapping is set, it's time to start drawing the glyphs. In order to do so, I'm going to teach you the two most important words every font maker ever learns. Ready? Here they are:

1. *COPY*

2. *PASTE*

You may think I'm joking, but I am deadly serious. If I haven't been fonting in a while and I return to it, I often forget these two vital words, to my detriment. I end up sitting there fooling around with the darn mouse and producing crap, when really all I should be doing is copying and pasting. More on this in a second.

While programs will differ, the glyph window in a font editor looks something like this:

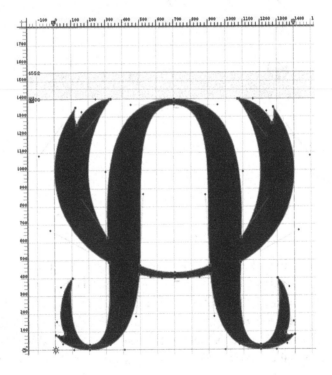

You've got a grid, an x and y axis with points, and a lot of space. The character shown above is the glyph for the [z] sound in Sondiv. The circles and boxes you see on the glyph are connection points, and the glyph does what it does all based on math. For example, the point at the very top, which I'll call point A, interacts with the two points on the right and left (points C and B, respectively).

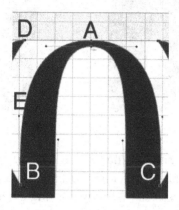

Each of these points (A, B, and C) have little lines sprouting from them with a plus at the end (the pluses for point A are very near to the two points that form the wingtips for the semicircle—ignore those). On the left side, there are points D and E. If you grab point E and drag it up with the mouse, the left side of the hump will get beefier, and will end up being taller than the hump on the right side.

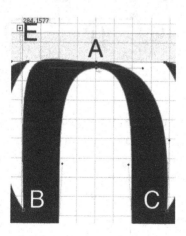

If you tug on point D, on the other hand, the hump on the left gets fatter, pushing into the territory occupied by the left wing of the [z].

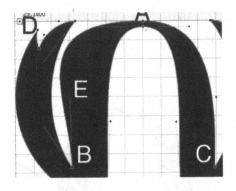

For this one character in the font for Sondiv, I produced ten different characters that were either variations on [z], or were built using the same pattern as [z], to say nothing of the characters that were very close in shape. If I'd had to draw all of them by hand, I would've invented a different writing system.

Instead, I just created the one and copied and pasted where relevant.

But it doesn't actually stop there. Just as you can copy a whole character and move it from glyph to glyph, so can you copy *pieces* of characters. There are probably twenty or so unique pieces that make up the Sondiv writing system, and most of them are shown below:

section	dieresis	copyright	ordfeminine	guillemotleft

twosuperior	threesuperior	acute	mu	paragraph

onehalf	threequarters	questiondown	Agrave	Aacute

Egrave	Eacute	Ecircumflex	Edieresis	Igrave

That probably looks like a whole mess of nothing, but the truth is you can use these pieces (or parts of these pieces) to build just about every glyph in Sondiv. The circle glyph that I stuffed under Agrave for this example shows up *everywhere*. And the best part is I only had to create it once. The top half of that circle forms the main hump for the [z] glyph, but the midpoints have been stretched. After that, I took a quarter of the circle, rotated it, and added it to the bottom of each half of the hump to have it curve outward. Bit by bit you can copy and paste a few small pieces into a full writing system, and render perfectly what one can only do imperfectly by hand (or by mouse).

Once the glyphs are built, what remains is extremely complex, so I'll simply mention it. **Kerning** is a set of rules that tell you how close one character is supposed to sit to a different character. If the rules aren't set manually, a word processing program will line all glyphs up at their edges. The difference is quite noticeable, as can be seen with the Sondiv sample below.

Above, the second glyph is supposed to nestle right next to the first, with its little dippy-doo on top pointing to the middle of the first glyph. Kerning is what tells the characters to behave in this way. Without kerning, the left-most edge of the second glyph touches the right-most edge of the first, resulting in an infelicitous pairing.

The second complex bit about fonting applies to abjads, abugidas, and cursive scripts. When we write in cursive in English, we have to learn four forms of each letter, depending on whether the letter begins a word, comes at the end of a word, comes in the middle of a word, or is sitting by itself. The reason is that the letter must connect to what's around it. That's easy to handwrite; very difficult for a font. In order to make it work, the font itself must make use of what are called **contextual ligatures**. A contextual ligature is a little bit of code that basically says "Change X to Y in the environment Z." Contextual ligatures are the difference between an Arabic word like /kita:b/ being rendered correctly, like so:

Or incorrectly, as below:

If you're someone who codes on a regular basis, creating a series of ligatures may seem relatively simple, albeit tedious. If you're me, it's rage-inducing. The darn things never work the way they're supposed to work! The reason is that a ligature is a bit of coded information that tells a word processor how a font should be rendered when two characters come in contact with each other. Since we have a fixed set of writing systems in the world, all Unicode-compliant fonts and all word processors are built to expect those—

and *only* those—ligatures. This is why you can write in Arabic, Hindi, Sinhalese, etc., without any problems on any modern word processor. An invented script will have invented ligatures. When *that* happens, most word processors are just done. They can't even. Just no. It's as if they have some problem with us humans using a tool for its unintended purpose! (And eighties folk thought computers would take over . . .)

Hope springs eternal, though, so if you want to try to use ligatures in your font, this is how to do it. As an example, I'll use the Yesuþoh script I created for the Væyne Zaanics language used in Nina Post's *The Zaanics Deceit*. The language is a conlang in the fictional universe of the book, and the writing system is invented, as well. The creators wanted a script that was hard or impossible to decipher, and so they built in a lot of odd rules. One rule sees a glyph for [k] change its form depending on whether it comes after a "light" or "dark" vowel (their terms for front and back vowels, respectively). The font, then, has to be able to detect whether the [k] glyph comes after a vowel from the group [æ, æː, e, eː, i, iː], or after a vowel from the group [ɑ, ɑː, o, oː, u, uː], and then change accordingly.

The first step is to teach the font what the groups are, since it has no way of knowing this. To start the process, I created a feature called rlig in the OpenType panel (where OpenType features are defined). This feature is recognized by most word processors (for those that don't, a different feature, liga, can be used). After opening this feature, I defined two groups by labeling them with an @ sign followed by their names (DARK and LIGHT) and listing the members for each group in brackets:

```
feature rlig {
#GROUPS
@DARK = [a alg o olg u ulg];
@LIGHT = [ae aelg e elg i ilg];
} rlig;
```

If I didn't know how to do this and saw that box, my head would explode, because it looks *super* computery. Basically, though, anything with # in front of it is just a note and isn't recognized as a part of the code (I use it to let me know what parts are what). Every line has to end with ;, otherwise it will all be treated as the same line. The curly brackets {} open and close a feature, and square brackets [] are used elsewhere to enclose other material, such as group members. The letters above are actual names recognized by all word processors, so a is always recognized as a lowercase *a*, etc. The ones that have lg after them are long vowels, and are names for special characters found only in this font. They won't be rendered without the ligature information. Thus, typing @LIGHT = [ae aelg e elg i ilg]; into the rlig feature is basically the same as saying the light vowels of Væyne Zaanics are [æ, æː, e, eː, i, iː].

Once those vowels have been labeled, they can be called as a group by their group name. So the next step is to tell the font what to do with the [k] glyph. Here's how the code is expanded to do so:

```
feature rlig {
#GROUPS
@DARK = [a alg o olg u ulg];
@LIGHT = [ae aelg e elg i ilg];
#SUBSTITUTIONS
substitute k' @DARK by kdk;
substitute k' @LIGHT by klt;
} rlig;
```

The code there says that in the event that k is followed by anything from the group @DARK, replace k with kdk (and ditto with klt when k comes before a @LIGHT group member). The syntax is precise, and the little apostrophe ' is the thing that tells the font what needs to be substituted out, but otherwise that's how it works. The result looks like this:

k [k]	+	ii [iː]	=	kii [kiː]

k [k]	+	o [o]	=	ko [ko]

On the left is what [k] looks like when it comes before a consonant (its default form). When you add a vowel after it, the character changes dynamically (on the screen) depending on whether the vowel falls into the class @LIGHT or @DARK.

Knowing the kind of power that these sets of functions have (and I haven't even come close to describing everything OpenType features can do), you can probably imagine any number of things that a font can do: change the form of a character at the edge of a word; change a full consonantal glyph to its reduced form in front of another consonant; make two vowel glyphs coalesce to form another vowel glyph; produce automatic smart quotes conditioned by the font. There are tons of possibilities, and really it takes a constructed script to take advantage of all of them.

To say I've just scratched the surface of font making is a gross understatement. The online manual for the program I use is *literally* 923 pages long—and that's just to teach you how to use *that* particular program! While the learning curve is pretty steep, it's possible to produce something minimally functional without getting too deep into the ins and outs of font making. And, from experience, I can tell you there are few things more satisfying than pulling up a new word processing document and typing in the font of a script *you* created.

Case Study

THE EVOLUTION OF THE CASTITHAN WRITING SYSTEM

When I realized there was a possibility that I could create writing systems for the languages I was creating for *Defiance*, I had to stop and take a deep breath. Creating writing systems is probably my favorite aspect of conlanging, and creating fonts is something that I'd been working on for over a decade. Even so, creating not just one, but *three* fonts for a major production like *Defiance* was daunting—incredible, but daunting. I had to think carefully about what exactly I was going to do.

As usual, whenever I start with any aspect of a language, I started with the people. The script I created for the Indogenes was a chance to just have some sci-fi fun. In the show, the Indogenes are a race of aliens that have, for centuries, been modifying themselves genetically to have superior sight, hearing, dexterity, etc. Their eyes can function as microscopes, and their hands are a thousand times more precise than the best human surgeon's. Since they're so keen on "improving" themselves, it made sense that they would have totally reworked whatever writing system they had to suit their new abilities. Consequently, their writing system is completely unnatural, and could never have evolved—and can't even be written by hand with any consistency, unless you have the keen manual dexterity of an Indogene. Their script is a series of interlocking hexagons that's featural, meaning that if you know how the pieces work, you can look at a hex and tell how it's pronounced, as shown below.

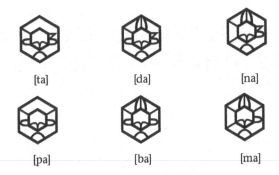

[ta]	[da]	[na]
[pa]	[ba]	[ma]

Both the Castithan and Irathient systems I wanted to be naturalistic, though, meaning I wanted the scripts to evolve the way scripts on Earth had. I had a bit of leeway with Irathient, since Irathients have an insular culture, eschewing technology in favor of reclaiming the traditional nomadic lifestyle they'd lost centuries before. Their people, though numerous, were not the type to go out and colonize other planets, which meant that their writing system would, for the most part, be used only among Irathients. This meant that it could look pretty wild and be a little less practical than a script that was used by many different people. Consequently, I evolved it to look that way.

Castithan, though, was an entirely different matter. In *Defiance*, the Castithans are the savviest, cleverest, and most well-connected aliens among all the Votans (the name of the aliens who came to Earth). Consequently, they're also the most powerful. Their cultural and political influence is vast, and though the Votanis Collective is supposed to represent all races equally, Castithans always tend to come out on top when disagreements arise. The upshot of this is that the Castithan language is the rough equivalent of English on Earth (everyone has their own language, but business is usually conducted in Castithan). The Castithan writing system, then, would be the Votan equivalent of the Roman alphabet.

Faced with this prospect, I made a couple of decisions. Of course, the Castithan writing system would have to look "cool" (it was an alien script), but it also needed to be versatile enough that it could be used *everywhere*. It had to look neat, but official—tame, compared with Irathient. It needed to be compact (Irathient is not) and easy to parse. But most important, it needed to not be an alphabet. Most invented scripts that had been created as set dressing up to that point for films and games (the Atlantean script for Disney's *Atlantis*, the pIqaD script for Klingon, the D'ni script used in the *Myst* series, the Dovahkiin script for *Skyrim*) were alphabets, and, while achieving a certain aesthetic, were rather simplistic and unrealistic. With my *Defiance* scripts, I was aiming to create something that could sit alongside some of the other outstanding conscripts that had been created by conlangers, like Carsten Becker's Tahano Hikamu, or anything by Trent Pehrson—something the like of which hadn't been seen on television, but only online among the conlanging community.

[Tahano Hikamu script text — six lines]

Ayeri's Tahano Hikamu (Carsten Becker)

The first step in the process was going back to Proto-Castithan, at a time when the script would have been developed. I decided to start at stage 2, rather than stage 1, since stage 1 for Castithan would have been so remote as to almost be erased by the passage of time. The sound system was very different at the time, with Proto-Castithan having an entire class of sounds modern Castithan had lost by the era the show takes place in, along with a host of other sound changes. This would have consequences for the spelling system, which I'll discuss later on. For the stage 2 writing system itself, which was an abjad, I decided to go with glyphs that could be etched on stone or imprinted on a clay (or claylike) tablet. I didn't know quite what the planet the Castithans came from would be like at this stage, but I figured that they would probably have the equivalent of stone or a substance that hardens like clay. The glyphs, while not completely devoid of curves (like Ogham), are nevertheless fairly simple, and wouldn't be difficult to carve or etch—certainly much simpler than hieroglyphs.

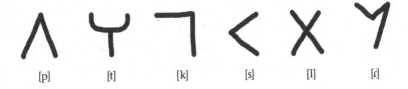

There's also evidence in the system that even at the time it was current, some glyphs were much older than others. For example, while [ɓ] and [kʼ] had their own glyphs, all plain voiced consonants are modified versions of their voiceless counterparts—as are prenasalized consonants.

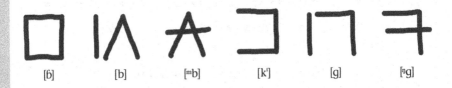

At this early stage, there were glyphs only for consonants. Vowels were indicated only where necessary, and even then, rather irregularly. Consonants were treated as the onsets of CV syllables with an inherent [a] vowel. Only a long [aː] was indicated in the writing system, as well as the other vowels [i, iː, u, uː].

| [aː] | [i] | [iː] | [u] | [uː] |

As a quirk of the system, the long [aː] glyph ⟃ would be used for both short [a] and long [aː] at the beginning of a word, once these vowel modifications started being used at the beginning of a word (they weren't, at first). A full word might have looked something like this, during the Proto-Castithan stage.

['zuː.^{n}da]
"storm"

The script changed when Castithans developed paper and the stylus, or their native equivalents thereof. My goal at this stage was to have Castithans not only write the script faster, but try to write each syllabic block with a single stroke, if possible. Several simplification principles were developed to achieve this goal. For example, the first was that all sharp, angled connections were rounded if they were approached from the bottom or left.

Proto-Castithan	Middle Castithan	Proto-Castithan	Middle Castithan	Proto-Castithan	Middle Castithan
⏄	⏄	∧	∩	Ɣ	ɣ
[k]		[p]		[ɾ]	

Next, full-length straight lines were no longer written starting at the top, but starting from someplace below.

Proto-Castithan	Middle Castithan	Proto-Castithan	Middle Castithan
[g]		[b]	

Above is also illustrated how glyphs that took more than one stroke began to be written with a single stroke.

The last step involved the introduction of the small loops that feature prominently in the Castithan writing system. Initially I was concerned about having so many characters with little loops, but I figured if Thai could get away with it, I could too.

พ	ฮ	ฏ	ฬ	ฆ	ษ
[l]	[h]	[t]	[tʰ]	[kʰ]	[s]

The basic idea behind the loop is that if an original line was deleted or not written out in full, it would be represented by a loop. For writers, it would be kind of a shorthand way of indicating that they had intended to write a more detailed glyph—like saying "Hey, I tried, but I'm a busy Castithan. I got things to do. Space things."

Proto-Castithan	Middle Castithan	Proto-Castithan	Middle Castithan
[h]		[ɓ]	

The major change, of course, was the inclusion of the vocalic pieces with the preceding consonant. Whether it was a long or short vowel, the additional glyphs were written with a single stroke, along with the rest of the character. Consonants followed by a short [a], again, were not modified.

Proto-Castithan	Middle Castithan	Proto-Castithan	Middle Castithan	Proto-Castithan	Middle Castithan
[pa]		[pi]		[pu]	
[paː]		[piː]		[puː]	

This period I'm calling "Middle Castithan" (which, incidentally, applies to the script only, not necessarily the language) persisted for a long time, eventually giving birth to the modern system. Once the Castithan equivalent of typesetting was invented, the system solidified, with a number of additional changes that occurred to stabilize and regularize the system. These can be summarized by examining the evolution of a few characters.

A small change was the use of the Castithan loop we've seen already as an initial element for orphaned lines at the beginning of a character.

Proto-Castithan	Middle Castithan	Modern Castithan
	[m]	

Certain characters added an additional stroke to distinguish them from characters that were too similar. Compare the characters for [ɓ] below to those for [m] above.

Proto-Castithan	Middle Castithan	Modern Castithan
□	𝑛𝑜	ᥑᥙ
	[ɓ]	

The vowel modifications for [i, iː, u, uː] got smoothed out a bit. In the case of [u] and [uː], the result looks almost like the inverse of the original glyphs.

Proto-Castithan	Middle Castithan	Modern Castithan
Λ-	↻	⋔ᖔ
	[pi]	
Λ=	⋔	⋔Ь
	[piː]	
Λʌ	⋔	⋔ᘁ
	[pu]	
Λ⩘	⋔	⋔ᗯ
	[puː]	

In certain vowel forms, characters that couldn't easily take a distinguishing stroke added a distinguishing dot, which was a modern innovation.

Proto- Castithan	Middle Castithan	Modern Castithan
	[mu]	
	[bu]	

Then, in addition to the remaining consonantal characters, a convention for writing diphthongs produced a new set of vowel characters that would come into play in the modern language, and would round out the system.

Proto- Castithan	Middle Castithan	Modern Castithan
	[pai]	
	[pau]	

Proto-Castithan	Middle Castithan	Modern Castithan
[pia]		
[piu]		
[pua]		
[pui]		

Now what makes the Castithan writing system fun is the fact that the spellings of most words were standardized at a time before the major sound changes that characterize the Castithan language began to take place, to say nothing of the grammatical and semantic changes. The result is a spelling system that's notoriously difficult to manage—almost as difficult as English, if not more difficult. The writing system, then, works hand in hand with the evolution of the language itself to produce a system that is complex in precisely the way that a natural system is complex. Some examples of the mismatch in spelling and pronunciation are shown below.

Orthographic Form	Original Pronunciation/ Original Meaning	Modern Pronunciation/ Modern Meaning
ᡃᏂᏝ	[ˈɾi.kuː] "to unearth"	[ˈʒe.gu] "to find"
ᏮᏈᡃᏝ	[si.ˈpʼai.li.kuː] "to spit"	[ˈʃpe.li.gu] "to joke"
ᏵᏈ	[ˈtui.hau] "bur"	[ˈkwi.o] "doubt"
ᏐᏂᏈ	[ᵐbiː.gau] "debt"	[ˈbi.ho] "credit"
ᏈᏈᏂ	[ᵑgai.li] "far"	[ˈge.le] "opposite"
ᏈᏋᏝ	[ˈpʼua.luː] "to enjoy"	[ˈpa.lu] "to use"

The complexity of the spelling system makes learning the Castithan language rather prohibitive—a source of consternation, no doubt, for the other Votan races for whom Castithan is a second language. Even though the writing system is a detail among the many facets of a large-scale production like *Defiance*, it can be used to further the artistic goals of the series. In this case, it becomes a part of the characterization of the Castithans—especially those in the upper echelons of society who continue to hold sway over the lives of other Votans.

As it stands, the Castithan writing system comprises more than eight hundred unique glyphs. Each consonant has sixteen forms, and I haven't even touched on the base-twenty number system or the punctuation system. Creating an alphabet with twenty-six glyphs, each one corresponding to an English letter, likely would have sufficed for the art department's purposes, and even for a majority of the audience. Productions today, though, have the ability to go above and beyond to maximize the authenticity of a world that doesn't exist—or even couldn't exist. And fans should demand nothing less. We can *do* immersive now, and do it well. When it comes to writing systems, I think the time has come to leave English ciphers behind. We can do better.

Postscript

If you've gotten this far, you now should have an idea what goes into creating a naturalistic conlang. This isn't everything, though—not by a long shot. I didn't even get a chance to talk about comparison. You know *big, bigger, biggest*? Many languages don't do that. Some languages say the equivalent of "The cat exceeds the kitten by bigness." Some do even stranger things than that. For every example I listed in every section there are a thousand more I didn't. This is just a toe dip.

But if I may, let me revisit the title of this book: *The Art of Language Invention*. What is art? Philosophy aside, we all know what it is: it's something original and creative that requires some specific set of skills to create that has been produced by a human. Thus, the *Mona Lisa* is art, but a computer printout of the *Mona Lisa* is not (though a photograph of a computer printing out the *Mona Lisa* might be). Is conlanging art? By any broad definition, the answer has to be yes. Some conlangs may be more utilitarian than others, but some painting is also more utilitarian than other types of painting. That is, just because I can paint a wall blue doesn't mean the *Mona Lisa* isn't art, or that painting itself isn't an art form.

Now, it's true that conlanging as art faces two real-world problems. First, it's questionable what form a conlang should take. That is, what is it that one presents when presenting a conlang? If it's a poem, is it the poem that's the art, or the conlang? It's a question that hasn't been settled partly because of the importance of money nowadays. You can buy a song; you can buy a painting; you can buy a novel. Can you buy a conlang?

Second, it's not clear how an audience appreciates a conlang. Is it by examining a reference grammar? Doing so takes a *long* time. Should that be a factor in determining whether conlanging is an art form or some other kind of practice?

Those questions aside, though, I'll tell you from personal experience that conlanging *feels* like an art to the conlanger. When I was a kid, all I did was draw. In high school, I picked up fiction, and then all I did was write. Finally in college I began conlanging, and all I did was conlang. For each stage, the drive—the motivation—was exactly the same: creation and expression. Inspiration comes from wherever it comes from and hits you, and then you're conlanging. Not for any specific reason, or with any goal in mind: it's to get what's inside you out into the world. I didn't know a thing about conlanging until after I was doing it, so I can say for myself, it felt no different from any other art I pursued.

Now if conlanging is just another art, one would hope that one could aspire to have a life like another artist in another field. Thus I have gotten many questions along the lines of, "How can I become a professional conlanger?," or "When did you decide to make conlanging a career?," or "What steps did you take to become a professional conlanger?" The honest answers to these questions are quite uninspiring. Asking what steps I took to become a professional conlanger is roughly like asking what steps Dumbo took to sign a Hollywood contract. There were no steps! Any conlangers who even suggested that they were seriously attempting to become professional conlangers would've been laughed off the internet as late as 2009. There were no professional jobs, let alone careers.

Nevertheless, we now live in a reality where there exists a vanishingly small number of professional conlangers, and an extraordinary amount of unpaid yet highly skilled conlangers. It's reasonable to ask how a highly skilled conlanger might get paid work. The problem is the only highly visible jobs have set unreasonable expectations. Projects such as *Game of Thrones, Avatar, Lord of the Rings, Thor: The Dark World,* and their ilk all have huge budgets and specific needs. There are countless other huge budget films that have absolutely no need of a conlang (where would one fit a conlang into *The Expendables III?*). Then there are millions more smaller budget films that have no need or would never spend the money on a conlang, even if the price were reasonable. There are simply not enough jobs to go around. Even so, creating languages specifically for television and film is the expectation. Could there be other ways to make money as a language creator?

Let me go back to Dothraki. It's true that David Benioff and Dan Weiss sought the help of a language creator when they decided their attempts at creating gibberish lines for the Dothraki were unsatisfying. But there was a very obvious first step they took that's rarely discussed. Specifically, they'd gotten the rights to adapt the whole of George R. R. Martin's *A Song of Ice and Fire,* so when they needed more Dothraki, where else would they go first? Their first step was to ask George R. R. Martin for his materials on the Dothraki language. Martin told them that all the information on the language that was in existence was in the books, which I detailed in the first case study of this book—hence, the need for a language creator.

That encounter, though, could have gone differently. If George R. R. Martin were a second Tolkien, he would've said, "These seven boxes contain my early notes on the development of the Dothraki family of languages, but all the up-to-date information is contained in these nineteen boxes here"—and, in that case, they probably would've hired a linguist and/or language creator to go through that material, organize it, and use it for translation, rather than create new material. This is what happened with the *Lord of the Rings* movies, on which linguist David Salo worked.

But now imagine if instead George R. R. Martin had said, "Well, I didn't create the language. I hired Amanda to do it, and when I need a translation, I just email her. Here's her contact information." If that had happened, I never would have gotten this job.

So. Undoubtedly there are language creators reading this book. There are probably also laypersons reading this book, for which I am utterly grateful (if you're in the area, hit me up for coffee—I owe you at least that much for dragging you through an explanation of ergativity). But I know there are probably also a number of writers and would-be writers of fantasy and science fiction reading this book right now. I would like to address the following remarks specifically to you.

Probably 0.001 percent of films and television shows would benefit from including one or more created languages. Almost 100 percent of fantasy works, and maybe a healthy 45 percent of science-fiction works, would benefit from including one or more created languages. While you, the writer, could give it a go and create the languages yourself, or go the George R. R. Martin route and create language-like bits, you know what else you *could* do? HIRE A CON-LANGER. There are literally *thousands* out there who are highly skilled and would take a bath in boiling hot, Texas-style ginger ale for the opportunity to see their work in print. I understand writers don't make a lot of money, but if you can't offer anything else, offer a percentage of the royalties. Offer to share authorship. Offer to name a character after their cat (that's how Nina Post got me to create a language for her book [and, no, that won't work again]). Give a conlanger the opportunity to improve your work and to prove themselves as conlangers. At the very least, you won't ever get stuck coming up with names.

The prospect of working on a novel that may or may not ever get published may not sound exciting to conlangers initially, but it's rare that a brand-new blockbuster springs whole cloth from the mind of a writer/director/producer. Adaptation is much more common nowadays, and both fantasy and sci-fi are hot. A small percentage of novels by fantasy and sci-fi authors will get published. Of those, a small percentage will sell well and become popular. Of those, a small percentage will get optioned. If those works have languages attached to them created by conlangers, those conlangers will get work over those who have more experience in the industry—after all, it's *their* work. And even if a novel doesn't become the next *Shadow and Bone*, the conlanger will have gained invaluable experience not just creating a language, but working with and for someone else. It allows them to build a résumé. Currently the only résumé a conlanger can boast is a page of links to their work displayed on a wiki or blog which no one will take seriously (for reasons that defy sense, mind, but which exist nonetheless).

Think of your favorite fantasy or science-fiction work not by Tolkien. Wouldn't it have been incredible if the various lands of Narnia had languages of their own? Or the four main divisions of the kingdom of Oz? What if there were an Eloi and Morlock language in *The Time Machine*? I think it's a bit much to expect a writer to spend their time working on their fiction *and* creating languages to boot, but a tandem can do it. And while not all readers would be interested in a conlang attached to a work of fiction, many would. It's a way to draw people into the world, and in fantasy and sci-fi, the world is a major part of what the author is selling. Why not flesh it out to the furthest extent possible? Make it huge! Make it a project so expansive, so all-encompassing that no publisher or screenwriter could *possibly* turn it down.

To the conlangers or potential conlangers reading this book, we're at a crossroads right now. The work that I've done and the place I occupy in the conlanging world is the end result of the collective work of the conlanging community that got together in the early 1990s. What comes next is a bit of a mystery.

It was easy to make yourself known in the early days of online conlanging if you had access to the internet and knew where conlangers gathered. It's very difficult to do so now. There are legions of new conlangers—legions of young conlangers—and they don't all know one another, or even know of one another. The community, in the broadest sense of the term, is larger and more diverse than ever, yet it feels as if it's less connected than it has ever been. That's a daunting task for a newcomer.

In such situations, it's always been my feeling that if you can't change the world, you can change yourself. As a conlanger today, you have to keep tabs on the evolving state of the internet, but focus primarily on improving your language skills. Even if naturalism in conlanging isn't your cup of tea, it's instructive to work through a naturalistic conlang—to learn what it is that makes human language unique. Consider it a foundation upon which to build.

But there's no need to stop there. My languages are naturalistic primarily because that's what I was working on throughout college, and that's mostly what I'm now called upon to do for the shows and movies I work on. But if conlanging is an art, then naturalism is a school, or a movement. Da Vinci, Michelangelo, Rembrandt—these are realist painters whose styles are unique, but whose paintings are attempting to be realistic. If naturalistic conlanging is the equivalent of realist painting, then what is an impressionist conlang? A surreal conlang? What's the conlang equivalent of *Guernica*? Who is the conlanging equivalent of Gauguin or Dalí? Suzette Haden Elgin intended her Láadan to be a strictly feminist conlang. Should it be the last? Can a language embody any other movement, political or social? And though there have been a couple good parody conlangs (Maggel is a favorite of mine), I haven't seen one in a while. We need more!

There's actually a lot of uncharted territory in the world of conlanging. Most conlangs that have attempted to stretch things have either focused on structure (i.e. what can a language potentially do that natural languages don't) or the speakers (i.e. what if cats had a language of their own). There are a lot of fruitful opportunities to craft new languages that instead try to make a statement to their audience by means of their content. What if there were a language that required all of its verbs to have a second person subject so that its speakers were forced to always consider what their listener was doing or thinking? What if a language forced its user to specify on the verb whether or not the action in question resulted in or was accomplished as a result of some living thing's death? Describing a meal would become far more interesting for meat eaters. What if, as a form of social commentary, there were a language that forced its users to rate the attractiveness of all human beings referred to by means of a mandatory set of scalar suffixes? Could there be a language conveyed through flavor, so that a meal itself could be a story?

Ultimately, a language is nothing more than a system to encode meaning. The possibilities of what to encode and how to encode it are endless, and in about one thousand years of active language creation, we've barely scratched the surface of what's possible. I look forward to seeing what the conlangers of tomorrow can do. Until then, I encourage anyone reading this to go out into the wilds of the internet and take a look at some of the work other conlangers have done. The only reason people know who I am or know a thing about any of my languages is because of *Game of Thrones* and *Defiance* and the rest of it. But if you enjoyed looking at my languages even a little bit, I guarantee you'll find others you like even more elsewhere. We haven't seen a conlanging masterpiece yet, but when we do, I guarantee you that it won't have been created for a show or film. A good conlang takes time to develop, and a conlanger who works on their own has all the time in the world. There's no doubt in my mind that the best is yet to come.

Acknowledgments

No human has ever done anything on their own. *Ever.* None of us would be alive if those who gave birth to us didn't feed and shelter us when we were defenseless. Humans exist and act thanks entirely to the charity of other humans. I exist because the entirety of humanity has allowed me to exist up to this point. For that, I thank everyone.

Among that group, though, exist a number of individuals whose help was instrumental in the writing of this book, and I'd like to thank them specifically. First, I want to thank the many people who've employed me to create languages over the years. Tom Lieber and Erika Kennair from Syfy were instrumental in getting me on *Defiance*, *Dominion*, and *Star-Crossed*, and for that I'll be ever grateful. *Defiance* continues to be an amazing experience, and I'm grateful for the insights of Kevin Murphy and Brian Alexander, who allowed me to do more than I ever would have dreamed I'd be allowed to do. That opportunity arose only because of my involvement with *Game of Thrones*, where David Benioff, Dan Weiss, and Bryan Cogman have long tolerated my incessant linguistic noodling. The series wouldn't exist without George R. R. Martin, whose work has changed my life in a profound and tangible way. I wouldn't have gotten the opportunity to work on *Game of Thrones* without the Language Creation Society (LCS), which, in turn, wouldn't have

gotten the job without Arika Okrent, whom Dave and Dan contacted first about the job. She sent them to the LCS after a positive
experience at the Second Language Creation Conference, which
never would have come to exist without the Conlang Listserv community. This book exists primarily because of the many conlangers
I've learned from and worked with over the years. I hope I've done
something that you can be proud of.

On the business end, I want to thank my agent, Joanna Volpe,
and author Leigh Bardugo, who introduced me to her. I hate
business-y/contract-y stuff, and Jo's value cannot be measured in
this regard. Thank you so much, Leigh, for putting me in touch
with Jo. And Jo, thanks for everything.

My editor Elda Rotor has displayed infinite patience with me, and
has been invaluable in helping to shape this work. In addition to
that, though, she contacted me initially about writing this book. It's
not as if I drafted this and shopped it around: Elda emailed *me* and
said, "Hey! Do you want to do what you've always wanted to do
your entire life for your favorite publisher in the world? We'll pay
you!" Not in those words, of course, but that's pretty much how it
sounded to me. What led her to decide that this was a good idea I'll
never know, but I am eternally grateful. Thank you, Elda.

For the book itself, the input of several people was instrumental,
including John Quijada, who told me not to lose my sense of humor;
Nina Post, who assured me the book could be profitably read by a non-
linguist; Doug Ball, whose work doesn't feature prominently enough
in this book, for which I apologize; and Sylvia Sotomayor, who noticed
a key error neither I nor anyone else had. Also thanks to David Durand
for filling in some detail about the history of the online conlanging
community. In particular, though, I'd like to thank Will McPherson,
who single-handedly rescued this book. I reached a crisis at one point,
not knowing how precisely to revise what I had, and his insights were
crucial in helping me to rework it. He also suggested the title of this
book, for which I'm grateful, and he even agreed to buy me Shubert's
ice cream the next time he sees me. Thank you to everyone, and of
course to Jo and Elda who also provided invaluable feedback.

Thanks to my many linguistics professors who helped to shape my
understanding of human language. In particular, thank you to (in

alphabetical order) Farrell Ackerman, Andrew Garrett, Sam Mchombo, John McWhorter, John Ohala, David Perlmutter, Maria Polinsky, and Eve Sweetser.

I'd like to thank my family members and friends who continue to support me: the Ishii and Ortiz clan, the McPhersons and the Tastos, the other Ortiz clan, who kept me plied with tri-tip and root beer, the Graebers and Laura's karaoke machine, and Jon, Kyn, and Harbor House. A big thank you to my mother Sandi and dad Steve who continued to support me despite devoting hours upon hours to creating languages, an enterprise which seemed, at the time, to have absolutely no practical application. Things sure change, don't they? And thank you to my little sister Natalie who's been my muse ever since she was born. Also thanks to my sister-in-law Laura who's sitting on the couch right now as I write this. I could be visiting with her, but . . . nah. I'm doing this. And she's just sitting there. Doing nothing. Because I'm not talking to her.

Thanks to my two little writing buddies Keli and Roman. They made sure I got up and stretched every now and then by meowing incessantly at me and tearing into something (respectively).

Finally, the biggest thank you goes to my wife Erin, my one and only love. Nothing I do in this life is worth anything unless I can spend my days with you. In addition to her endless support and love, though, Erin also has the exact same linguistics background as I do, and has been instrumental in helping with every single one of my professional languages and in proofreading this book for both typographical and linguistic accuracy. She does everything. I love you so much, babe.

Thanks for reading! I hope you found it to be a worthwhile experience.

Dothraki Phrase Book

M'athchomaroon	Hello
Fonas chek	Goodbye
Hash yer dothrae chek?	How are you?
Anha dothrak chek.	I'm good.
Sek	Yes
Vos	No
Athdavrazar!	Excellent!
Me nem nesa.	It is known.
Ei mahrazhi'th drivoe.	All men must die.
Shekh ma shieraki anni.	My sun and stars.
Jalan atthirari anni.	Moon of my life.
Hash yer astoe ki Dothraki?	Do you speak Dothraki?
Anha garvok.	I'm hungry.
Anha zhilak yera.	I love you.
Hash yer nem akemoe m'anhoon?	Will you marry me?

High Valyrian Phrase Book

Rytsas	Hello
Geros ilas	Goodbye
Skorkydoso glaesā?	How are you?
Sȳrī glaesan.	I'm good.
Issa	Yes
Daor	No
Rōvēgrior!	Excellent!
Gīmissiks.	It is known.
Valar morghūlis.	All men must die.
Vēzos qēlossās ñuho.	My sun and stars.
Ñuho glaeso hūrus.	Moon of my life.
Udrirzi Valyrio ȳdrā?	Do you speak Valyrian?
Merbun.	I'm hungry.
Avy jorrāelan.	I love you.
Ao ynoma dīnilūks?	Will you marry me?

Shiväisith Phrase Book

△8)\V◹△Ŀ *Äshlimär*	Hello
⊤△◸△W∨8 *Näkäthish*	Goodbye
V△Ŀ△Ŀ⋇△ △)\△)\≡ *Jäärärljy yväl?*	How are you?
◸△W⋎Ŀ— *Käthiär.*	I'm good.
)\△W *Vääth*	Yes
W△8 *Tjäsh*	No
≾△)\∨୮Y— *Gyvidhe!*	Excellent!
)\XW ⋇WX8�YW—⸌ *Vath uathashoth.*	It is known.
◸△◹∨)\ )\X⊤∨)\ ≾Y⎍∨X⊕∨)\∨)\— *Kämil vanil gorjapsivil.*	All men must die.
Ŀ⋎)\∨◸ + ⋇Ŀ∨⊙∨)\∨◸— *Reevih u uurisilih.*	My sun and stars.
W�Y)\Y V△⎍∨୮Y⊤△⊙◸∨— *Tove jääridheenäski.*	Moon of my life.
�X⊙△)\ 8∨)\�X⊙∨W△Ŀ≡ *Äisäl Shiväisithär?*	Do you speak Shiväisith?
◸∨Ŀ⅄X Ŀ⊹⊤W∨W ◹�Y Ŀ⅄W— *Kira ruthith mooreth.*	I'm hungry.
◸∨Ŀ⅄X)\∨)\⋇⋇X)\ ⊤⅄)\— *Kira liljal nol.*	I love you.
⊤⅄)\ X)\ ◸⅄)\X◸∨V ◸∨Ŀ⅄XW≡ *Nol al kevahi kirath?*	Will you marry me?

Castithan
Phrase Book

ᘑᘘᘗᘖᘕ
Religwo — Hello

ᘑᘘᘗᘖᘕ
Religwo — Goodbye

ᘏᘑᘜᘛᘚᘙ
Zwore i she? — How are you?

ᘏᘑᘜᘛᘞ
Zwore ya. — I'm good.

ᘟᘠ
Su — Yes

ᘡᘢᘣᘤ
Gao — No

ᘥᘦᘧᘨᘩ
Furíje! — Excellent!

ᘪᘫᘬᘭᘮᘯ
Hinjudhala je. — It is known.

ᘰᘱᘲᘳᘴᘵᘶᘷᘸᘹ
Pombune foja re vuzukswe je. — All men must die.

298

ᯜᯜᯜ

Ichuko veraho ki shiralino. My sun and stars.

ᯜᯜᯜ

Isho shinovano dwokeno. Moon of my life.

ᯜᯜᯜ

Kastíthanwa nggo erustali she? Do you speak Castithan?

ᯜᯜᯜ

Nirizhiwa do yenda. I'm hungry.

ᯜᯜᯜ

Noraka do deta. I love you.

ᯜᯜᯜ

Famiya ksa nevitsa do kufyunje she? Will you marry me?

Irathient
Phrase Book

ᘓᖇᖚᑎᐷᑫ
Eseneziri

Hello

ᐷᑫᑐᘓᘛᑫ
Tha rikisa

Goodbye

ᘓᘓᖉᐃᑐᘓᘛᑫᐃᑐᑫᐷ ᘓ ᘛ ᘛᐃᑊ
Avoshə rikisa pa-wazazə?

How are you?

ᐃᑐᑫᐃᐷᘓᘓᘩᑐᑫᐷ
Pa-nuba.

I'm good.

ᘓᘓᘧ
Thei

Yes

ᑫᑊᘩ
Me

No

ᐃᑫᘧᐷᑐᘓᘠᑐᘧᐃᐃᑫᑊᑫᐷ
Nabaktə kima!

Excellent!

ᐃᑫᑫᘩᑐ ᘛ ᘛᐃᘧᑫᐷᐃᑫᑫᘩᑫᐷ
Nanizizagba nuna.

It is known.

ᐃᑎᘓᐷᑫᑫᑊᘧᐷᘩᑐᑫᐃᑫᑎᑫᐃᑎᑐ ᐷᘛᘧᘛᑫ ᐷᘩᘛᘧᑊᘩᐷ
Ezegnə tei ememə zushon zweigyu.

All men must die.

ᐃᑎᐷᘩᑫᑫᐃᑊᑐᑫᑊᘩᑎᘩᐷᑫᑫᐃᑫᐃᑊᐷ
Uzidme s'utegməmu.

My sun and stars.

ᐷᐷᘧᑐᑎ ᐃ ᑊᘧᑐᑫᐷᑎ ᐷᐃᑎᘩᑫᑫᐃᑊᐷ
Zugyire pathezuhme.

Moon of my life.

ᛉᚢᛈᚲᚾᛟᚲᛗᛁᛋᛖᚷᛟᛈᛃᚲ𐰒ᚲᛈᚲ

Letha analaktə Thwelu l'Irathi?   Do you speak Irathient?

ᛈᚲᛈᚲᛒᛖᛟ

Emak enurwa.   I'm hungry.

ᛉᛈᚲᛒᛗᛟ

Lemak ewei.   I love you.

ᛉᛈᚲᛈᚷᚲᛖᛟᛒᚢ

Lemagyi shreke?   Will you marry me?

Indojisnen Phrase Book

Eydakshin   Hello

Iovenan   Goodbye

Ellasema?   How are you?

Ellahen.   I'm good.

An   Yes

Tu   No

Lyurinjetlen!   Excellent!

Heytlat.   It is known.

Vowtalzinnek bashrachotlek.   All men must die.

Lewsitanani meysannekani.   My sun and stars.

Ellastatalla duokena.   Moon of my life.

Indojisnedma koyshistusama?   Do you speak Indojisnen?

Apahen.   I'm hungry.

Sayatranguhan.   I love you.

Ellantezhuhesfe?   Will you marry me?

Kamakawi
Phrase Book

ᵀᵛ
I elea   Hello

ᵀᵋ
I nikula   Goodbye

Ai a kopu ia ti kane ai?   How are you?

A eyana ei.   I'm good.

Λ
Ea   Yes

Oku   No

Feya!   Excellent!

A fe'a'u amo.   It is known.

Au li'u hopoko uila ea ima. All men must die.

ᘓ᙮

E eili oiu inivie oi'i.   My sun and stars.

ᘓ᙮

E uomo oi'ala'iki o ei.   Moon of my life.

Ai a oala ia ti Kamakawi ai?   Do you speak Kamakawi?

ᘓ᙮

A imo ei.   I'm hungry.

ᘓ᙮

A eli ei i ia.   I love you.

Ai a male oine ia i'i ai?   Will you marry me?

Væyne Zaanics Phrase Book

ꝗ꓄꓂ꒉꓴ꓃	
Dolne	Hello
ꝉꓴ꓃꓂ꓴꝅ꓀꒒꒐꒒꒒	
Isalnæælæ	Goodbye
ꓫꓑꓶꓠ ꓂꒐ꓻꓮꝗꓮꝗ ꓂ꓓꓶ꓂ꓴꝗꓴꓵꓮ	
Jur nachehoh sunen?	How are you?
꓂꒐ꓻꓮꝗꓮꝗ ꝗꓓꓶ꓂ꓴꝗꓴꝉ	
Nachehoh hunen.	I'm good.
ꝗꓴꓠ	
Ter	Yes
꓅ꓮꝗꓠ	
Cor	No
꒑꒒ꓮꝗꓕꓴꓵꓮꝗꓮꝗꝉ	
Þornehoh!	Excellent!
ꓰꓴ꒐꒑ꓕꓵꓴ꓇ꓕꓵꓴꓴꝉꝅ	
Vamemenaw.	It is known.
ꓚꓲꓓꓶꓵ ꝉꓓꓵꓠ ꓂ꓵꓠꓮꝗꓠ ꓐꓚ꒒꒒ꓵꓴꓵꓕꝗ ꓰꓴꓚꓶꓴꓵꓮꝗꝉ	
Mun izir sebor waatheneh vinen.	All men must die.
ꓮꝗꝗꓓꓶꓑ꒒꒒ꓮꝗ ꓕꓮꓴꓮꓴꓕꓵꓶꓠ ꓮꓴꓮꝗ꒒꒒꒒ ꓕꓴꓵ꒒꒒꒒ꓴꓴꓮꝗꓴꓶꓠꓭ	
Ohuþo eloove yæ esæyne.	My sun and stars.

ᚠᚾᚱᚢᚴ Ᏽᚦᛁᛚᚪ ᚾᚾᏟᚢᚢᚴᛄᛏᚢᏟᏟᏟᏟᚪ

Oloovo huþo yesvarnenec. | Moon of my life.

ᚡᚩᚻᚾ ᚢᚪᛁᛁᛁᚾᚾᚢᚻᛁᛁᛁ ᛎᚾᚢᛦᛎᛎᚢ ᚢᚾᚠᛏᚢᏟᚢᚪ

Jur Væynæ Zaanics sornen? | Do you speak Væyne Zaanics?

ᚪᚾᛁᛁᛁᛁᚳᚾᚢᚪᚢᛁ Ᏽᚾᛏᚢᚾᚠᚢᚪ

Dræpova hornon. | I'm hungry.

ᏵᛦᚢᛁᚾᚢᏟᚢᚾᚠᚪᛁᛁᚪ

Hisalnenos. | I love you.

ᚡᚩᚻᚾ ᚢᚾᚠᚢ Ᏽᚦᛁᛁᛁᚾ ᛞᛦᛦᛏᚢᛦᚾᚾᚠᚪᛁᚢᚪ

Jur son huþar tacirnilos? | Will you marry me?

Sondiv Phrase Book

ᲒᲐᲑᲐᲑᲗᲘ᳒ *Alyakson*	Hello
ᲒᲐᲑᲢᲦᲡ *Aldovos*	Goodbye
ᲝᲝᲐᲜᲒ ᲒᲐᲑᲐᲠᲦ ᲒᲐᲑᲢᲱᲠ *Sogdon ildis ili?*	How are you?
�᳐ᲑᲐᲐ ᲒᲐᲑᲐᲠᲦᲡ *Tezur ildis.*	I'm good.
ᲧᲐᲑ *Di*	Yes
ᲒᲜ. *Jen*	No
ᲒᲢᲦᲔᲘ *Ameku!*	Excellent!
ᲒᲗᲦᲑᲐ ᲒᲐᲑᲡ *Ipikev iji.*	It is known.
ᲒᲐᲒᲘᲐᲑ ᲒᲜᲢᲒᲐᲑ ᲗᲦᲑ ᲐᲮ ᲧᲱᲒᲡ *Jivur umyuki pil usayad.*	All men must die.
ᲒᲐᲑᲝ ᲜᲐᲒᲝᲜᲒ ᲒᲐᲑᲐᲡ *Aksemu nigayana yala*	My sun and stars.
ᲒᲐᲘᲝᲒ ᲒᲐᲑᲝᲐᲐᲒᲐᲡ ᲒᲐᲑᲐᲡ *Ewaganu husoljivi widi.*	Moon of my life.
ᲒᲐᲑ ᲒᲝᲐᲑᲐᲑ ᲒᲐᲑᲐ ᲒᲐᲑᲔ *Yen asondiv inira isi?*	Do you speak Sondiv?
ᲒᲐᲑᲢᲧᲑ ᲒᲐᲑᲡ *Irbik idi.*	I'm hungry.
ᲒᲝ ᲒᲐᲑᲐᲑ ᲒᲐᲑᲡ *Asa ijita idi.*	I love you.
ᲒᲐᲑ ᲒᲐᲑᲢᲑᲐᲑᲐ ᲒᲝ ᲒᲐᲑᲐᲘ *Yen ukuvuji usu idi?*	Will you marry me?

Trigedasleng Phrase Book

Heya	Hello
Leidon	Goodbye
Ha yun?	How are you?
Krei os, you.	I'm good.
Sha	Yes
No	No
Bos!	Excellent!
Em ge get in.	It is known.
Hef-de ogeda souda wan op.	All men must die.
Ai deimeika en skaifaya.	My sun and stars.
Nashana ona ai sonraun.	Moon of my life.
Yu mema Trigedasleng in?	Do you speak Trigedasleng?
Ai ste enti.	I'm hungry.
Ai hod yu in.	I love you.
Yu na soujon we gon ai?	Will you marry me?

Méníshè
Phrase Book

Azwànò	Hello
Súlènò	Goodbye
Lwadèír lujè jìnà?	How are you?
Yèlá ùmáì.	I'm good.
Yéò	Yes
Ut'àú	No
Padèírkà jè!	Excellent!
Kat'îzénzhí.	It is known.
Shówòr úrrà nagaghàà.	All men must die.
Imé jìpón jè wèdís.	My sun and stars.
Yu'ánk'è mé azwà.	Moon of my life.
Lúdèír Méníshè jìnà?	Do you speak Méníshè?
I'ózè.	I'm hungry.
Lóù imé wèlá.	I love you.
Lújèzò imé apáné jìnà?	Will you marry me?

Ravkan Phrase Book

Ꝡꝇꞇ ꞇꞇꞇꟋ
Sho sol

Hello

ꝑꝗꝡꞇꞇꞇꝗꝍꝇꝡ
Zyeshostash

Goodbye

ꞵꞇꞇꞋꞇꝍꝕ ꞃꞃꝗ:
Zhorvat kei?

How are you?

ꝗꝍꞇ Ꝥꞃꞇꞇꞇꝍꞇ
Eya brova.

I'm good.

ꞇꝍ
Da

Yes

ꞇꝇꝗꝕ
Net

No

ꝩꞇꝕꝤꞇꞃꞇꞇꞇꝽ
Razbrovi!

Excellent!

ꝗꝕ ꝗꞇꞇꝭꞇꞇꝣꞇꞇꝘ
Et etsilanya.

It is known.

Ꝙꝍꞇꝭꞇ ꞇꝍꞇꝗꝭꞇꝭ ꝣꝇꞇꝘꞇꞇꝩ ꞃꝩꞇꞇꞇꞇꝘ
Vyoni bleini nolas chovad.

All men must die.

ꝩꞇꞇ ꞇꞇꞇꟋ Ᵹꝗ ꞇꝭꝗꝣꞇꝨꝨꝥ
Moi sol ye tselai.

My sun and stars.

ꝑꞇꞇꝓꝍ ꝗꝍꝝꝍ ꞇꞇꝗꝣꝥꝍ
Zyoma maya olya.

Moon of my life.

ꞃꞃꝗ ꝩꝗꝓꝔꝍꞃ ꝩꝍꝝꝤꝍꝝꝍꝡ:
Kei ryezich Ravkayash?

Do you speak Ravkan?

ꝗꝍꝍ ꞃꞃꝗꝽꝍꞃ
Eya chela.

I'm hungry.

ꝗꝍꝍ ꝴꝗꝽꝍꝍ ꞃꝩꝣꝍ
Eya fyela chi.

I love you.

ꞃꞃꝗ ꞇꞇꝘꝣꞇꝘꝕꝍꞃꞃ ꝝꞇꝘꝣ:
Kei onolich yash?

Will you marry me?

Chakobsa
Phrase Book

𐎧𐎧𐎧𐎧
Tuli rush

Hello

𐎧𐎧𐎧𐎧𐎧
Ekkeri hiyash

Goodbye

𐎧𐎧𐎧𐎧𐎧𐎧𐎧𐎧
Is-kiftha chaiya huraaha?

How are you?

𐎧𐎧𐎧𐎧𐎧𐎧
Sa gif cheshii.

I'm good.

𐎧𐎧𐎧
Charra

Yes

𐎧𐎧
Ats

No

𐎧𐎧𐎧𐎧
Cheshaiza!

Excellent!

𐎧𐎧𐎧𐎧
Ledaas-ha.

It is known.

𐎧𐎧𐎧𐎧𐎧𐎧𐎧𐎧𐎧
O riidh hiili uzzulatha.

All men must die.

𐎧𐎧𐎧𐎧𐎧𐎧𐎧
Fizii hi esshaidhii.

My sun and stars.

𐎧𐎧𐎧𐎧𐎧𐎧
Gevi eddemayi.

Moon of my life.

𐎧𐎧𐎧𐎧𐎧𐎧𐎧𐎧
Vii jaraagash sa Chakobsa?

Do you speak Chakobsa?

𐎧𐎧𐎧
Yulii.

I'm hungry.

𐎧𐎧𐎧𐎧
Bariisha.

I love you.

𐎧𐎧𐎧𐎧𐎧𐎧𐎧𐎧𐎧𐎧
Vii hiyaashash ekkerash hi chaskii?

Will you marry me?

Engála
Phrase Book

Sainyun	Hello
Selúlu	Goodbye
Lai kaubi ko 'n is?	How are you?
Kaubyun.	I'm good.
Chemí	Yes
O	No
L'ungwéda!	Excellent!
Yemés.	It is known.
Papaha zos kaimé linyús taníma.	All men must die.
Izi keli kayén un.	My sun and stars.
Ulu a ihu un.	Moon of my life.
Lais yemésis linyá Engála?	Do you speak Engála?
Wimon.	I'm hungry.
Zhavyun lu is.	I love you.
Lai kanises ne un?	Will you marry me?

Glossary

Adposition An independent word with grammatical function that modifies nouns.

Affix A phonological string attached to an independent word often resulting in some sort of semantic or grammatical change.

Artlang Portmanteau of "artistic language." A conlang created for artistic purposes.

Aspect The manner in which the action of a verb takes place.

Auxlang Portmanteau of "auxiliary language." A conlang created to facilitate communication among a multilingual group.

Case The morphological reification of the grammatical function of a noun.

Circumfix The simultaneous addition of a suffix and a prefix.

Conlang Portmanteau of "constructed language." A language intentionally created by one or more individuals.

Creole A complete system of communication which began its existence as a pidgin.

Derivation Changing the grammatical category of a word.

Engelang Portmanteau of "engineered language." A conlang that is created to achieve a specific, often unnatural linguistic goal.

Gap In a relative clause, a gap is the place where the modified noun would ordinarily appear.

Glyph An individual character in a writing system.

Grammatical Category The part of speech of a word (noun, verb, adjective, adverb, adposition, auxiliary, conjunction, particle, determiner).

Grammatical Number The amount of a noun as grammaticalized by a given language (e.g. singular vs. plural, singular vs. dual vs. plural, etc.).

Infix An affix that is placed inside of a word.

Inflection Changing the grammatical function of a word without changing its grammatical category.

Interrogative Pronoun A pronoun used in questions that requests a specific type of information (person, place, time, manner, etc.).

Language A complete system of communication.

Linguistics The scientific study of language.

Morpheme *See* AFFIX.

Morphology The sum total of a language's systems of interrelatedness between word forms of a given type (e.g. nominal number or verb tense).

Natlang Portmanteau of "natural language." A language that arose spontaneously on Earth.

Negation A linguistic strategy to show an event didn't occur, or that a state is not the case.

Object The noun that receives or is affected by the action of the sentence.

Orthography The writing system of a language and its prescriptive usage.

Phoneme A sound used to distinguish word meanings in a language.

Phonology The sound system of a language.

Pidgin An incomplete system of communication. *See also* CREOLE.

Postposition An adposition that appears after a noun.

Prefix An affix that attaches to the front of a word.

Preposition An adposition that appears in front of a noun.

Question Word See INTERROGATIVE PRONOUN.

Relative Clause A full sentence that modifies a noun.

Romanization A transliteration scheme that utilizes the Roman alphabet.

Semantics The collected meanings of the various words of a language.

Sign Language A complete system of communication that uses the hands and/or other parts of the body rather than sounds as tokens.

Sketch An incomplete conlang.

Subject The noun that enacts or gives rise to the action of the sentence.

Suffix An affix that attaches to the end of a word.

Syntax The rules defining the order in which words are allowed to be placed in a clause in a given language.

Tense The time in or at which the action of a verb takes place.

Word Order The linear order of the subject, verb, and object of a sentence.

Index